MOSTLY W.

MOSTLY WATER

Selected
Memoir & Essays
Rural & North

Mary Odden

Book design by Mark E. Cull

Library of Congress Cataloging-in-Publication Data

Names: Odden, Mary, 1955– author.
Title: Mostly water : selected memoir & essays, rural & north / Mary Odden.
Description: First edition. | Pasadena : Boreal books, [2020]
Identifiers: LCCN 2019042642 | ISBN 9781597099196 (trade paperback) | ISBN 9781597099189 (ebook)
Subjects: LCSH: Odden, Mary, 1955- | Authors, American—21st century—Biography. | Alaska—Social life and customs—Anecdotes. | Country life—Anecdotes.
Classification: LCC PS3615.D426 A6 2020 | DDC 814/.6—dc23
LC record available at https://lccn.loc.gov/2019042642

The National Endowment for the Arts, the Los Angeles County Arts Commission, the Ahmanson Foundation, the Dwight Stuart Youth Fund, the Max Factor Family Foundation, the Pasadena Tournament of Roses Foundation, the Pasadena Arts & Culture Commission and the City of Pasadena Cultural Affairs Division, the City of Los Angeles Department of Cultural Affairs, the Audrey & Sydney Irmas Charitable Foundation, the Kinder Morgan Foundation, the Meta & George Rosenberg Foundation, the Allergan Foundation, the Riordan Foundation, Amazon Literary Partnership, and the Mara W. Breech Foundation partially support Red Hen Press.

First Edition
Published by Boreal Books
an imprint of Red Hen Press
www.borealbooks.org
www.redhen.org

For Jim and Kari

CONTENTS

MOSTLY WATER

1
GOING TO THE HILLS

Looking for the heroic in all the female places

My grandmother Mona was missing an index finger on her left hand because she cut it off with an ax when she was a little girl. The part of her hand that should have been a finger ended at its big round knuckle with not even a scar. That my straight-backed and elegant grandmother with her black shiny shoes and blue-and-white printed jersey dresses had ever been in proximity to firewood was a wonder to me. I was even more impressed after she explained the concept of firewood.

Mona lived in Portland at the end of her life and didn't visit us very often, but the absent finger, which I noticed at about age four, set me on an entirely new course regarding my family. After that, when Mona came to visit, there was a whiff of old cowboy times around the house and enough silences to make her mysterious as well as loved.

Due to some fortunate indiscretion on the part of my grandfather, Harry, I had two grandmothers on my father's side and cousins in descending ages all over the West. The old hurts had shrunk up to slight pauses in the stories told by the first and second generations, and the meaning of those hesitations was entirely lost upon me in the third. What I knew for sure was that I had two grandmothers who had known horses and wild Indians and cowboys. My other grandmother, Margie, lived close to us for years and was a grandmotherly figure in every way. She grew flowers and sewed aprons and upholstered her own chairs. She baked cookies and muffins. And when she was in her seventies and we'd bought an intractable Appaloosa mare named Candy who liked to throw herself over backward to squish the rider, Margie climbed on and taught the mare to behave.

Until I was a teenager, I never learned any names of plants in eastern Oregon where I grew up, except for the few plants that my parents talked me into tending in the garden and the weeds they showed me how to dig out of the yard. As a result, for years the only plants I could identify that grew where we lived were buttonweed and Russian thistle. When I got old enough to read Zane Grey's novels about the west at Mona's urging, I learned about a few of the desert plants. My favorite Zane Grey heroine was Sego Lily. Lovely words, I thought, and one day I found her namesake. I was riding a horse around the Owyhee Desert margins in spring, probably in dampish and still-green May, when I came up to a flower all by itself on a pale-green stalk. It was surrounded by nothing but the pebbly brown desert soil and a few clumps of sagebrush standing back in admiration. A frail tulip shape, a goblet for an elf—each delicate petal started out pink but reached upward to a nearly transparent white tip. It was like meeting an angel. There was not a doubt in my mind that I was looking at a sego lily, and also that she was a girl.

Some ranch families still needed their horses, but that wasn't our story. We owned a small grocery store, and my father hadn't ridden horses since he was young. In our family, I was the caboose and the only girl. With my grandmothers' stories and in the company of a handful of young friends who had horses, I was doomed to be horse-crazy. By the time I was nine, over the worried objections of my mother and the annoyed bemusement of my older brothers—all three of them deeply engaged with the second half of the twentieth century—there was a roan pony in our pasture. Several horses would follow as my dad indulged my interest and explored his own affection for a ranch culture he'd never actually had much chance to enjoy when he was living in it.

Dad's first order of business was the acquisition of the roan pony, Comet. Comet was rumored to be part Standardbred and part Welsh Pony. He'd sometimes pace, the classy smooth parallel gait of the Standardbred show horse. Dad had asked Rollie McKinley, who knew a lot about horses, to buy me a large pony, so Mr. McKinley brought the sturdy little horse all the way from a sale at Twin Falls, Idaho. He said

Comet had been raised by the Blackfoot Indians, a fact that interested me greatly and excused Comet's odd color. He was a red roan, a coat color of mixed sorrel and brown and white hairs, but he was also a pinto, with a normal brown eye on the roan side of his head and one blue eye on the white-patched other side. This was very much out of fashion at the time. Now you see pintos all over that country, and even pinto mules, but there were hardly any when I was a kid. None of my friends had one. The country around there was still getting over being a working West and was not yet aware of itself in flashy horses and cowboy poetry.

Comet didn't like men to ride him. He'd evidently had some bad experiences, and he had some health problems too. He'd gotten into too much grain and was slightly foundered, which left his front hooves in terrible shape. He came to us with gigantic rope burns cut into the back of his hocks from being kept on a rope hobble. On someone's advice, we rubbed bacon grease into these wounds every day until they closed. He was a gentle soul and allowed us to do this without fidgeting. We trimmed his hooves carefully for months until the spongy and sore red areas from the foundering worked themselves out. He was docile when I rode, but he was feisty with Dad and threw my brothers off his back at any chance they gave him. To tease me, they called him "Vomit." One day my middle brother Cliff was going to "ride the kinks out of him" for me, but as soon as he swung onto Comet's bare back, Comet took off down the hill toward the Snake River at a run. About eighty yards into the ride, Cliff didn't make the same sudden ninety-degree left turn as the agile little horse. Comet ended up at Mrs. Williams's house, and Cliff ended up in the ditch. After a while Cliff came back up the hill leading the horse. Giving me a leg up, he delivered a too-hard push that sent me clear over Comet's back and piled me up in the gravel on the other side. "Whaddya do *that* for?" I asked him.

Comet and I explored the sagebrush hills and ditch banks around Adrian. There was Brown Butte, where the big letter *A* is painted white on the rocks, and little Rattlesnake Butte in front of it. Rattlesnake is just a pile of basalt boulders you can climb on, not more than a few hundred feet high, but there was a cave in it we called the "Indian Cave," about which was told our local version of the story of how the guy from the university had found the Indian skeleton. I'd go to the cave with a playmate or two, however many it took to be brave. We'd gallop up bareback and throw our horses' reins around sagebrush and scramble up the moss-eaten rocks and then pull ourselves on our bellies back into the acrid, thick dust of the cave. If we had a flashlight along, we'd go clear to the end, where the passageway widened into a "cavern" probably ten feet wide and three feet high. We'd cough until the sour-tasting dust settled so we could look around for Indian bones.

My dad let me join the 4-H horse club, and in the late summer I'd take Comet to the county fair. All of us kids would make our horses shiny with soaps and oils and then lead them or ride them around to be judged by the officials and admired by our parents. All of us got ribbons, blue or red or white. Other kids' horses were bigger, with eyes both the same color, but Comet had become my friend. One morning I went down to the horse barns early, before anyone else was awake. I lay down in the straw next to Comet and went to sleep with my arms around his neck.

When I got older, I lobbied for a taller horse. This was a gigantic mistake, but of course I didn't know that. Riding with my friends, I'd begun to feel silly on a pony. Dad said he'd buy a horse for himself, a horse he could ride when he rode to the hills with me. He said I could ride that horse when he wasn't along. We went over by Meridian to a fellow who crossbred Appaloosas and Thoroughbreds, and Dad picked out a three-year-old, a light bay gelding with a vividly spotted rump blanket. Dad told me to take a ride around the corral, but as soon as I got in the saddle the young horse crow-hopped and knocked me off against the fence. Even before I got back on, I heard Dad tell the owner, "We'll take him."

I'm not sure what my father saw in that horse at that moment. I don't think anything was ever really interesting to him unless it was a challenge to be overcome. All I knew in those days about my father's interior life, if I supposed he had one, was that he always seemed to want me to do things he hadn't been able to do—graduate from high school, be the best athlete, know the right word or answer. And whenever I didn't, his disappointment in himself spread over me, too, all the more as I got older. I didn't know about my mom's family thinking that an uneducated, rootless young man might not be good enough for her. I don't know if they really thought that, only I know now that *he* thought he might not be good enough, and now he wanted some turning point back again, maybe a time before his folks split up, the time when he had family all over the green creeks and the sunburnt hills. He had these pictures of perfect horses, perfect achievements and prizes, perfect families, of how it would be if he had them. Sometimes he'd forget that he'd grown up and done well, that he already had what he wanted.

Dad never rode his new horse much, which had the unfortunate effect of putting me in charge. I was only saved from Comanche's sullen nature by his laziness. He threw his head and nearly knocked my teeth out. He reared, lay down in canals, and rolled on my saddle. Sometimes I couldn't control him; other times I couldn't wake him up. But the increase in altitude was exciting. Deciding one spring that I would be a barrel racer, I practiced every weekend—but not nearly enough—and then signed up to ride in one of the local rodeos. I remember my dad took me down to register for the race, and we were a few days too late, but Dad talked them into putting me on the list.

When we got to Nyssa for the rodeo, there'd been a big thunderstorm and the sky was still so dark that they turned on the stadium lights. Comanche got us around the first barrel, and we were on the way to the second when he noticed the lights. He stopped dead in his tracks, throwing me up over the saddle horn and against his neck. He stood and shook for endless seconds until I could get him headed out of the arena. My face was burning up with shame. I'd overheard one fellow by the gate tell his son, "Let's watch this little girl on the spotted horse ride," but they weren't there when I rode out of the arena. When I got back to the stands I couldn't look at anyone, especially my dad and my 4-H leader, Gladys, who'd come to the rodeo to cheer me on. My dad could barely talk to me after the rodeo, his mood as dark and stormy as the sky. A few days later, back at my practice barrels at Big Bend Park, I timed myself riding Comet and tied the race winner's time.

Dad, born in 1912, sometimes blamed my mom for dragging him toward convention and dull middle-class values, which was pretty ironic given that he never stopped pushing us kids toward our own dull middle-class values. He loved my mom a lot and told my brother David at one point that Mom had been the difference between success and failure in his life, but at times he didn't give her much credit. When he felt bad and had a couple of extra beers, he liked to use my mom as an example of the opposite of whatever quality he was trying to shore up in himself at the moment—intelligence, compassion, wisdom. At those Oly-pop-influenced moments, his descriptions of the lost Edens of who he might have been, minus my "mercenary" mother, were colorful and discouraging in an eastern Oregon, old Irish sort of way. If my dad was talking about a woman he respected, it was usually one of the grandmothers, those bastions of his lost youth, or often an outsider to us, like the mother of his old friend Clarence. In those descriptions, he pronounced *woman* with the letter *o* long and unfamiliar—the *woe* over the *man*, the word nearly too strange to say.

His occasional lascivious mentions of women made me uncomfortable too, sideways grinning comments about bosoms or butts made *sotto voce* to uncles or my now-adult brothers. When these were accidentally overheard by me, I was bothered and puzzled because I couldn't really determine how he felt about women—my purported future identity. There were no grandfathers in my world, all having exited by one curtain or another before I was on scene, and my mom's mom had died when I was very young. The surviving grandmothers on Dad's side were loved and admired by him, but were part of a mysterious female past to which I had no easy access.

I liked my dad a lot, and when I was a child I took his general appraisal of the world without question. Since his attitude toward women seemed ambivalent, I struggled with this problematic fate of growing up female. Horses were emblems of his treasured early boyhood and of my capable tomboy present. Horses were possible.

As we got horsier and Dad gave more thought to the fact that he could actually claim to have lived in a cowboy family, the old connections and people started popping up around us. Gladys, the leader of the 4-H horse club, was someone Dad had known since his childhood. Although Dad hadn't given Gladys much thought for forty years, he began to speak about her like she'd been one of his close friends, and they both seemed to enjoy suddenly having a cohort from the long ago. When we went over to her place, Gladys said, "Your dad is a pal of mine," and my dad said, "Gladys is a good old girl." I was intrigued by this cross-gender camaraderie—that a grown woman, an old woman, would have been a pal of my father's. It contradicted what I knew about him. She fascinated me because she seemed to have devised a way to scoot around being female and get to the real stuff, which was horses.

From day one, Gladys was on my side. At the ill-fated barrel-racing event, Gladys acted like I hadn't made a fool of myself in front of half of Malheur County. The day after the rodeo, she got her horse trailer and took me and the horses out to her ranchland above Succor Creek. She didn't really have much to do out there, but we took care of a few of her horseback tasks—wonderful fun for me.

That day would be the sum total of my career as a working cowboy as we chased Gladys's cows away from where they had collected themselves around little potholes of trampled water and up to where there was grass left for them to eat. We checked the fences, making sure none of Pete Bishop's white Charolais cattle could get in and mix with Gladys's Black Angus, causing ugly mottled-gray offspring. Pete was even older than Gladys and shared her early-century cowboy background, but he was an enemy as far as the fence line was concerned. She complained about him, how picky he was about his "precious white cows."

After that pleasant work, which required no dismounting, we rode around the gullies admiring her now-placid cows and then made our way up onto the high basalt ridges where we could look over at the Owyhee Canyon and down on the water backed up by the Owyhee Dam. The water was a bright blue, in contrast to the yellow and red canyon that held it. I'd been down there fishing with my dad, and I knew the water was a milky green and that the blues were just an illusion of distance and sky.

Gladys showed me a place where a hillside had newly slipped down, a tear in the sagebrush fabric about a hundred yards long, fifteen or twenty feet deep. It was strange to learn that the ripped earth in ribboned layers of browns and reds was still moving, that the faces of ancient basalt and shales were whitecaps in a sea of stone. I have a picture of Gladys from that day, above the torn ground. She is turned sideways on her big mare Tahoe, made aware of herself as both myth and flesh by the picture taking. She is wearing her red shirt, only one shade brighter than the deep-red horse. She took a picture of me, too, a skinny kid in a stocking cap and an old green cowboy shirt with the sleeves torn off. I probably thought I could look like Gladys if I did that, or that having brown arms meant I deserved to be there.

Let me draw you a picture of Gladys when she was in my world. She was a tall woman for her generation, maybe five foot six. Not skinny or fat, she had a big stomach. It was not a beer belly, because she never touched alcohol, but a hay-bale-bucking belly, a horse-breaking strong belly. It was a bit old and folded up when I knew her, like a pile of towels.

She wore jeans—Wranglers, not the "Can't Bust 'Em" Levi's that were popular in the 1960s and which most real working people found too tight-legged. She used a thick leather belt with no tooling, no name on the back of it. She had a variety of plaid short-sleeved cotton cowboy shirts, but in the hot weather she usually wore just a turquoise tank top. You could see all of her large arms, sun-browned, darker than walnuts. Every hair on her head was either black or white, a kinky blue-roan bush of hair that she cut off straight all the way around, a couple of inches above her shoulders. She parted her hair not quite in the middle and held it back with a barrette on the thick side. In the truck or outside she always wore a hat, not a cowboy hat exactly but a felt hat with a broad flat brim. It was a milk-chocolate-colored hat with the sides of the brim rolled up from years of being grabbed off the wall and pulled down on her head without thought as to how it looked. It had a narrow leather strap for a hat band and was sweat-stained around the band, but other than that it was a noticeably clean hat for a rancher.

Gladys would never have been dirty for effect, but only because she was doing dirty work and couldn't clean up. Even out at camp in the trailer—which was not the pre-fabricated affair suggested by the term *trailer* but one of the old half-domed wooden boxes you used to see at sheep and cow camps all over that country—there was a metal basin and a jug of water for washing up. The inside smelled of bacon grease and coffee and unpainted wood and the wool blankets on the bunks, a good old smell. In the trailer, Gladys always kept a clean shirt to wear when she drove back to town. She wore boots, but not so high-heeled and not so pointy-toed as the cowboy boots you see in the stores now. Gladys's wire-rimmed glasses sat on high cheekbones in a wide face, and her black eyes darted around behind them, looking right at you, looking at everything far and near, and fitting it all into a sturdily fenced version of the world.

One strata deeper than the corn and sugar beet farmers were the old ranch people like Gladys and Pug, the Bishops and Skinners, the Camerons and Timmermans. These were the grandparents of the kids I went to school with. Nearly subterranean now, people of ancient trucks and auctions, owners of the old horses standing swaybacked in small fields, white spots bright on brown withers where the old saddles had rubbed. Mom's and Dad's parents and grandparents were of those same people, which miraculously made them my people too: Parkses and Looneys and Botts and Hendersons. They had all been part of this older country, friends and enemies of the Bannocks, miners, and ranchers. Now, though, we were band boosters, owners of a stereo and a Naugahyde couch. Vietnam was still happening, and Woodstock hadn't happened yet. I wasn't going to be a girl teenager for a couple of years, and Mom and Dad still had the grocery store, though they were getting tired and looking for a way out.

Dad and I were just trying to finish off my childhood and put off the next big changes. I think now that what Dad was getting out of palling around with Gladys was that he thought she'd let him return to the parts of the past he'd admired and missed out on and had therefore reinvented. He wanted to reclaim the little green valleys with broken gray homesteads in them, rebuild the broken corrals.

For Dad, hills and horses were a lump in his throat he couldn't get over, so the way he talked about the old places and people was as if they were characters in medieval plays, standing for qualities of mind and heart, and as if the eastern Oregon hills were some great healing theater. He could have been a playwright, my father, and he'd have made the long ago turn out right. Standing out in the sun wearing one of the gray cowboy hats he bought when we started having horses again, looking down at the ground with his thumbs tucked into his belt, I could feel the deep contradictions grinding in him like the plates that split the earth and pushed up the hills. Like all good playwrights, he never finished getting out what he wanted to say. He'd see the remains of a rock corral or a broken cabin in some little gully and the tears would come down his cheeks. "You know what I mean, Mim," he'd say.

Well, I did and I didn't. The trails and springs had belonged to people he'd known before he got yanked out of childhood with his mom and then put back into the country with his Grandmother Parks. He had farmed for a few difficult years with his dad, where a cow kicked his leg and broke it, killing his baseball dreams. Now he felt like he should remember how to get to places that didn't even exist anymore. He hated that the old ranches were gone, and he loved to find a ruined cabin poking out of the sagebrush in the bottom of a gully. Until he was very old, he'd drive to the Owyhee Dam the back way, over Cherry Creek Road (when was there ever a cherry tree in that country?) that had mostly washed off the side of the steep hill. I'd be so scared he was going to roll the Jeep that I'd get out and walk, which made him mad.

There was always some challenge or contest he had with himself, and none of us ever knew how far he was going to take it.

From when I was small, I knew the best gift I could offer my father was to remember places in the hills, some of which I'd never been to, and say their names: Lone Willow Spring, the Rock Corral, North Fork of the Malheur. When I run my mind over the texture of those place names, I can feel my father's deep regard for them. I learned that from him: to feel the buried stories beneath me wherever I go.

Apparently, Gladys had no such complications. She knew everybody would come out to go riding in the hills, out the old trails to Three-Fingered Jack, Rimrock, Round Top, Lone Willow Spring, and she knew how to get there. She knew where to cross the creek on a horse, to find a pretty view or a little seep of sweet water. She knew how to get to the bleached bones of a ranch community that was long gone, killed when the highway looped around it or the price of cows went down or the water from the dam came up over the top of it. She knew where there was a willow tree tall enough and shady enough to eat a sandwich under without even having to get off your horse. Gladys was on a first-name basis with all the geography of my parents' past, like the trails in and out of the pocked and golden spires of Leslie Gulch, trails that used to run up and down the Owyhee River to ranches and old towns before the dam got built in the 1930s.

It surprised me whenever I ran into the fact that my parents' distant past stories were Gladys's present tense. My mother and my aunt were the last schoolteachers in tiny Owyhee ranch communities Watson and Hot Springs before the water came up in 1934, covering the house of the moonshiner with his same load of whiskey-hiding grain he hauled to Homedale and back up the canyon again. The water covered the house where my mom boarded, where the wife thought my pretty eighteen-year-old mom was after her ugly husband. Mom didn't have any door to her room in the attic of their house. At the Watson schoolhouse in 1933, one of the Fisher kids told her the world wasn't round 'cause his daddy said it wasn't. Mom cut sagebrush to heat the school, and no one helped her until the second year because they were just waiting for her to give up. But she never did give up until the water came up and they all had to leave—ranchers, moonshiner, teacher and kids, and all. I had these strong secondhand memories that came from my mother's stories, all under thirty or so feet of water by the time I heard them, greenish milky water you can't look down into. Standing on the Owyhee lakeshore, though, you can look up at the same red-rock rims that have always been there. You can climb up there on foot, but you have to watch for snakes. Snakes are always present tense.

Gladys had always had cows running out on the Owyhee and always would have cows as long as she lived, so there wasn't any past tense to it. I found that I liked to go with Gladys, instead of my dad, to the places my dad knew, because she was a cheerful encyclopedia of ways to "make a day of it," getting from some old stone corral to a rim-rock where you could sit and eat a candy bar and still get back to the truck and load the horses before dark. If she felt the names draining out of the country, it didn't make her sad.

She never saw things in terms of the good old days. In the late 1960s she got a pre-fab trailer house and electricity and an indoor toilet, but those things didn't make any difference to her. That new stuff was just what there was to replace the old stuff when it wore out. She never saw anything in terms of progress; it was only just whatever she wanted to do next. I can't remember her ever telling me that electric lights were better or that it was nice to have a flush toilet or a new truck. What happened inside a house didn't concern her much, and trucks were for getting horses from one trailhead to another, or to and from the auction house. She might have considered this last item to be a modern advantage.

Gladys didn't see any contradiction between horses and jet airplanes, though she knew other people did. She just liked horses. She knew about and enjoyed her popularity as anomaly and western relic without really considering herself unusual, making a pretty clean division between what other people thought of her and what she knew about herself. There were cruel stories about her, like the rumor that she'd had her breasts cut off so they wouldn't bounce when she rode a horse.

When word got around the school that I was friends with Gladys, my schoolmates immediately told me those mean stories. I don't know if she would have been puzzled or would have laughed. One or the other I think; she was good at disregarding petty attitudes. This was an ability I fervently aspired to. Discovering Gladys was to deny expectation and fate. It was like finding out, in a canoe, that you got control by keeping yourself slower or faster than the current, as opposed to matching the speed of the water and being carried along helplessly on other people's opinions, pouring over the rocks and whirling in the pools.

I didn't just want to know what Gladys knew; I wanted to be like her, to take a form in present time like she seemed to be able to do. As I snuck up on puberty, I must have been curious why my father was not standing in front of me to supervise my advance in this direction. Finding Gladys was like discovering a mysterious tunnel in my own backyard, and I set out to explore how this woman might stretch the term *woman* out for me, make it something a girl could crawl into.

I liked almost everything Gladys said, and she said a lot. People said that after she died, Pug learned how to talk. That may be true, because I don't remember the sound of his voice. He was busted up from ranching, and he hobbled around the chores at the home place. His face was bent into a smile, wrinkled and handsome from being outside all his life—the way you want to look when you get old. Gladys always said there was only one good man in the world, and that was Pug. They'd had no children, so it was just them and the horses and dogs. After Gladys died, Pug married again, which surprised everybody who knew him. We just thought the dogs and Pug would go into the grave with her like the attendants of a Chinese emperor.

Riding in the truck with Gladys made me feel that we could do anything. "Anything" was comprised of going to the hills on horses or to the auction in her old truck, but Gladys treated me like an old friend, not the daughter of an old friend.

Gladys went to the livestock auction in Caldwell every Sunday in the turquoise Chevy pickup, a fifty-something, with a metal rack around the bed for hauling livestock. Or it was a Ford. I can tell you it smelled like sunburnt rubber and gasoline when you crawled into the cab. I can see the Mexican blanket she kept on the bench seat for "the boys," her little dogs. The black-and-white dog was some sort of boxer crossed with some kind of cow dog. Maybe his name was Tippy. The other dog was one of those noisy little scrub brushes that couldn't do much but yap and curl up wherever you would have liked to sit. Gladys said she preferred them to most people, but there was room enough on the seat for me too.

"Let's you and me go look at those horses," she'd say on the phone, and pretty soon she'd pop in our door with her hat on, with some remarks of friendliness but little content for my parents, saving the real stuff for me, and we'd hurry out to her truck and scoot the dogs back into the middle of the seat: "C'mon now, little boys, let's let Mary get in." On the way to Caldwell, she'd tell me about what she was doing with the cows, or what Pug thought about some pasture project. Often we talked about which horse she wanted to trade in for another.

We sometimes took a horse with us to the sale, and we often brought one home. Because of this practice of Gladys's, she and Pug were known to be "horse poor," with a pasture full of varying horse shapes nibbling grass and twitching off flies. We'd try to get to the sale early so we could walk around out back in the corrals, climbing up on fences to look at the sale animals and to talk with all the people Gladys knew, which was everybody. We'd feel the legs of horses and look at their teeth, then go up and sit in the sale arena, where Gladys would chatter and consult with me about every horse that came through the ring, though she knew how little I knew. "Look at that ankle. That horse is a little down in that ankle, isn't he? Sometimes you can't tell till you get 'em walkin'. I looked at him, but we don't want him." She'd say *we*, like that.

The auction hall was a little amphitheater with plywood terraces for seats, smooth with many years' applications of thick white enamel. A sweet, vinegary smell rose from the dry sawdust and old manure on the floor where the animals came through below us. The seat area bent around and above this little arena with a gate at either side. On the last Sunday of every month, a steady stream of Malheur and Canyon County livestock (one county was in Oregon and one was in Idaho, but that was only a paperwork detail) would pour in through one gate, be prodded around the ring to the auctioneer's popcorn syllables, and head out the other. We'd wait until all the pigs and sheep and even cows had gone through before we went in to the hall to sit down. Gladys seldom bought cows, so she wasn't much interested in the cow transactions unless she was selling.

Gladys was a smart bidder, too, a nodder, raising her hand only when the auctioneer wasn't paying attention. She'd talk to the other bidders under her breath to me, "Now, you don't want that horse. What would a big fat man like you want with a little mare like that?" It bothered me when she talked that way, or when she'd size up some man who looked at us, at me. She'd say, "I wouldn't want something like *that* hanging around, would you?" With these comments, she alluded to the sexual and physical threat of the male-heavy world around us, as if she was accepting other people's view of herself, a broken bone that's gotten stronger than the bone around it, or a scar. But I didn't want her strength to be a response to injury. I wanted Gladys to be a regular thing, an option that would *solve* the limitations I felt. I thought then that self-respect was like being saved—if you got it one time you were in forever. I hated those indications that Gladys, even with the truck and the horses and the ranch and the talk, still wasn't powerful enough.

Sometimes she was outbid, and she always gave up if the bid went a dollar more than she had decided the horse was worth. She'd give up the bidding without much comment, and I'd feel disappointed that we weren't going to have the excitement of that new horse. Money to Gladys was purely utilitarian, and she never talked about it—the lack of it or how much other people had. I never saw her spend a single non-horse penny she didn't need to spend, though we always had a hamburger in the auction house café before we went home, with or without a horse.

She had a weakness for Appaloosa horses. At one sale we bought a little mare that was a speckled apricot color, some combination of Appaloosa, POA (Pony of America—a pony version of an Appaloosa), and grade stock. The mare tried to bite us while we were looking at her, but she had been bred to an Appaloosa stud and Gladys wanted to see what came out.

Gladys named her Chippy, and I remember the naming conversation because it played into my identity crisis about which Gladys had not a clue. She was an enthusiastic mentor in all things, including what could embarrass me, in the way that you can become embarrassed about things you've never thought of as embarrassing until someone else dances around a topic or uses a euphemism. *Chippy* was one. At some point in history the word referred to prostitutes who accepted company coupons earned on the job by miners or loggers in return for sex, but it was a word from my grandparents' generation. When Gladys first used it in a description of someone, I'd never heard it before: "She's a little bit chippy," for promiscuous. Gladys wouldn't tell me straight out what the word meant, except that it was just for "some women," and that made me squirm because I was always trying to figure out what kind of a woman I was going to be. She got tremendous fun out of naming the Appaloosa mare Chippy because the mare was with foal. Then she would laugh whenever she said the mare's name, "My Chippy is a little chippy." Her voice and her laugh were a high music, sometimes insistent as an electric drill.

Then there was the term *pee pee*. Gladys had useful advice for a girl who had to pee when she was out driving cows with a bunch of men. "You just hang back a little," Gladys told me, "then you find a sagebrush to pee pee behind. If a man's any kind of gentleman, he knows not to look back at you." I had been worried about this on trail rides and felt comforted by the advice, but I did wish she'd limit herself to one syllable.

Like those squirmy terms, most of Gladys's observations on the world outside Pug and ranching were a little after the fact. She had already sorted out what mattered to her in the society and dismissed the rest as insignificant or trouble to be avoided, like a buzzing snake. She tried, for my sake, to be observant about what was going on so that she could be a friend and warn me. She'd say, "Men want you to drink wine, and then they think they can do whatever they want with us girls. But we'll show them, won't we?" And I'd say, "You bet," though I was a bit intrigued at that time by the thought that drinking wine might turn me into something anyone would want.

Gladys and Pug lived less than a mile away from old Big Bend Park so it was easy for Gladys to hop on a horse and ride over to preside at the meetings and practices of the horse club. We'd taken over the old park because it was empty and it was there. Its ownership was so old and uncertain that none of the local farmers had cleared it for pasture or potatoes. A grove of huge elms stood at one end and at the other end was an open area where we had the barrels for racing.

There had been a dance hall at the park in the 1930s, and my mother met my father there at a dance. But the hall had fallen down years before, and the park was all gone to weeds and fallen branches. The park held a few older family stories I knew about. My own experiences there, of untangling brush piles and clearing space for horse games, would cause a strange little dust devil of an argument with my mother years later. After my father died I was talking to her about the park, which had become a potato field at last. Mom told me I could not have possibly known where the park had been, so we got in the car and I took her there. Her odd anger at me changed to puzzlement: "How did you know where it was?" She had known the place for sixty years, the dances and the giant elms that had guarded the grassy space where Big Bend school had stood. I remember my uncle Gaynor, my father's older brother, describing those long-ago days when Mom and my aunt Anna had come down from the Owyhee and taught at Big Bend together, in 1935 and 1936. He said the sisters were so beautiful with their bobbed hair and dark eyes: "Those Henderson girls. You should have seen them."

Mom could tell you the names of the children in that Big Bend school, and she kept track of them later, too: who they married, where they lived. She taught their grandchildren when she went back to teaching second grade in Adrian many years later. As far as she was concerned, by then, the park belonged to *her* past, not mine. My few summers there with Gladys had slipped through the sieve of her memory; I was my very own ghost.

With Gladys, we kids had wanted to clean up the park, maybe even build a club house. But that never got done. For one thing, we didn't have the right kind of people. The kids in the club didn't have Jaycee or Lion's Club types of parents. Their parents had to work too hard or they drank too much. Some were "jack" Mormons, too rowdy and independent for the church so that no one from their wards ever came to help them. Instead of having horses because they had money to burn and it was fashionable, they had horses leftover from when horses were important—which is an indication of how lazy they were about moving forward with the world. They weren't up to clearing the limbs and old boards in the park on Sundays. "Not exactly a ball of fire," was how my mother described one of the dads.

In fact, the kids in the horse club were people I wouldn't have been with if it weren't for the horses. They were invisible at school, didn't get good grades, and didn't hang around for sports. If they weren't mousy and quiet, they were in trouble. But to Gladys, any kid or horse who showed up was a good possibility. She never blinked an eye at what her western renaissance was digging up, and I never heard her complain that fixing up the park was a pipe dream.

Personally, Gladys had plenty of dreams, and she generously gave me a part in them. She wanted to ride the Pacific Crest Trail, from California up through Washington, on an organized ride with a club that only allowed Appaloosa horses. Since I had Comanche, Gladys intended that she and I would do the ride together, a plan that seemed wild and beyond hope to me, like being an astronaut. But Gladys was serious, and I watched with fascination someone who could methodically take all the steps to achieve something she wanted to do.

There was a kind of retro movement for ranch people starting up when I knew Gladys. The Oregon Trail Grange Hall hadn't been used much for decades, but when the 4-H horse club started up with Gladys as the leader, we put on skits and parties there. The hall had an oak plank floor, soaked with the sharp, sweet smell of ancient cookies and coffee. I went to dances there, once with a boy from Nyssa who rode in the rodeos. I mostly danced with his dad, a Mormon bishop with a belly so big I had to dance a couple of feet away from him. After that, the son kept inviting me to go to church, but I didn't want to go, so the dance invitations stopped. I was a full-blown teenager by this time and more likely to slow dance in a dark school auditorium to "Crimson and Clover," over and over. It would take many years to realize I'd loved the "Little Foot Waltz," an old fiddle tune.

The normal way the story goes at this point is that the old friend gets gray and drops out of the picture while the young person becomes an adult and launches out into the brave new world on her own, leaving the creaky old friend behind. But what happened was more wonderful. Gladys, at the age of sixty-something, had gotten notoriety for being a great 4-H horse club leader, and several of the still-agile ranch grandparents woke up from their naps. Gladys found even more old horse pals, mostly women, who were just as sturdy and determined as she was to enjoy the hills. They became the Oregon Trail Grange Hall Riders and rode all over the Owyhees together. And Gladys had Tahoe, her soul mate.

Gladys hadn't ever been interested in the big-butted quarter horses with their short ears and even tempers. At all those auctions she was looking for something else, something around the scrap heap of expectations about mixed-breed horses—called grade horses—that might turn out to be good. Long before I met her, Gladys had found her Tahoe, an exceptionally tall mare with a deep, wide chest. Tahoe was a blood-red bay whose coat darkened into long brown legs, the hooves black and hard as flint. Tahoe wasn't a friendly animal; she was more likely to strike at you with a front foot than to nuzzle you for a rub. By this a few will know her for a mare. She had big ears for a horse, ears that moved every which way, taking things in. Her owners hadn't been able to train her, and because she was no breed in particular she

wasn't valuable as a brood mare. She ended up at the sale when she was
about three years old, and that is where Gladys picked her up. I always
stayed out of reach of Tahoe's teeth and her front legs, but she liked
Gladys, and Gladys could do anything with her.

Gladys had a way to get a horse to walk, really walk, that nobody
else could follow. Gladys hated it when a horse would trot with her. "I
hate that jigging," she'd say, then she'd pull the horse down to a walk
but just keep agitating or clucking her tongue a little bit—just loud
enough for the horse to hear—and in a few days that horse would shift
into a fast walk whenever Gladys wanted him to. She even taught Comanche to walk like that, though I could rarely get him to do it.

Walking races were just becoming popular when I was in high
school. Tahoe and Gladys won every race they entered around our
country, usually held out at Zerbel's runway, and they did it for years.
It got more difficult to squeeze in a Saturday or Sunday with Gladys.
The races would be written up in the Nyssa paper, the *Gate City Journal*, and Dad would have the article cut out and on the kitchen table
when I came home on break from college. Gladys got her long fifteen
minutes of glory in a lesser known region of Malheur County.

I loved Gladys and I loved horses, but I was getting distracted by the
rest of my life, and sometimes it was scary to be on a horse. There were
dangerous lightning storms and flash floods in the desert. My dad and
I were famous in our family for liking to watch thunderstorms, sitting
together in the doorsill at the back room of the store. No words passed
between us in those times, just the love of wild light and plentiful disorder. But it was one thing to watch the sky from the back door of the
store with my dad and another to pick my way through boulders, alone
on a horse in the bottom of a funnel of clay and sandstone while the
sky was black and splitting overhead.

One day when it stormed, I was on a ride with Gladys and the kids
and parents from the 4-H club. A summer storm came up out of the
heat in the afternoon, and we knew we'd be caught in it. I expected
Gladys to say something about riding up out of the flash-flood-inviting
gully, but she just said, "Looks like we are going to get wet," then kept

on chattering to the parents. It got yellow out and started to hail, not the huge kind that knocks down the grain but on its way to that kind of destruction.

My mom would say of thunderstorms that thunder means "the devil is beating his wife." Many years later I was listening to audio tapes of a Koyukon Athabaskan woman in Alaska, and she startled me by using nearly the same expression about thunder: "The devil is mad at his wife." Words get around, or storms bring them. In eastern Oregon, you knew you were about to be in a storm when the sky would glint yellowish gray and the filmy veils of virga would start to descend. The rough ground, the hills, showed the violence of these storms in washed-out gullies and boulders planted in the trail and creek bottoms. There was nothing for the soil to hang onto when the water came down, nothing between the sagebrush and greasewood clumps but the barest, most fragile latticework of grasses and wildflowers. Running water cut like acid through the hills, cutting all the way down to the farms and into the cultivated fields of corn and alfalfa, busting through the big irrigation canals, driving the farmers and the ditch riders crazy.

That day I thought we were going to get it. Everything around us began to look bruised, booming and flashing, and after the hail a hard, cold rain came down. The horses couldn't stand the electricity in the air, and we kids couldn't either, so we let them run up a gully in the rain, over rocks and holes, not completely out of control but barely hanging on to it. We let the horses run until they were breathing in heaves, a stupid thing for us to do. We were breathing like that, too, soaked and glowing with heat. Gladys didn't say a word to us when she rode up, which meant she was truly angry.

Despite what you see in the movies, horses can't run all the time. Dad and Gladys would both say this and I paid attention, mostly. A fast walk was how we rode anywhere, and if we wanted to race the horses we had to be out of sight of the adults. One of the few times we did that, I ended up in a barbed wire fence, with trouble explaining the holes in my arm when I got home. Another time I knocked Rich Oca-mica clear off his horse when we were chasing a coyote and both horses decided to meet on the same trail. There was always this real barbed wire and sharp rock world out there, beyond the cautions of my father, and whenever I came up against it I was surprised.

And there were the snakes. Gladys said she and Pug had killed thirty-five rattlesnakes a day when they ran their first cows out on the Owyhee. I'd never seen even one rattlesnake up close, except the one my brothers caught in the yard and put in a big jar in the back room of the store. My dad hated rattlesnakes, and "Watch for snakes" was a litany I'd absorbed from him.

I was probably a sophomore in high school when some other kids and I took hot dogs and cans of pop and stayed in the hills with our horses one night until the moon and the rattlesnakes were both out. On the way home, I came close to being thrown twice when snakes buzzed under Comanche and made him buck. The parents were frantic with worry and met us at midnight with trucks and cars where the paved road ended under the canal by Brown Butte. We all got a solid tongue lashing, especially me from Dad. Afterward I never admitted how scared I'd been on that ride because anytime it came up Dad immediately started in with how stupid I was—"What a knucklehead." He was as hard to agree with as he was to have an argument with.

Later on that summer, Gladys took me on a ride with the Oregon Trail Club, her cronies. I expected this to be a tame affair with a bunch of old-timers telling stories, leaning over their saddle horns, and letting the horses eat grass down along the creeks. But that isn't what we did. We rode up in the Owyhee Breaks on the far side of the reservoir, and those old codgers took their horses down the steep faces of bluffs a thousand feet above the dam, looking right down on the spillway. The Owyhee Dam was the highest in the world when it was built, and I could scare myself standing on my own two feet looking down at it just from the top of the dam itself. So I got off Comanche halfway down the hill and led him down the rest of the way. Like the other horses, he was scooting on his butt and working his hind legs on the pea gravel slope. It was hard to hold onto the reins and stay out of his way. All the other riders were still in their saddles, enjoying the view and their confidence in sure-footed mounts. Dad wasn't with us, but I know he would have been as terrified as I was.

My friendship with Gladys never wore out, but the shine wore off it for my mom and dad. Gladys was too loud and "mannish" for my mom, and Dad had found out he couldn't really talk to Gladys in the flesh, despite his being proud of having known her for so long and approving of her as a non-woman woman. He didn't agree with anything she said, but he couldn't get a word in edgewise to say so. They'd be in the same room or leaning on the same fence, and she wouldn't stop talking long enough for him to get a run at the subject. If she did let him talk, she'd complain to me later, "He just wanted to talk about those old things."

Gladys was still trying to guide me on the right path in life. We talked about the Pacific Crest ride off and on, but I was getting booked up. I'd gone backpacking with a church group, and I brought home some new enthusiasms to share: backpacking and becoming a preacher. These ideas raised winds of violent objection from her. People said Gladys wouldn't walk to the outhouse if she could catch a horse, which wasn't true, literally, because the outhouse was closer than the corral. But she didn't understand that there could be any benefit in walking when there were horses in the world, or any benefit in preaching when people were just what they were going to be forever no matter what. She said, "You wanna spend your whole life pretending you're better than everybody else and gettin' the rest of 'em to pretend they're better than everybody too?"

Dad went on a few rides with us, but his back hurt him, and he didn't feel as at home on a horse as he thought he should feel. Working at Big Bend Park drove him crazy because it made him hurt and because we weren't doing it right. He wasn't much fun to have along on the rides either. He was more cautious than Gladys and would ride around a hill while she'd walk Tahoe right up its face. He was always telling me how to hold the reins and how to sit in the saddle, though by that time I thought I had spent as much time on a horse as he had when he was a kid. I'd enjoyed coming out with Gladys as an escape from this critical attention, so it grated on me.

I still loved driving out in the Owyhees with my dad. He'd stop the red-and-white Willies Jeep halfway down into a gulch and turn it off so we could look at a little grove of locust trees someone had planted to grow fence posts a hundred years ago when there was a ranch there, or a line of cottonwoods along a creek. "Isn't that pretty, Mim?" he'd say. One time we saw a mountain lion jump from one rim to another; another time I caught a little trout in a creek and felt his pride on me like sunshine. There was always a six-pack of Olympia or Budweiser beer, and a half-full can rode on his knee or in the open window at the end of his sun-freckled arm, as we swayed up and down the rutted two-track trails. But then he'd throw the empty can out the window. One time I got out of the moving truck, teenage Puritan, and fetched the beer can and threw it in the bed of the Jeep with him screaming at me the whole way, "Goddamit, I said leave it there!" That was a quiet ride home.

All the extra strength Dad could muster was spent on an acreage we were trying to fix up in Big Bend, a few miles away from the park, where he thought he and Mom would retire after the store, raise a couple of calves every year. Dad and my brother David dug holes and built a corral and stock chute. I'd hold boards while Dad scratched pencil marks then scratched them out and measured again, swearing "Hell's bells," his favorite profanity. He was not happy with how the ground went up and down and how it made his fence look. He was a bugger to work for, so I kept my ear phone in and my little transistor radio tuned to the rock-and-roll station.

With all the hats and horses going on, Dad had begun to wear cowboy boots again. He'd always had a pair of nice ones in the closet, and by the last years of his life he wore them all the time. When he and Mom gave up on their retirement ideas for the Big Bend acreage and moved down the hill to the little house her parents had owned, he complained about cold feet in the winter. He couldn't work out in the shop in the winter because of his feet. By then I'd lived in Montana and learned that you could have warm feet if you changed your footgear. So I came home with a big pair of shoepacs and liners for him and advised against the cowboy boots. He thanked me and said the new 'pacs were just the thing he needed. He kept them on the porch for the next seven years, spider habitat. The only time he ever wore them was the first ten minutes after he opened the box, just to please me. The cowboy boots never left his feet unless he was sleeping, and one of the last things we did together, a week before he died, was to pick up his rebuilt cowboy boots at the shoemaker's shop in Vale.

Gladys had given me an opening into the ranch world I admired and the unfairly subsumed tradition of tough women who have always inhabited it. I continued to pry it open with high school trips to my teacher Carol Shultz's ranch. Shultz was born into a western Idaho ranch family and became the primary operator of her father Harold's land and Forest Service grazing leases. She and partner Bev Martin packed salt for the Payette Valley Cattle Association with horses and mules for nine mildly famous years and then ran cows on the high mountain meadows for decades more, protecting the stream environments and the grazing lands. The anti-government ranch rebels beating on their chests these days could have learned civility from Carol and Bev's professional relationships with both the U.S. Forest Service and the rancher organizations. With other girls from our high school, I made trips to Carol's ranches and became a fence post and barbed wire packer as well as a huge fan of elk steaks. Later on I sought out tough women like Ma Hill from Trout Creek, Montana, who was notoriously as familiar with a D-8 road-building Cat as with her string of outfitter horses. These women had apparently always been in the world, without raising much dust about whether they had families or just partners, whether they were old maids or idiosyncratic loners. They were characters in a western landscape filled with unusual and admirable people. Grandma Mona told me that she had known a quiet and capable cowboy named Little Joe Monaghan when she was growing up in Jordan Valley, Oregon, before 1900. When Joe died, people found out he was a woman. This was no big deal to Mona, who told me she thought it was a pretty good trick.

Thanks to people like Gladys and Carol and my grandmothers, I learned there were all kinds of ways to be female, though it also became clear that the trails were a labyrinth. Gladys gave me a taste for self-motivated people who did what they liked and hadn't given a great deal of thought toward what was considered regular. In a cable-TV culture of Dallas Cowboy cheerleaders and Botox, that attitude has been a friend.

As he felt his control over me diminish, Dad pulled harder and I scrambled away from him, leaving behind obligations I see now as belonging to me, though his presence was all around them. Dad told me one day that he was going to let the neighbors take care of Comet. Their little girl, Annie, would ride him. Another day, he told me that he'd sold Comanche to Gladys. He'd tell me these things, how Gladys was winning races, how she said to tell me hello, and her passed-on greeting became an accusation about my neglect. But I couldn't sort out who I was neglecting. Then one day he told me, "Annie really loves Comet. You kind of lost interest, didn't you?" When Comet died, Annie was home from college. While Comet was dying, she spent the whole night in the barn with him, with her arms around his neck. When Dad told me that, I was glad to allow it a painful pull on my heart. I am very much like my father, and I never lose interest in anything, just save it in some subterranean place and go on.

Gladys would have thought my sensation of loss and separation was nonsense if I had tried to explain it to her. What I'd guess now is that Dad and I were wrangling over the hills and who they belonged to, as if it could only be one of us. We never did figure it out—where the one of us stopped and the other began. I still don't know, but now I'd just like to lay all these things out, watch the storms come and blow them all around. Just sitting beside each other in that doorway would be all we need.

I didn't spend much time with Gladys during my high school and college years. By the time I went off to college, Gladys had lots of friends I didn't know anymore—from the races, from all the auctions I missed. She and Pug slowly drew down their population of black cows, giving her more time for walking races with Tahoe. Often I wouldn't even see Gladys when I came home, but my sense of her life was that she was plenty busy without me. The auction house was in the same town where I was going to college, but it might as well have been on the other side of the moon.

Gladys died of a heart attack on a summer morning. One minute she was standing by her truck, talking to the guy from the hardware store, and the next minute she was dead is how the story was told. Hers was a consistent and enviable performance on earth it seems to me, but then we see most people from the outside—see the gullies but not the storms that made them. It's usually only between parents and children that the troubles are palpable, that the separateness of our bodies and our will to remake ourselves can't quite pull the bone and blood of our shared histories apart.

I'd never visited either of the horses after they weren't mine any more, but one time I went up on the State Line Road where I could look down on Gladys and Pug's place. I could see Comanche out in the field, swishing his long Thoroughbred tail. Later, when I saw Gladys in town, I asked her about him and she said, "Well, he's a little lazy."

She said she thought about taking him to the sale, but she never did. She kept him around their place for years. She might have been doing that for me or for Dad, but I doubt that very much. She just liked him because he was pretty with that bright white blanket and black spots, and because she could get him to pay attention.

Mincemeat

Decide to allow meat to be dessert, but then refuse to eat your own piece after the holiday dinner that features it. The next morning, eat it for breakfast: take the thick slice and warm it in the cookstove oven until it is crisp. Don't let it anywhere near the microwave or the crust will turn to mush.

To make mincemeat, start with the neck of something wild: venison, elk, caribou, or moose. The neck is stringy and boney, but flavor lives between the muscle and the bone, which makes the neck a place of opportunity. Put the neck in salted water in a big pot and boil it for several hours until the meat comes loose. Take the bones out and discard them. Separate the meat from the broth, keeping both. Let cool. Run the stringy cooked meat through a grinder with twice as many apples as you have meat—some tasty tart kind—and a third as much suet as you have meat. Use a whole orange or lemon for every five pounds or so of meat. Suet is not just fat but kidney fat from inside the animal. Few butchers' counters think that you know this. If you didn't save the suet when you butchered, then get fresh real beef suet from a butcher shop. Argue with them if you need to.

Now you are ready to cook the mincemeat, probably in the same large stock pot where you cooked the neck. For every 5 pounds of meat you originally got from the neck, you will need 1 ½ pints of apple cider vinegar; 1 cup of broth from cooking; 1 cup of molasses; 2 cups of sugar; ½ cup of butter; 1 tablespoon each of cinnamon, cloves, and nutmeg; ½ tablespoon of mace; and 2 cups of raisins. Combine ground meat-apple-suet mixture with all the other ingredients and start cooking and tasting. The mixture should have a very sweet and sour character.

If you have an Aunt Anna, this is where you throw the recipe away and stop measuring. She and you will keep tasting the mincemeat and move it toward your own ideas of delicious: adding sugar, vinegar, salt, spices, or lemon rind as needed. When you are satisfied, can or freeze the mixture in quarts for pie-making. When assembling a mincemeat pie, slice a fresh apple on top, with a pat of butter, before applying the top crust.

Gather the family. If you grew up eating mincemeat pie at holidays, some of those present will be dead, but they will invite themselves and they will be welcome. Remember that eastern Oregon farm ladies wore those printed aprons that hung around their necks with the strings tied in back and they hardly ever sat down. Remember that the men had waited a long time to eat this pie, coming in from fields that are gone now. Don't worry if your father pushes his chair back; he's the one who taught you to save your piece of pie for breakfast. You belong to these people. Set a big table.

2
MARCH

for Norman Wilkins

Who am I in relation to the things that don't need me?

The stillness of early March is an illusion. It is the stillness of runners poised in their stocks at the starting line, waiting for the gun. When some tipping point of sun and instinct is reached, chickadees and grosbeaks and redpolls will suddenly be joined by sparrows and juncos, nuthatches and restless clouds of white snow buntings. Owls will call for mates in the night. Resident ravens will be annoyed by returning eagles. Swans will pass overhead on their way to the opening mouths of lakes. Even the trees will start to breathe. In this month we go from ten to fourteen hours of sunlight, confusing our bodies and waking our memories of green.

March is a cusp, an edge, a phase change in the odd physics of living in Alaska. Landscape that in summer seems impassible, wet, and many brushy distant miles away from us, gradually becomes accessible over the course of the winter by the miracle of ice and snow. By December even the surface of a big lake is solid enough to traverse. By midwinter, the cushion of white is deep enough over the rough holes and brush that we can ride on it with skis or snowmachines, follow the straight lines of seismic exploration trails cut out in the 1950s or the curvy hand-cut trails of earlier trappers and travelers through the country. In March, we open our coats and switch heavy mitts for leather gloves, drink the air that flows around us when we travel. We can ascend the frozen overflow of creeks and little valleys to the summits. With time enough, we could travel over the white top of the earth.

There's more country out here than we see from a road or a house. Just on the other side of my garden is the lake, and just on the other side of the lake is a mountain. But get on the snow and start traveling to that mountain and you will find yourself crossing wide benches full of poplar groves, alder tangles, and stands of spruce. At the top of each ascent are high lakes you never knew existed. It takes an hour to reach a ridge you thought was right in front of you. The mountain, when you finally get there, is several mountains, with valleys and lakes in between. Beavers live up here, and moose. Big bears have left scratch marks high on the trees. Wolf tracks, twice the size of a dog track, are on every trail. Every mile you travel has a vertical dimension too, deep with detail to draw your attention. The distance you were hungry to cross gives way to looking at this tree, at that marten track.

In March you can still cross even the widest lake right across its middle, but if you are crossing the river on its ice, you'd better follow a moose track. The channel is running somewhere beneath you, too muffled to hear, wearing your bridge of ice too thin. Be careful. Travel for hours, and you are deep in the folds of country where you are a guest, not an owner. Relationships swing to a normal that is unfamiliar. In this cold air like flavorless water, I'm just another animal, admitted by the season and the snow to my animal life. Only my kind of watching makes clear the kind of animal I am.

In March I know I'd better enjoy these strange privileges, because they are about to melt away. The easy admission will be over, and we will be locked out. It starts with deep, snowless holes melted away from the bases of trees, then the trails go away and all this country expands away from us again, becoming a distance we can cross only with great effort. It will dissolve into water that cannot hold us up. Danger from precipitous surfaces, bears, swamps, and stranding will return. It will be a different country entirely, in spite of what the map says. Beauty, now spread wide and quiet over a pastel palette, will bloom into greens and the noise of birds. The land will smell like hot Labrador Tea plants and mud. Little rips in the mossy fabric will reflect the sky. In summer, I won't be here.

On a March day on the top of Slide Mountain, I looked at four distant mountain ranges, each with its own storms. High enough to experience the perspective of a tilted map, I could see lakes and valleys I knew about but had never seen together at the same time. Looking down from the mountain top, my house tiny as a toy in that view, I realized I'd dreamed over and over about a small lake beside the house and a steep hill leading down to it—neither of which actually existed. After gazing across the real landscape, I don't think I ever visited that dreamscape again. The view of us from the mountain showed me it wasn't there and I couldn't get there, didn't have to take care of that other life.

Fifty miles north and decades ago in March, traveling with Norman Wilkins, hundreds of caribou are coming through the eleven-mile trail. We sit on the snowmachines and watch the animals cross into the black spruce, a continuous stream of mostly cows and calves for long minutes. Norman calls it a "caribou carousel," says the animals are just making a big circle down on Hole Lake and coming around again. A bunch of youngsters trots and jumps across the trail a few feet in front of us—heads thrown back, noses in the air.

Jim says, "Looks like school's been let out."

We are not hunting. We are just along with Norman as he sets his traps for the last time this winter. My husband and Norman are thrilled to be standing on this last white edge of the season, and I am along to watch them. I am a young wife, but with my Jim in the woods I've always reverted to a role I like even better than wife: I'm a kid playing house in the wild country, following a dad or older brother and making jokes and small trouble even as I learn to drive, walk softly through brush, hold a gun and shoot it. When I was a dozen years old, I was the .410 to their 12 gauges, the .22 to their 30.06s.

Jim and I hunted grouse along a road in Montana before we were married, and I shot one I shouldn't have from the roadway, just as a pickup truck came along to see me do it. I kept my head down and stood in the barrow pit alongside the road, the dead grouse in my hand. The driver pulled up next to Jim, rolled down the window, and, laughing, said, "That's okay. I like to see a kid get a bird." Jim of the gigantic red beard and blue eyes held his mirth until the truck was out of sight, then came over and lifted me off the ground like I was that kid.

I have some terrible stories too. Another new hunter and I shot whitetail deer from too far away and then had to find them and kill them. The ruined face of a fawn struggled up at me as I cut its throat because, horrified already at what I had done, I'd left my gun down the hillside when I had come running. And I once shot a moose I couldn't find. A friend on that trip said, "It's good for the ravens. They got no knives." But those tragedies have risen through all the clean kills of my life until I'm not much interested in pulling the trigger anymore. My mother, distracted by my small brother she had in tow, once walked across a cornfield with the safety off and a shell in the chamber. That moment scared her so badly she would never again pick up a gun or go hunting. Like her, I can imagine being the agent of awful harm.

But I love the shape-shock of seeing a big animal. When Jim or a hunting companion kills an animal, I like knowing that it has died with a smaller suffering than what ends most lives out here. After its death, I'll thank the animal for its meat, slit the skin up the belly to roll out the guts, help to take off the shoulders and legs and ribs, get my gloves and pant legs bloody kneeling in the moss. This is the blood that brings forth life, the kind of blood I know. We play by the rules as we understand them and bring everything home that we have been taught how to use. Nothing is ours, so we are grateful. I believe in give and take. I believe in liver and onions.

With Jim and Norman, I ride a sled towed behind one of the two old snogos—snowmachines. These men are best friends in the pursuits they've loved since they were boys. We are a ragtag trio, lots of wool and stained Carhartts and a scarcity of haircuts. Once in a while I feel a tinge of jealousy or exclusion when they dive into some farming or trapping subject, but mostly I am wordlessly included. As I hang on to the hoop of the sled, I watch the frozen land go by as if the land was moving and not me. I accept that Jim and Norman will do most of the navigating, deciding, chopping, even most of the cooking while we are out here. All I have to do is reach out for a big cup of coffee or cocoa when Norman hands it to me. There won't always be these big broken-knuckled hands. I know this even then.

Just tens of miles from the roads, we feel like the only people on earth and at the same time we bask in the luxury of our unimportance. There aren't any phones in our pockets yet.

The Ahtna people were here first, for thousands of years. Morrie and Joe Secondchief were still living here when we came. Morrie was born at Tazlina Lake and her husband, Joe, came from Tyone Village, north of here. He was the last of the Secondchief brothers. Morrie and Joe trapped here all of their lives. They took a lot of beaver and otter out of this water-soaked country.

One time, Morrie traced the otter's circle through the country in the air for me, a map for my imagination. She said the otters hunted all the lakes and creeks for fish, traveled from Snowshoe Lake down Cache Creek to the Nelchina River. The otters went down the Nelchina and worked the country around Tazlina Lake, then traveled up Mendeltna Creek, over to Old Man Lake and up into Mendeltna Springs where the Old Man Lake water comes from. From there they went over to the lakes above Snowshoe and came down to Snowshoe again. It was over seventy miles, that circle. This revised what I'd thought of as Otter Disneyland, all those little squiggles in the trails and down the banks. With Morrie's story, I realized it wasn't an amusement park after all but a big serious commute. I asked Morrie if she thought the otters had any fun. "Oh yeah," she said. "They have fun."

Morrie had me clean her cabin for her and carry boards and tubs around the yard, things she and Joe couldn't do anymore. She told me I was strong, but when she felt my hands for calluses she mock-frowned at me. "Too many books," I told her.

When we start up the machines again, we are going so slow that we don't startle the caribou cows still trickling across the trail, jogging their calf-big bodies. From behind, their ballooned bellies have an exaggerated swaying and their huge angled hocks and hooves flail out sideways.

Unaffected by our presence, they stop to paw the snow for lichens, and a few lie down next to the trail without even glancing our way. Perhaps because we are not wolves or bears, they don't recognize us as beings from up the food chain. But we are, and even though we are not hunting, I pick out one without antlers, which in March means it is probably a dry cow or a bull. I silently tell it, "I could eat you if I needed to," practicing that. In another layer of this moment is the beauty of the animal. And in another is the animal in its own life, unknowable by me. Sometimes I wonder how long this wildness can exist, and when it ends how long it will have been without us.

Norman is at home on a March trail. Before he moved north he was a Minnesota dairy farmer, important to his peers for innovations in milk barns and handy with all things mechanical. He's from the generation before Jim and me and served in the army with the U.S. occupation forces in Italy after the Second World War. He met Sylvia there, a young woman who had walked through lines of Nazi soldiers on her way out of Slovenia. Norman promised to return to Italy and bring her to the States. Sylvia's family told her he wouldn't keep his promise, but he did. They raised a family together and picked stones off of rocky Midwest farms. She couldn't believe it when they'd finally built all that and then he wanted to give it up to come north and live in a cabin. But she came too, and eventually they built a house and filled the role of parents for us and our neighbors. Just down the road with cookies on the table, they were grandparents to our children.

Stormin' Norman, his friends called him, for his temper and his partying, but the storms receded. Today on the Blue Lake Trail he's quick to smile and full of droll humor, though he can still be a booming baritone when he's excited. When we were trying to get him out the door of his house for this trip, he was grabbing and swinging gear, ducking back inside for items he'd forgotten. He stormed and thundered, whined like a braking train.

One time I met a British fellow who had ridden his bicycle all the way from Patagonia to Nelchina. He'd blown a tire in front of our driveway; I found him there fixing it. We talked long enough for him to share his wonky theory that English people were quiet and reserved, Australians were louder, and Americans were way too loud. I tried to argue with him about that, but Norman came by in his truck and pulled over to join the conversation: "MAN, ARE YOU EVER ON AN ADVENTURE!" I had to concede the argument.

Norman settles down in the woods. He usually traps and travels alone, but today he shares his familiar routines with us. At noon it is time to pack snow into a beat-up aluminum coffee pot with the guts taken out. He says, "A guy needs a little coffee and a cookie." We break some of the dry widow wood off the bottoms of the black spruce where the March sun has already shrunk the snow away from the trunks. In an open spot we dig down through the snow to the evergreen cranberry and pale lichens and make a little fire. Sylvia has packed gigantic cookies for us, full of coconut and chocolate chips and nuts. After we eat and warm up with the coffee, we'll close our eyes for a little while in the sun.

We start up again at the same pace, going very slowly, staying on the one trail, and making only the same mark through the snow that Norman started in November. I have a strong impulse, after miles and miles of this, to want the machines to throttle up, pull off the trail, and carve fresh snow. But there is something to learn from following an already used path, this slow deliberate looking, and I am here to learn it.

Farther on, or "fuh-ther" in the midwestern speak of Jim and Norman, we come to the scattered bones of a moose, one of its thickest leg bones crunched open by a wolf's jaw. Bits of hair, patches of blood, and the tracks tell a detailed story of how the moose died—if you are a student of this language. Jim tells me how many wolves there were and how big they were, which also indicates age or gender, and he says they must have been hungry, judging by how they ate on the carcass. I can't see this for myself, but Norman and Jim talk about it for several minutes without rancor or politics. This is just life and death out here. Wolves don't always eat what they kill, especially if they are teaching the pups to hunt. Other creatures—ravens and foxes and weasels on down to the tiniest creatures—will clean the wolves' plates for them, and in doing so will survive in their turn.

Norman often asks Jim a question he already knows the answer to, just to keep a small exchange going: "Looks like that calf got away," or "Think this was an old break in this rib? Look how it's healed over." The signifiers of this gracious exchange still confuse me, because I am a westerner. *No, that's right* is an affirmation that begins with a negative. *Yes*, with a pause after it that is not followed by *but*, can precede a dissenting opinion, of course rendered gentle with that peace-making *yes*.

Here's an example: I say, "That looks like a fresh moose track." Jim says, "Yes, maybe a week or so ago."

There are shallow lakes of every size, curiously held up on top of a plateau. There are no creeks in or out of them, just rends in the cloth of moss and black spruce, ragged basins held aloft by permafrost. Look west to the Talkeetnas, north to the Alaska Range, south to the Chugach, and east to the Wrangells. Mount Drum stands out from its companions; although at 12,011 feet, it is smaller than Mount Wrangell and Mount Sanford behind it. In the cold clear air, it looms gigantic in front of them, like a fish held out toward the camera at arm's length.

This section of the trail is a high, flat, frozen sponge, cupped in a wide circle of those mountains and etched by crazy little trees with growth rings no bigger than the grooves on a vinyl record. I think these off-putting trees protect this country in the way that dryness protected the West until cities spilled onto them. This homely ground, happily for itself, is not a human paradise. If trees are the memory of the earth, these memories are old, twisted by frost and fire, and inscrutable.

Up on top along the eleven-mile trail is where Norman looks for muskrats to trap. In the spring the snow settles down around the "push-ups," frozen bumps of dark roughage the muskrats have dredged up from the bottom and pushed through the surface of the lake during the winter, making comfortable little sitting rooms for themselves above water level. The caribou paw some of them up for dinner salads and then the muskrats have to build them all over again.

The white expanse of Bear Lake is dotted with a few push-ups, not enough for Jim and Norman to get excited about making sets, skinning and stretching only a few muskrats for all that work. They say they'll wait for a muskrat bonanza some other March. It's pretty clear they are just taking an inventory of everything they can notice, storing it up for stories when we get home.

By this time of year, fur on the land animals *singes*, changes color because of the lengthening exposure to sun, and the animals feel itchy in their too-warm winter clothes. They begin to rub off their fur along their sides. Because of this, trapping season for marten and fox and lynx closes at the end of February, and it is only these swimmers left to trap, the water mammals who slide in and out of the tea-colored creeks and lakes beneath the ice. Those movies with the trappers walking around with furs in the middle of summer are a bunch of hooey, and so are Disney's trappers with their lust for blood.

Sylvia and I both sew some fur, warm hats and mitts for our families and a few extra hats to sell. Word of mouth brings business enough for the few items we make, and neither one of us can stand to charge enough to make the long handwork profitable. I think of Morrie Secondchief long ago making beaver blankets to sell for people's beds. She told me she charged just thirty dollars for an entire blanket, the product of weeks of hand-sewing thick hides together. I think of her poor hands twisted by polio and then arthritis, the hands she had when she was old.

After we explore some new creeks, we'll go to Norman's little cabin. Jim and Norman will find some paper that hasn't been used on both sides, which they'll employ for scribbled drawings of tree sets and cubby sets. Plans for the future are properly made in a cabin, the jumping-off place to the wild, where the chores of water and wood are basic, where your feet are cold and your head is hot as you sit at a piece-of-plywood table and look at a map in the dim light, sipping coffee and drawing.

When he says his bones are tired, Norman leads us to the cabin. It's up here on top, next to where the high wetland drops off to a lower and oddly drier geography. The cabin is hidden from the people who don't know about it already. It is built away from handy water and off any established trail and made of the trees and moss the country will soon eat up again, spitting out the rusty log spikes when it has finished its meal.

To build a cabin in this country, most people look for trees straight enough and thick enough to stand upright for the walls, seven to eight feet high, palisade style. The trees have so much taper here, you can't find many that will give you more than one log. Two-sided with a chainsaw mill or just eyeballed for the saw cuts, the way Norman sliced these sides, logs are spiked together and set into a sill log at the base with sixty-penny nails. By the time you get three logs set up this way, you already have the start of a firm wall. Spike your logs together around a corner and not even the wind can bring them down—not yet. Old cabins stand until the rot comes up from the sill where it touches the ground, or the roof fails and moisture gets in from the top. A generation or two of people use a cabin, then the people and the cabins crumble into the earth. In a crowded world, scarcity gives this place a rare balance.

To converse with curious grizzlies, Norman nailed an exceptionally sweaty T-shirt onto the cabin door. We see that so far his claim has held—no torn-off door, no mess inside. He says, "I guess the bear must be disgusted with me for that T-shirt," and grins at us.

He tells me, "I used my drill on this," pointing to the hole where the rope runs through the spruce-slab door to lift the bolt on the inside. I know he's still joking around, because he's got no power and no generator out here to run a drill, and battery drills were not in our world. "My drill was a three-eighths log spike and a vice grips," he says and tells us how he heated the spike red hot on a Coleman stove then quickly pressed it against the thick wood of the door. He walked back and forth doing that over and over for half a day, burning the point into the slab and scraping the soft black ash out with his pocket knife, happy with himself.

After supper the coffee pot comes out again. Miraculously, the coffee and the warm fire make us sleepy. I get the narrow top bunk because I am smaller and still the kid, Norman takes the bottom bunk, and Jim rolls out a sleeping pad and bag next to the stove. I go to sleep in the hottest layer of dark, listening to them talk.

I've been drawing pictures of cabins all my life. By the time my best friend and I taught ourselves the Russian alphabet so that we could pass secret notes in our high school social studies class, my cabin habit was full blown. I told my typing teacher that I didn't need to learn to type on an electric machine because I didn't plan to have electricity when I lived on my own. "What are you going to do," he said while wrinkling up his nose, "live in a cabin in the woods?"

One time I stayed in a cabin out on the east fork of the Owyhee that was made of juniper, those corkscrewed desert trees. It was woven more than stacked, and every twist that led to a gap outside had to be chinked by the builder. When I lay down to sleep there, it felt like hands were clasped around me.

When Jim and I came to Nelchina, it was forty years after the Glenn Highway came through, several years past the Alaska Pipeline boom times. Norman and Sylvia didn't even know us yet, but they brought us a load of firewood and a bag of fresh cookies.

We hadn't had electricity in Montana, so we didn't know the power worked when we got to the half-built cabin that would eventually be our house. We burned a few gallons of pearl kerosene before accidentally flipping a switch that turned on the lights.

Just before we came up here, we'd made a journey back in time to try and find one of Jim's family homes in Sweden. We started at our little cabin in the Montana woods and traveled through London and Paris and Frankfurt and Copenhagen in search of relatives who had been lost to the rest of the family since Jim's grandfather, Carl Erickson, was killed in a Wisconsin car accident in 1935. We had three words on a piece of stationery paper, towns or place names—we didn't know which—from Jim's mom, who had gotten them from her mother but didn't know what or where they were. We found one of the words on a map, finally, after crisscrossing Varmland on successively smaller and smaller trains until we were on a train that was just one car that could drive either way. It brought us to "Arjang," a town. In Arjang, we asked about "Silarud" and found someone who knew it was a parish church, seventeen klicks away on a dirt road. We pedaled old rental bikes deep into a spruce forest very much like the one we'd left on the other side of the world. We found the church and a caretaker named Gunnar digging graves. He knew Jim's grandfather's name—it was in the church book. He pointed us to an even smaller road that led deeper into the woods. He told us that the word we had not been able to find, "Intaka," meant "taken from the forest." The small road led us into a thicker, darker forest that opened up a mile or two farther into a small clearing with a house, Jim's grandfather's childhood house. There was a spring, covered with old planks. We reached down into its darkness for handfuls of cold water. The little one-story house looked modestly lived-in but no one was home. It was Intaka, an in-taking for us. No other Swede we've asked has ever known that word.

Later we made Jim's parents a sign that said "Intaka," and they hung it on their house in Wisconsin. They traveled back to Sweden a few years later and met Manne, the elderly great-uncle who lived in the clearing we'd found. We tried the name Intaka on our Montana cabin and later on the cabin we built at Boot Lake with Norman's help. It would as well fit on our Nelchina house, land carved out by someone else and with a house eventually finished by us. The word fits everywhere we have ever lived, which is probably why it never stuck anywhere. Of course this is the forest; of course what we have has all been taken from something else. It's just our turn to have it for a little while.

Norman helped all of us with our houses, clambering around on the rafters as if he wasn't a quarter-century older than the rest of us. And when we all got tired of building houses, we took off into the woods to build cabins. When Norman and his friend Darrel went to stake remote land, we followed them to check it out. The enterprise was full of high excitement and ill-conceived notions—for example the release of a male and female Chinese pheasant. After we let them out of their little cage, the pheasants did not seem very wild or very romantically inclined. They hung out around the fire with us as we made coffee and were still standing there when we went home. Some fox probably ate them as soon as we were out of sight.

The next March, we staked our Boot Lake cabin land next to Norman's. Sighting down our arms toward the flagging hung on distant trees, we cut lines across the hilly spruce and birch knobs. We located our cabin site scenically on a lake too small to be of much interest to pilots. This would be a winter place, accessible by its trail. I was aware during every moment of the measuring, sighting, cutting, and sweating that there was deep privilege and deep disruption in what I was doing. We were turning the unowned into the owned. We called the lake "Boot Lake" because of its shape, like a Puss in Boots seven-league boot. Immortalized now in the notes for the state survey of our properties, the name is not on any map and may outlive us or be lost. The lake is deep enough that it won't become a meadow in our lifetimes.

Before Nelchina and Boot Lake, we'd already spent summer work seasons in Alaska places where people remembered the "firsts": first white guys, first English, first talk of Jesus, first miners, first roads, first airplanes. In the Kobuk Valley, we knew people who had talked to those who had talked to those who knew Maneuluk the Prophet. Inupiaq elder Louise Wood's grandfather had met the first missionaries. We gratefully felt the past through these firsthand voices, even got to experience one ambiguous first of our own: we were there when television arrived in the Kobuk villages in 1980. On that day *The Mary Tyler Moore Show* gathered a circle of schoolgirls around the TV in postmaster Guy Moyer's house.

The Copper Basin felt different. We weren't suffering under the illusion that we were the first of anything, and our stubborn white-person chauvinism had been knocked about enough by then that we knew we were also strangers, a new migration overlaying older lives. Thousands of years of Ahtnas and two hundred years of white guys had done it better, deeper, and more, walking all over this place in all seasons and laying down names with every pass. Just before us, Lloyd Ronning and Al Lee and Don Deering and Rick Houston had flown in and out of more lakes and river bars than we could ever count. Rick and Sharley lived in the Honeymoon Cabin at Tazlina Lake in the 1940s. Junior Hunt had trapped before Norman, and the Secondchiefs long before him, Johnny Tyone before the Secondchiefs. As we claimed our lives here, no matter how far or large we reached, we knew our time on the land followed those people we knew about and all the ones before them. "First" couldn't be the point.

We weren't looking for the nobility that comes from isolation either. There was plenty of chicanery around the solitary wilderness myth even by the time we got here, decades before legislature-subsidized Alaska "reality shows" would turn every discerning stomach. We knew several actual ideologue fathers who had taken their brainwashed wives and unfortunate broods into isolation in order to control them. These guys existed before the infamous Papa Pilgrim made it popular. Even in our short tenure, tens of examples present themselves that a solitary existence is just as likely to make people weird as it is to make them hardy and wise. Pretty much, what you get from living in the woods is a more intense version of what you brought in there. We'd also watched the trade-offs that the remote settlers had to make for their goods, their kids' education, their medical care. Those could be round-trips of hundreds of miles to adjust braces or buy a chainsaw, a trip maybe involving a trail and a boat and an airplane. Romantic certainly, difficult always.

Our compromise was to willingly put ourselves under the spell of the rural—close to a road but far from a town. Jim wanted the access to the animals and the wild, woods wrapped around him and a little homestead cabin. I wanted plenty of trees around me, too, but also neighbors and a garden—some of the simple goodness I naïvely associate with the past, thanks to my parents and Laura Ingalls Wilder and her Big Woods. I never understood why Papa moved them to the prairie.

At times, my eastern Oregon mom and dad seemed heartbroken about the loss of the promising world they occupied in their young adulthoods. Never mind the Great Depression and then the stateside hardships of raising young children during the Second World War. Their heyday was a western America with empty land and undiscovered fishing holes, opportunities to build farms and businesses and families. Although my parents were unhappy when we moved our household goods to Alaska, instead of just working here for a few years and then coming home with the stories and setting up a regular life, my mom visited us often and told me our little gatherings of people and music were like her family picnics fifty years before.

Jim's dad, Lester, often told us how his parents, first-generation Americans from Norway, farmed in northwestern Wisconsin to feed and raise their family, the need to make money a secondary motivation. At the start they logged the white spruce, then burned the stumps to make farms, then "farmed to live." While the memory of those fires hung over them like smoke, their part of Barron County was called Brunland, literally the "burnt land." Increasingly, there was cash in that system from milking cows, but the garden and other livestock were still crucial. Lester and Lois raised everything they could eat, but public health scares over tuberculosis and brucellosis banished pigs and chickens from the Grade A dairy farms, an unhappy day Jim remembers from his childhood.

Lester always wanted to be a farmer. On the eve of the Second World War and after he'd finished his farmer's course down in Madison, the farms in his part of Wisconsin weren't earning enough to support the families so he traveled out west and down the coast looking for a job. He got turned down for job after job and then finally had to give in and lie about his work experience, as people had been advising him to do. It makes me grin to think of Lester Odden consciously lying—he always exuded honesty and plain speech. It must have turned him inside out to tell the Consolidated Aircraft Company that he could read aircraft blueprints. Lester had never seen an aircraft blueprint, but he got the job. He made parts for experimental airplanes during the war, a protected industry that kept him working and stateside. As soon as he could, though, he went home to farm.

Our parents' old rural days helped give us permission to fling ourselves far, find a place where "to live" was the idea. In the early 1980s, we'd been coming up to Alaska in the summers to fight wildfires. Wanting more—a place of our own in the woods—we caught the tail end of our generation's homesteader migrations and started looking for land.

When I'm cynical about what people do, how people poison everywhere they live, I think of our house and gardens and the cabins we've thrown out beyond the houses. They are like spores of civilization, for good and for ill. In this northern land, you often see places where people have reached out too far, their dreams overshooting and collapsing finally into an overgrown place when they are gone, leaving tangles of fallen gray logs. I should be grateful to be reclaimed by moss, but it is a lonely thought. While Jim and Norman are at the table following a lynx track between the salt and the butter, I stretch out on my back in the bunk, wondering if the season at this altitude is too short to grow carrots.

Recently I opened a magazine to photos of the refugee camps in Turkey where Kurdish families have fled from ISIS. Rows and rows of tan rubber Quonset huts stretched across the desert, and there was no green plant in sight except for in front of one of the Quonsets. In that photo there was a patch of green grass the size of a dinner table, a canopy of flowering vine, and blooming pots of flowers. At this tiny outpost of human hope, a man on his knees was cutting the grass with a pair of scissors. That man is my brother.

This is a complicated love. I see root cellars and gardens, and I leave straight lines, squares, and rectangles wherever I go. Carried to my logical conclusion, I am kin to the bulldozer. Homesteaders bring cleared land, tractors, schools. The animals have a smaller piece of the diminishing earth.

Sometimes I feel for the squirrels. They are little acrobats, jumping so far from tree to tree that they only catch themselves by a claw, swinging wildly beneath a branch that bends perilously down toward a waiting dog. They chase each other, chatter warnings and nonsense and destroy our insulation, our wooden doors and window frames, our cabin logs. They are far from gentle seed eaters. They eat the baby birds alive in whatever nest they can scramble to. Sometimes there is a resident squirrel who acts like a guardian, keeping the others out of his area and out of trouble with us. If he does not feel the need to destroy buildings, we let him live. At times there are no squirrels around—never because we've done them all in with the .22, because we can't—but because of some mysterious shifting of the creature populations around us. When the squirrels aren't here, the birds do not miss them, but I do. Our little community of grosbeaks, chickadees, redpolls, summer sparrows, and voles and all the larger predators those bring—the shrikes, the goshawks and eagles, foxes and ermine—are incomplete without the scamper and chatter of red squirrels.

I don't have to shoot squirrels because I am quite sure I am already slowly killing them: the sheer numbers of me, a species escaped from all constraint, released by myself from any restraint. Breathing, shitting, building our middens, puking our poisons. The poison drifts north, salting the fish in the lakes and changing winter. I am a northern "me" now—endangered as I also endanger. I bless what moves and chatters and flies around me; these are not just words, but it is only my one heart, not so important or true as I want it to be.

The swans and loons seem gracious to come back here, though their imperative is not for us humans. A bit earlier this year? I am afraid to count. The swans trumpeting in the night are music. How many more years will they come? Each summer they can only stay so long, teaching the cygnets to fly as they turn from gray to white. Did they leave a bit later this October? They take their youngsters south to a country where changes come even faster. You, swan, might find your lake has gone. You didn't keep the title or the deed.

All the summer birds will go somewhere, but I trust that they still exist when I don't see them. The squirrel stays in winter, along with the gray jays and grosbeaks and the tiny vole under the snow. I stay too, and I value them as companions even while I betray them with my industry and privilege. I am the Judas of this world and its witness too. The raven with the white wing feather visits the unfinished top of our airplane hangar and the dogs bark at him; they seem to hate him for knowing all about their good deal contract with humans. I try to speak to him in his own language—Caw! Caw! or Coke! I am an occasional source of embarrassment to humans and always an amusement to ravens.

Great horned owls roost in the rafters when the vole and rabbit populations are high and shit wads down on our old airplane wings. One footfall on the porch, the click of our front door, and the owl departs nearly silently to the trees on the other side of the runway—just the *whoooooooooooo whooooooooooo* of her giant wings pushing air and then she's sheltered by the dappled coat of invisibility.

I don't know where any of them are when they're not here. When any of them are here, even a spider now, I try to say, "Yes, you can build the world back without me. Invent someone new, take two or three of the billions of years before all of this is eaten by the sun. Make someone who can watch and love but not invent the wheel."

Beyond the culpable house is the cabin, like a question. For some people, our log house is already teetering on the edge of nowhere. They will say, "Jim and Mary's cabin," which is funny because where we live is definitely a house. A house is a place where there are too many buckets, too many tools, too many pictures to hang on the wall, too many cups, and too many things to do. The house is a staging area for all of our work and clutter, but a cabin is a leap away from the familiar—harder to arrive at and more spare. Where do we think we are going?

Scandinavians understand the concept of a separate cabin without question. A person needs a *hitte*, a place to go. For Jim, it's a place he could trap or hunt from, a place with animal tracks and a woodstove.

For me it is a place to play house in the woods and make coffee, read, and write. I know where I'd put a garden out at the cabin—there where the land slopes a bit to the south, sheltered from the prevailing weather by that long ridge, but I never start digging. For both of us it feels so good to be reminded how little it takes to live, how little we really have to think about in order to live.

The cabin narrows us down. What we hear on the windup radio, who wins the game of cribbage, what we have for supper—if it happens at the cabin, we will pay attention to it while it is happening and remember it longer. The cabin wakes us up. The cabin has matches and a jar to keep them dry, some old clothes and sleeping bags, and my favorite hat that says ERA, given to me by a helicopter pilot in McGrath. Even though it is just the name of an aviation company, it makes me think of the Equal Rights Amendment that never passed. This disappointment is important to me, a caution about the bone-deep reluctance in both men and women to allow women to conduct their own lives or to lead men and women. In spite of everything, we are still a prey species with our backward-glancing eyes, our parenthetical speech. So I hang the hat on a peg and look at it every March, in the cabin where I enjoy my great luck and my great loves. I never want that hat to wear out.

We built the Boot Lake cabin in two separate Marches in the 1980s while living in a wall tent. We arrived at the beginning of the first March with sleds full of tools and camping gear. It was late when we pulled up to the bottom of the little hill, getting dark and the temperatures were hard winter, far below zero. A friend with a Super Cub on skis had arranged to fly in and camp with us for a week. He arrived just a few minutes after we did, and what he saw was a pile of bundles and boxes in the deep snow, surrounded by "the land of little sticks," as he has always called our part of the country. Seeing no tent up and no warmth in sight, he made quick apologies, got back in his Baldy Bird, and flew home to Palmer. We still laugh with him about this. It did feel grim for a few hours more after he left, until we got the snow shoveled away, tent poles cut, and the tent stretched up. But then the little Air Tight stove steamed away a square section of the cold.

Living in a wall tent is intense fun, with spruce boughs spread on the ground and the fresh smell of pitch each time the cabin warms, with hot food in a pot on the stove, dogs to play with, and work to do every day. We hauled and cut logs for a twelve-by-fourteen-foot foundation and shorter ones for the walls. We bathed in a bucket, made nightly forays out of the tent to pee and to admire how the light glowed orange through the canvas, like a big Chinese lantern nestled in dark blue snow.

The second March, when we got to the point of actually putting up the cabin logs and building the roof, Norman came out to help us. Jim and Norman milled two or three flat sides on the logs, depending on where they were going to go, and then I peeled the remaining round sides almost as fast as they could nail the logs in place. Log-peeling takes an IQ of twenty-five, but you never have to wonder what you've been doing all day. After a couple of weeks it makes your arms tough as tree limbs. Even better, Norman once boomed out, "Hey Jim, I wouldn't mess with her by the time she gets done with that pile of logs."

Some years in this country, we can't remember seeing a cloud in March. We worked in bright hot sun with the snow disappearing around us and went to bed exhausted every night. Roof on, we traveled the snogo trail home at the very last minute the snow would hold us up. The remnant of the trail was just a white line through a brown forest, about to vanish into summer—the other season in Alaska.

Boot Lake is a good place to go in the winter, best in March, although we have walked around the little lakes and slogged through the swamps to get there in the summer too. A *hitte bok*, "cabin book," hangs on the wall and documents thirty years of trips with brilliant creative writing by ten-year-olds, snarky cartoons by ten-year-olds turned into teenagers, journal entries obligatory for all visitors, with most of the notes lovingly addressed to the cabin itself. There are only a few rules at the cabin: keep it clean, bring in some wood, and write in the book. Because we document our life carefully at the cabin, we know that the winters since 2000 have been warmer, and that March is beginning to feel like April. We may have to start March earlier in the coming years.

When we go on trips to Boot Lake in the winter and the early spring, we take the chainsaw to restock the wood pile. We take cookies in case we have a visitor. By March, we have become eager to be lonely enough that the sound of a snogo coming along our trail draws an exclamation of pleasure. We'll put the coffee on.

For several years we and a few neighbors volunteered as first responders for the Copper River emergency medical service. When there were vehicle accidents at our end of the highway, and there were many in those years, we would go to the scene to try to stabilize the victims until the ambulance arrived, usually forty-five minutes to an hour behind our arrival. Those minutes were long and terrifying. A man who had been thrown from his pickup died in spite of our CPR, leaving us standing there in a ripped-open morning in March. After the ambulance and trooper arrived and the medical detritus was cleaned up, we three couples unanimously decided to go to Boot Lake for the rest of the day. We took tools but never used them; we just rode out to the cabin and drank coffee, sat around in the sun all afternoon. We spent the time talking about how we felt: harmed and dissatisfied before we got there, whole again by the time we left. Whatever that is, is also what a cabin is for.

Norman doesn't live here anymore. He and Sylvia moved back to Minnesota in 2004, and he had some sweet time with his kids and grandchildren down there, going deer hunting in those woods again. Now he's lost his memory, though he is still living, but we spend many of our hours remembering him.

Norman loved trapping, and the woods barely knew he was in them. I am conscious when I write *killing trap* that a reader will not find *humane* in those words. But however you visualize a wild animal's last hours, when the trapper is gone, the land is still here. There is no net loss for the animals until the land falls to some other kind of human hammer—not the snare but a road, a house. Trapping does not remove forests, drain wetlands, encourage human "improvements." Ours is the first American generation to find "improvements" ironic— contemporaries of Mark Twain found him just cynical. Trappers like Norman thrive in the health of wet and rough and wild places. People who trap well learn something every day from the animals. Their human tracks mix with those of the wolf and the fox and disappear at the end of March.

There is some wild margin we need, that has us in it only barely. The trappers I know would not trap along a road or anywhere close to houses or where anyone else was trapping. I think Norman would say there is no point in having a trapline next to people. To be a trapper means visiting, participating in an extravagant and fascinating universe that thrives without us. I heard on the radio that there is a town in Greece, famous as a processed fur capital, selling fur clothing to Russians and Europeans. But those furs come from North America— the United States and Canada. Our emptiness, our wild land, is the actual valuable and rare commodity.

Many places in Alaska can take your breath away with their absence of us. You can follow a trail to the headwaters of the Delta River until there is no trail. The one time we were there we stood in an ankle-deep sea of blueberries and cranberries on a hillside and watched beams of light pour through a hole in the clouds—a "Jesus hole"—down into the canyon miles below. Albert Bierstadt would have painted it just as we saw it. Fly over McCarthy and the Kennicott Glacier beyond is just as big as if you were standing at the foot of it. There are plains flooded with caribou. Why do we want to be there when it is so good without us?

It is a relief to walk in places where the world has survived us and grown back. In the far north a cabin or a farm or a mine can lose its way and disappear. The wilderness is most visible when seen against the broken outline of a gold mine or around the square pit of a trapper's cabin. Our hopes have lived in such places, in ghostly gardens we planned or we made—in our old trams and railroad tunnels, in our poisonous mistakes.

The old trappers talk about falling under the spell of the country. By the second day with Norman, it feels like we have moved off the edge of the map. We leave a few things at the cabin and start down his trails, following creeks and clearings rather than survey lines.

Almost immediately, we drop into land with gravity so strong it sucked the water out from under the ice of this lake, so the ice is bent down like the inside of a spoon. We swing around the smooth margins with the machines, carefully, watching for empty air below us.

Down on Hole Lake, with the steep banks all around, I feel like I've been dropped into the bottom of a white sack. It is ten degrees colder down here, and the snow is deeper, making it impossible to find this beaver's food piles. We look for a silhouette of a lodge, for a likely slope of bank, for aspen or at least alder and willow—any non-spruce treat he'd have munched on. Finding willow, we cut a hole in the ice and send some debarked willow sticks down the hole attached to the Conibear 330, a large square killing trap. These stripped sticks will attract with their brightness. Beavers swim with their eyes open, their noses closed. In March, the holes stay open and won't freeze your traps, and the fur is still sleek and thick and dark.

Here, too, there are a few caribou, and they seem curious, as if we were the Alaska Trapper Repertory Theater performing for their benefit. The amphitheater shape of this place adds to the effect. As we finish the set, they turn and file away slowly up and over the ridge—a sedate audience retiring after the matinee performance.

We pick our way down the drainage, following the trail Norman cut with an ax years ago, finding some open spots in the tiny creek and one lovely otter hole, shiny with slick ice but small. We optimistically place a Conibear over the opening, but there is no way to interrupt the visual outline of the device. It remains hopelessly square and unlike tree or stone or ice. In the deep layered cold of the creek bottom I raise my beaver mitt to my face and brush the silky loft of beaver onto my eyes and nose and mouth, feel the instant warmth that blooms back against my skin.

We leave the trap fixed as well as we can fix it, but I can see that it is as square as a cellar door. Norman says, "I sure hope that's the otter's back door and not the front."

Next we come to a place where the freezing flow has swelled up like the back side of the spoon, a laminated mound of frozen overflow. At the top, the highest circle, the hump is cracked, and you can look down into the book of days this creek has kept on itself—a fat edition this year. When we look at the spruce on either side of us, we see we are standing halfway up their thirty-foot trunks. This is a winter show of muscle: see this teeny little trickle of tea-colored water lift a hundred tons of ice over its head!

At this far end of Norman's trapping circle, we are in a hidden country distinguished mostly by Norman's eagerness as he leads the way along the creek. Suddenly we are in big trees—white spruce. The annual wildfires started by lightning haven't gotten down into these drainages, and the permafrost lenses haven't stopped the roots or held up water to drown the trees from below. The size and numbers of the tall trunks here are all the more surprising because of the sparse country around them.

Norman stops us when the trees open around the small lake he calls Pristine, a lake he could have built his cabin on but didn't. That's all he will say about that, like Forrest Gump, so that means he had reasons wide and deep for not building here. Norman is like that—quiet when the thing is hard to explain—and if you wait long enough you might learn what went unsaid. Or not. The lake doesn't have any name on the map, so Pristine it is for us. A hundred years ago there were trappers and travelers out in this country. Jim and Norman have read and listened to every story they can find, but mostly the stories died with the people.

A lone bull caribou is out on the ice and he makes several great leaps while we are watching, his forelegs tucked up and all of him pushed muscularly through a high arc by his back legs. He lands to look around—we are now the audience—and then does it again. Norman names him Prancer the Dancer of Pristine Lake. Other caribou in the trees stare placidly at us and at their very own performer, a prophet in his own country.

On the far side of the lake, on a bench above the shoreline, we walk around in big trees that have a sanctuary feeling. The place is quieter than the quiet land around it, and the settled incense of spruce needles and Labrador tea rises through the shallow snow the canopy has allowed to fall. We find a square hole in the ground and the remains of cabin logs. Digging around in a likely eruption of moss reveals old bottles and tins, garbage gone to artifact, stories gone to silence.

On the way home, we visit Mendeltna Springs above Old Man Lake, where pressurized groundwater has percolated up into the layers of ice and snow all winter to make crazy pale blue and tan layers, some squishy and some hard as glass. We stop the machines away from the creek and pick our way on foot along the solid meanderings of overflow above the creek channels until Jim finds an otter hole that looks like it's been in use all winter. "Look at this," he says to me, and I cautiously peek over the edge into a translucent cavern. I ask Jim if he will hold my legs so I can get my head down under the several inches of ice and have a look at the otter's universe. There is a foot and a half of air between the undersurface of the ice, which forms a green sky, with a black riffled sea below it. The sea is this branch of the creek on its way down to Old Man Lake, tinkling like crystal through stones. I look upstream and down this musical, half-lit cathedral highway of otters. Strange and unknowable, fluid as the days of March, the wild cradles us. And when it's gone, it's us we will miss.

Lingonberry Sauce

After Chernobyl, the berries were injured. It happened in the spring, on April 26, 1986, my husband's thirty-fifth birthday.

Native women in Alaska sent meat, fish, and berries to Laplanders in the fall because during the event, Chernobyl poisoned the ground with radioactive Caesium-137, a water-soluble isotope that plants and animals take up like salt. The people closest to the Chernobyl reactor and all the people downwind of the shifting plumes being emitted by the ruined power plant could not safely subsist off the land.

Lingonberries are lowbush cranberries that grow in forests all over the top of the world. The Kobuk Inupiat call them *kikmiñak,* and women's hands stroke them from the hillside into deep birchbark baskets. Finlanders call them *puolukka.* In eastern Canada they are foxberries or redberries. In Norway and Denmark they are *tyttebaer,* and the Swedes gave their *lingon* name to us. They are in the genus *Vaccinium* with blueberries, which their stems often touch, but when blueberries are soft and shriveled and their red leaves have vanished in the fall winds, the lingonberries are ready to pick and their tiny, waxy oval leaves will be green under the snow all winter.

In the summer, we watch the clouds of Russian forest fire smoke drift over our short forests, until the wind shifts and we send them our Alaskan smoke, waiting for the smoke from Canada's Yukon to drift in from the east. The world is small at its top, the center of a spinning disk.

Pick the berries after one or two frosts, after they are red all over but before too many frosts have softened them. Pick bucketfuls. Pour your berries from one bucket to the other in a stiff wind or while your friend flaps a big piece of cardboard to blow away sticks and leaves.

The berries will sound like hard rain as they fall on each other, filling your bucket with red opaque jewels. They will keep all winter in a cool room; use them by the handful when you need them or make a sauce for meat. You can eat the sauce on bread, too, or stir it into pudding. Morrie Secondchief told Norman to eat a spoonful every day to stay healthy. To eat lingonberries is to taste the bright sour heart of spruce and poplar woods in the late fall, when the winds that blow across the north have turned cold and the ground is waiting for snow.

I am comforted to know that wind does not belong to anyone. The mercy we could give the forest is for ourselves. Beauty and danger and comfort are human things, and they will not outlive us.

3
FROM THE AIR

This was those people, and that time.

We worked as firefighters in the Kobuk River Valley for six summers—from the receding of ice and snowbanks in the spring, as on this day in May, to the September snowlines marching down the Cosmos Hills around us until the ground was white. There is a visual pun I could share with you: the huge British-made Argosy cargo planes we used were painted white and dark gray, with the white on top. I have a photo of N1430Z sitting on the Dahl Creek runway, exactly echoing the paint job on the September mountains around it. Unlike the mountains but very much like me, it would fly away.

I say we worked, but I was a puppy and didn't know the difference between work and play: loading a helicopter or making a pie to take to someone in the village or singing songs until dark. Dark happened in August. My roots desperately wanted to be planted in this northern country that seemed so austere in its distances, smelled like sour fish and smoke in its warm houses. I would spend winters reading and studying the voices of elders and historic travelers through the Kobuk country. Like all wannabes, I would come part of the way toward the authentic life of the place, stitching the air to the ground. Trying to see beyond the apparent, I would constantly measure the depth of what might be below the surface—adding constantly to the ways I knew I was a stranger.

On this day I am the only person in the airplane besides the pilot, so the prized seat—front right—is mine. When you ride front right, the pilot gives you the other set of headphones and you can look at the sectional maps too. You're not just a passenger anymore but a privileged confidant who can look down as you cross a little pass, at the

next headwaters, and see the village places on paper and below you for
real. You can peer through the cockpit window at the weather in the
next valley that might make the airplane go around it or turn back.
A respectful front right rider waits until the pilot is done talking to
the tower and setting the throttle, waits until the altitude levels off to
cruise. She waits for the pilot to talk, or takes the temperature of the
silence before breaking it. If it feels warm between you—and there is
nearly always an intimacy up there in front created by your common
destination—you can ask for a life story framed special for you, told
between radio transmissions.

Sometimes you just can't stay awake though. Av-gas doesn't smell
good to me today, so very soon after the Cessna 402's gear clunks up
inside her, I retreat, letting the drone of engines draw my eyelids down
into a deep, druggy, time-killing sleep. I am probably snoring, possibly
drooling, undoubtedly happy, held tight like a baby on a cradle board
until some traffic over the Koyukuk River statics through the headphones and wakes me up.

The disorientation I feel is familiar. I had a childhood idea that
every time I went to sleep in the daytime, it would separate me from
who I'd been when the day started, so that when I woke up I'd be with
strangers in a different place. I'd "remember" them but with brand-
new fake memories, like the fossil record nineteenth-century Christian fundamentalists believed God put in the earth to make it look
old. My real family, my real house, would be back there somewhere
I'd never be able to find again. This explained the feeling of loss I had
each time I woke up, even sometimes after a night of sleep. Taking a
nap in the daytime made it worse because I didn't even get to finish
one day in the same family.

Waking in the airplane today, there is no trace of where we've
been—Fairbanks or the slate gray sky above it—but I don't mind. The
cloud ceiling has disappeared into a blue we could climb into forever.
Below us the Koyukuk is running high and muddy, carrying a scattered cargo of ice and broken trees. I was sleeping as we flew over the
Tanana and Yukon Rivers dumping their floods together. I started to

wake up over the squiggles of the Tozitna and Melozitna Rivers north of the Yukon. They say you travel three miles to every mile you advance on a river because of all the turns, but the ratio in these feeder creeks must be closer to six to one. They are as loopy as Christmas bows and some are still frozen, little squiggles of white icing through the already bare tundra waiting for green.

We're headed for a small plywood camp next to Dahl Creek at the foot of the Brooks Range, three miles from the village of Kobuk. This camp, established by the BLM's Alaska Fire Service, is where my husband, Jim, and I, with a few others from our agency, work all summer extinguishing, diverting, or just watching lightning-started wildfires for the federal government. There are a hundred or so of us in little airplanes this week, headed for stations scattered around northern Alaska. We are mostly very young, in our twenties. In Fairbanks for our training classes, we've recently been reunited with friends from other summers, so of course we've been dancing and drinking beer every night, maybe falling in love, probably talking about what we are going to do when our pockets have money in them again.

At Fort Wainwright, where the BLM stages us for our training weeks, the smokejumpers and helitack crews are staying in shape, running alongside the roads on base. I run a little too, because there are also physical tests the rest of us have to pass, even if for me fighting fire means talking on a radio or riding in an airplane to look for fires. I like to run in the woods by the Chena, but I'm soon distracted by the beauty of the pussy willows coming out along the bank or a beaver working the narrow strip of water where the ice has melted back from the shore. I end up just walking, wonderstruck by the slow explosion that is spring in the Tanana Valley.

Not long after we get to Fairbanks, though, I'm anxious to get out to Dahl Creek because at Fort Wainwright we are just military folks "lite," barely associates of the uniformed people running the gigantic army base and airfield around us. Though we have no ownership of the place, we are under the influence: we go to the officers club, we call the kitchen "mess," we use the terminologies for gear and numbered codes instead of clear text (simple plain talk) on the radio, and we refer to ourselves as pogues and crew.

On the military base we sleep in one of the cloned barracks buildings, in a cloned barracks room with paper-thin walls and pipes that bang all night, where a much-washed wool army blanket can't cover a person's shoulders and feet at the same time. The room and even the water in the toilet is hot—you forget about this until you sit there for the first time—because boilers in these World War II–era buildings push hot water year-round through ancient pipes and radiators so that the Fairbanks winters won't break them.

Beyond the barracks, there are hangars full of knobby airplanes that are here to protect us in general but don't care about me in particular. I feel the blindness of the military clear across its great Alaskan reserves, an entity that touts the billions it spends in the state—but with the notable exceptions of the rescue units—does not live here. The Alaska military is a web of military operations areas, or MOAs, with radar running like celestial windshield wipers hundreds of miles long in the air above the landscape and rows of drab green aircraft— this one bristling with weaponry and another large enough to contain all the houses and boats of a small river village. The military's Alaska is a map without rivers, without trapping prices and goose foot soup. Its collegial thousands associate predominantly with each other, live with their families on base, go to movies and to school on base. Arguably, they "occupy" more than "reside." Even fire doesn't touch the military unless smoke shuts a runway down or we wildfire people run out of helicopters. Often, a summer lightning strike will ignite the trees or tundra inside the miles of practice target areas where so much ordnance has fallen that the land is too "hot" for firefighters to enter. Dear old John Adams, never mind the Bill of Rights, we have finally garrisoned those soldiers in all of our sky above huge tracts of our "empty" land.

Outsiders to the military on base, we wildfire-fighting people are also strange to the permanent employees of our own agency, who regard seasonal workers an incongruity to put up with for a short time, like chicken pox. An agency manager once asked a roomful of firefighters in Galena how many of us would continue our careers by seeking year-round positions. Not a single person raised a hand, which of course was rude and would prove untrue but was likely payback for perceived slights by the "regulars." Most of those in the room were spending the winters like gypsies, scattered on beaches around the world or in some little woods they'd found. They were already what they wanted to be when they grew up.

I've never been a good gypsy because I am always trying to dig in and have a neighborhood or a clan, stitching the aunts and uncles I know to the aunts and uncles I can find. I want to have coffee and hear the news and feel loved and love back, which is what I was used to growing up and what I expect everywhere I live. If it is human and small, I want to know about it. How did you make that? Will you show me? Where does this grow? How do you eat it?

I increasingly loved our mission at Dahl Creek, which we and our supervisors at Galena refined to an informal efficiency. With our boss, Brian, a durable and loved friend of those days, we learned to build ourselves into a busy miniature firefighting base in half a day after a lightning storm first spread its fires. The fires around villages and mines were our first concern. We expanded into twenty-four-hour coverage of dispatch and operations, with mess hall, staffed warehouse, camp areas for crews and bosses. Spotter planes were often Aero Commanders, and smokejumper airplanes were Volpars, converted from old Beech-18s. Cargo and retardant airplanes were World War II fly-ins to our airstrip refueling operation, with the PBY the strangest and most exotic of the bunch. Really it was all about the airplanes.

On the side, between fires, I installed new aunts and uncles from Dahl Creek, the Bornite mine, and the village people we grew close to in Kobuk and Shungnak. And I tried to garden. In the first year, we scratched out a nearly soilless garden that soaked in the cold breezes flowing down out of the Cosmos Hills drainages each night. Almost nothing grew, but I have the memory of six-foot-three Greg Podsiki bent over nearly to the ground, saying to a white crown sparrow, "Don't eat those little seedlings or Mary is going to be mad at you." Exploring abandoned mining camps with their old steam machinery and ditches for the water cannons brought us closer to the miners who still worked in the country. Sometimes they would come over for coffee and blueberry pie. Amazing to me, Jim has always been able to look at an old machine and know how it had operated: leather gaskets, rocker arms, pressure fittings. Growing up on a Wisconsin farm where he learned to fix machines alongside his dad gave him a deep interest in all things mechanical. He and our new friends talked hammer mills and steam donkeys until I could nearly see the old iron things too, clanging and chugging in the long-ago camps on the creeks.

In this clear weather, we don't need the little pass between these rivers to find our way around Indian Mountain, pointing up above four thousand feet—the highest rock between the Alaska Range and the Kobuk River country. Pilots told me that Indian Mountain has a curious effect, caused by some hard or shiny magnetism in the rock that folds the electrons around itself, skews compasses, gives little airplanes a fling in the wrong direction.

In a clear sky like this one, the mountain is a friend, an unmistakable landmark meaning when we pass it we will still know where we are going. Seeing it on the way to the Kobuk, I try to look beyond it for the canyon of the Koyukuk below Hughes, for Hog River camp, the Pah River, the break in the Zane Hills where the Koyukon Athabaskan people sometimes went to trade with the Kobuk Inupiat people. Knowing that, looking for the storied places gives this view ghostly layers of time periods, each of the layers with its people traveling, their tales known and unknown.

We are coming down, through three thousand feet now, to land at Hughes. The slopes show bright patches of snow and an emerging dulled tapestry of last fall's color. I press my fingers against the scratched plexiglass and imagine that I feel the mountain changing from the shape that tells us we are almost to the river to the shape that tells us we are above the river. What does "same" mean? It's not the "same" mountain from the Tanana side, or from the sky here and there above it. Without a paper map, with only the moving map created in our minds, we recognize not things but relationships, like Mark Twain's river pilot Bixby in *Life on the Mississippi.* Explaining navigation by landmarks, he says, "That's the main virtue of the thing. If the shapes didn't change every three seconds, they wouldn't be of any use."

The rugged and valleyed shape we are passing doesn't look much like the little elevation dot on the aircraft sectional on my lap as the land shifts in my view. Still, I have to believe in a map that lets me count the drainages running away from each mountain. Because of the map, I can locate myself on the airy, imaginary lines cartographers use to grid the earth, then recognize the actual place as we pass above it. Now there's another way: Earth stations talk to sky and radio signals to triangulate with satellites to find us within this space. Above Indian Mountain, the Global Positioning System display in the instrument panel reads out: "n66 04.12w153 39.50," word to flesh. But I like my old boss's advice: "Don't forget how to use the map." I can find us if I count drainages and contour lines and compare those with the gigantic rocky pyramid out my window. I recognize this mountain and this place on paper, even though all I really see through my eyes is the approaching and receding shapes of ridges and slopes. A map is more than coordinates; it teaches a place to me before I see it. It allows me to recognize where I am, a place I've never been, as I see it out the window. "Oh, there you are!" This is an abstraction, an equation, and a human magic.

In the summer, usually June but sometimes later, the tundra can dry out and be touched off by any lightning bolt that reaches clear to the ground or one that starts in the ground and reaches clear up to the dark blue bottom of a cumulonimbus. Then the brittle dead branches at the bottom of the black spruce will lead fire up to their crooked crowns. After the fires start and especially if a fire grows too fast in the direction of a village, we will look down into flat maps as if they are oracles. The fires will run up those paper contour lines, slow down on the bare ridges, back themselves into the daily wind that will arrive by 10:00 a.m. We'll lean close over the paper to look for drainages and little ponds and then send the pilot out to see if that green on the map signifies spruce or hardwood or if that pond has become grass since 1956 when this old quadrangular survey map was made. When we are fighting fire, we call trees and brush and grass "fuels." Villages, even the aunts and uncles, flatten out to a plan, a place to protect, a system of hose lays. A big enough town might have a trained crew we can hire. They have been waiting for this day. We'll know which crew and how many crew members are there. In the excited, noisy-with-propellers, and routinely dangerous days of fighting fire, our chunk of Alaska will transform to its avatar the plan, a busy one-dimensional map.

At Hughes we drop off groceries. Despite the mud, a crowd meets the airplane, mostly Native youngsters and some grandmothers on wheelers. One white guy picks up the groceries for the school in a pick-up that doesn't have any dings in it. The pilot starts into a conversation with a man I recognize from the fire crew, so I get out and stretch my legs, grin at the kids, and ask them to tell me about the fishing. "There's no fish now," a tall boy says but points at a girl who caught one a few days ago. The girl looks down and the other kids giggle. "Through the ice?" I ask, and they say no, "By the ice."

I remember what they mean: the way the ice comes away from the bank before it goes out and the grayling run up the margins looking for their creeks. An early photo in the collection of missionary nurse Amelia Hill from the Episcopal mission at Allakaket, called St. John's in the Wilderness, features some miners sitting on the bank very near here in the early springtime, little piles of grayling beside them.

The miners weren't old then. It was nearly a hundred years ago, and just like now half of the people in the world were younger than the other half. There was fiddle music here and mission boats and supply barges on the river and long black stockings like the ones my mother told me she wore when she was a girl in western Idaho. Sometimes when the manifest destiny mood falls on me and this country of rivers and lakes seems empty—or seems to belong to me in any way—I remember how many times it has been opened up and lived in. I think of Bob Marshall staring at his horizon of peaks and declaring the country empty of names—at his airy level this would have seemed true. All the countries of peoples in his view, each with place names and camps, were invisible. Later on, in *Coming into the Country*, John McPhee declared that no white man before himself had stood on a certain ridge near the Salmon River, proximal to Dahl Creek, one of a plethora of Salmon Rivers in Alaska, but who's counting. The BLM had firefighters on that ridge the summer before McPhee walked there.

If you cannot claim to be the first man to be somewhere, then it is an interesting fallback measure to name yourself the first white man to be there. My husband and a village fire crew had used a very noisy Mark 26 pump to put out a fire on the ridge that McPhee mentioned, but the activity left no human trace. When Jim came to the place in the book where McPhee describes the ridge, he started laughing. He said, "I wondered the same thing! Was I the first white guy to walk around there?" An answer: who knows but maybe not, given the exploration and mining and the incessant wandering around of the last two hundred years—but the question is troublesome. When you think about it, that kind of first is a "first in breed," like we were at a dog show. What about women. What about redheads. What about the nearsighted. The question is irrelevant, mistaken. It isn't the *country* that's new, when we first look at it. It's *us*—the great hopeful makeover of ourselves, courtesy of the remote, the awesome, the seemingly empty.

Tucked up alongside the upper slopes of Indian Mountain, the mining district called Utopia comes into view. Hughes village, on the river at the base of the mountain, was at one time a place where the little horse barges could bring supplies to those miners. Now the USAF calls their station Utopia. I think this is probably a little joke for the Air Force people stationed here, although some may mean it. I wonder if it was a joke when the gold-seekers named it, maybe to the ones on the bank in the springtime with the cranes already back and the ice melting off all the pay dirt.

Flying over Utopia—"UTO" on the sectional map—Norutak Lake will come into your view at the far right, over several folds of hills. From here, it is a shiny coin on the old portage between the Alatna

River country and the Kobuk River. For people whose families have lived here for centuries, places along that trail have songs and stories that belong to them, waving in memory like flags.

On a tape I listened to at the university, I remember that interviewers asked a Koyukon elder if she knew a certain place, and she said no. "But," objected her interviewers, "we know you camped there."

"Well, yes, I camped there," she said, "but I don't know the stories that belong to that place." After that, it seemed to me the interviewers took special care to explain themselves when they used the word *know*.

And if you know the story, you still may not get the joke, because you are not listening in the dark, as the Koyukon people once listened to their winter stories, or because your memory does not provide you with the same map of the land.

One of the stories I remember was from a very old category of tales, in which animals interact with each other like humans, setting up initial relationships in the world that can be told to teach us how to behave. It is about Wolf and Otter trying to build cooking fires for each other, but the damp wood Otter brings can't cook anything for the wolves. Wolf finally has to go out and get some dry willows to start a fire. Otter then wonders out loud what kind of fire this is that Wolf has made and says his children are going to freeze to death.

This is a funny story, and the teller laughed. I think about this over and over, and I finally start to get it. My expectations of fire and water turn over slowly. I think of the story, or the story thinks of me: Otter is stranger to me than Wolf. Can my children be warmed by the stories of another people?

My understanding of the people who have fed me and told me stories at their tables sometimes seems less intimate to me than these recorded voices, listened to in solitude and then carefully stroked, a few at a time, onto white paper where they will hopefully live long and prosper, or better yet, drive the reader back to the voices. If there's a pause after a question—why the pause? A voice raises, it softens. An odd side comment becomes clear later, or forever covers a thought that is never shared. Listen again, make a note. I was no one to the storyteller but a ghost from the future, an eavesdropper. But Wolf and Otter live in me like grafted branches.

When we are back in the airplane and in the air again, off the gravel strip at Hughes and over the bluffs, I begin to see places I've touched with my feet, though I know only a few of the stories that belong to them, and, of course, only in a lone way, like the bear who has no community. According to some elders, that's the danger of the bear—not his claws or teeth but that he acts and lives alone. Just saying the name of the bear or looking in his direction can drive his anger and aloneness into the womb of a woman, tear apart the sinew strings that a woman sews—with food, with husbands and children, wood and water and stories—to hold her people together.

I see the gap where the tea-colored Pah goes through. I recognize it from standing in the river on the other side of that hill. We were at the mouth where it flows into the Kobuk. In the low water of fall we stuck the boat on a gravel bar and climbed out to push. Cussing and laughing, we scooted the johnboat, a bit lighter without us in it, into a deeper current. I watched the ribbons of green Kobuk water and brown Pah water flow together around my legs. Just up the Kobuk is a cabin built by a white guy who liked to trap in this country. He built his cabin a little late in the century—past the federal homesteading act that closed in 1976, past the mining claim time. "Owning" the land along the river was still a new idea to many people in Kobuk, so a trapping cabin was no big deal at the village, but the Native corporation and the National Park Service seemed to think the fellow had a lot of gall. Before he built the cabin, he had made himself a pit house built down into the ground like a traditional *ivrulik*, with a sleeping shelf around the fire pit and sod walls sloping up to a smoke hole.

After we pulled the boat off the gravel bar, we explored the bank to find the old pit house and see what it was like. It was damp and cold and empty, with only a little light coming down through a piece of dirty plexiglass boxed into the thick dirt of the ceiling.

Before the cabin, we heard about a hired cabin-sitter living in the pit house one winter and taking care of a little dog team. He was going crazy from being alone and living in a hole in the ground. Harold Lie told us he flew up from Dahl Creek and pulled the unfortunate caretaker—a stinking matted hairball of a human being—out of there. "It was a good thing it was so cold," Harold said, "or I couldn't have stood the smell of him in the airplane." He said the dogs smelled better when he brought them out.

Louise Woods told me there is a graveyard on a bend just down river from where the Pah comes in, on the Brooks Range side, but now it is overgrown and as invisible from the river as it is from the air. But invisible things were once real. Louise is a Baptist now, but she says before Christianity came to the Kobuk "it was danger," an "evil time." A shaman was jealous of the power of one of her ancestors, a successful trader. The shaman said all the men in her family would die young and so they did. Jesus superseded the power of shamans, said Louise, but Jesus couldn't change what happened before he arrived on the scene.

This is something quite different from the typically western idea that the clear light of science, or Christianity, or any other kind of explaining that can illumine all the way backward and "solve" the past. In the culture I grew up in, ghosts get explained as marsh gas or perhaps Christian ghosts, allowing us to revise and correct those earlier ignorant or pagan folks (please do read irony in that). In Louise's view, and the views of some others we talked to or read about in the Native north, powers are exchanged only at the point of introduction. Rules and retributions are in effect for those who believe in them, at the time they believe in them. In her *Tales of Ticasuk*, Eskimo writer Emily Ivanoff Brown said of the Ogre baby crying in the caribou herd, "And when the Gospel came, the crying ceased forever." Or of different supernatural events, an elder says, "We have noticed that these things do not happen anymore." Even more carefully, one elder often reminds her listeners, "That was those people, that time," which is a very considerate thing to say. The storyteller refuses to tread on what was true for the others who came before her.

Watching the rivers run together from the air, I wish to learn to be this careful, as if I could feel the distance between the air and the ground as voices, as if my feet could know the distance between the surface of a sandbar and where the river ran before.

"I love white people," Louise says. And I love her back, since I *am* "white people," and I always have tea with her at her cabin in Kobuk before the fires come and again afterward, just before the snow. I shot a caribou for her one fall and rammed my ego directly into the culture cutbank. Louise pushed her little knife into the top of the rump and pronounced the bull a poor animal, "not much fat!" Maybe noting my fallen face, her footnote comment was, "Good for my dog!" Her big grin healed the status of my gift.

The sky is so seamless it is no place at all, and it is easy to forget that you have a body, that you have friends or family. Like an astral projection, all your strings are cut; the obligation to bring a pie to the potluck supper is officially discontinued. I am slightly afraid of small airplanes, which make occasional unplanned contact with the tundra, but this fear goes away as soon as the plane leaves the ground. Anywhere starts to be familiar, even the near-touching of flying in airplanes. The mind wishes to recognize a pattern, a story so big that it not only locates by triangulation but looks into the intersecting histories and explains the present moment.

When we came to work in Dahl Creek in 1978, there weren't any maps with the miles gridded off, just unmarked 1:63,360 quadrangular survey maps, some of them from the lovely colored topographic relief series the USGS discontinued after the 1950s. We were making our station sign for Dahl Creek out of big expensive redwood boards, routing out "Northernmost Fire Management Station in the U.S." in the spring of 1979 when the USGS brought in a survey crew to fill in the lines on the quads. The survey crew lived in Harold Lie's cabin, so Harold had to spend most of the summer at Kotzebue, his other home. We missed his stories and the vaudeville Norwegian accent he put on for us every time we walked in. We missed the pot of coffee that was always sitting on the oil stove. It wasn't much fun to go over to Harold's cabin that summer because, besides the fact that Harold wasn't there, the USGS crew had a cranky helicopter pilot who hated the cook, so the place was always full of sarcasm or swearing or sulky silence.

In one of the odd coincidences that happen so often they aren't really odd, the crew chief was a man I'd been in love with back in Oregon when I was eighteen, a sweet-natured and reclusive person too many years older than me, last seen flashing mirrors from ridge to ridge in the Owyhee Desert. This should not happen in a regular world, that people you have cared about can start popping up in front of you thousands of miles away in remote river valleys. At Dahl Creek he always looked tired and sad. Besides having to manage a fractious crew, a task he hated, his technical job was to compile data that would finally lay section lines over landscape that had never had them before. He spent hours bent over his notebooks in the cabin, turning the asbestos spires of the western Brooks Range into numbers, numbers. I know he would have rather learned the names.

Names can save you, when the ceiling is low or the sky is all smoke and you are with a pilot who hasn't flown in that country. One time we flew out of Fairbanks into scattered layers of fog and clouds. It was getting darker and the weather seemed to be closing in behind us while it was still lighter ahead. But as we approached Indian Mountain, the weather started to come down and I felt the pilot freezing up beside me, nervous hands moving over his gauges, watching the little craziness in the compass from the mountain below us, unseen now. He kept asking me, "Do you see anything you recognize?" And occasionally I would, a twist of water or the edge of an old forest fire burn whose shape I recognized because I'd drawn it with different-colored markers as it burned outward, day after day.

We turned around once, but the route looked worse, less familiar, so we headed back north and I could just barely see a layer of the Kobuk country far off, lighter than the sky we were in, with the Brooks Range riding across the northern horizon behind it. I showed the pilot the gaps where the rivers and lakes pushed down through the foothills range, chattering a litany of names to him from the USGS maps—Koliaksak, Koguluktuk, Cosmos, Ruby Creek—twisted orthographies from Native place names alongside the names of miners and explorers, names of the lovers and financiers of miners and explorers. I was a person who could see the road but couldn't drive; he was a driver who found himself suddenly blind, having to trust the directions of his passenger. I borrowed the power of names, the iceberg tips of stories, to help him: "A little left, that gap beside where the mountain looks flat on top, that's Cosmos, that's where the runway is." And so we "lucked out," as Grumman Goose pilot Jim Pickering used to say, meaning that we'd gotten where we were going. I saw the pilot a few times after that and we smiled at each other like we'd once danced a slow one.

In a July fire season, I was in a Cessna 207 with another pilot hired by our agency to deliver several of us to country he had never seen. We entered a cloud of smoke when we came into the Kobuk Valley. Incredibly, the pilot turned right when we flew over the Kobuk River, heading upriver and away from the airfield at Dahl Creek. I was in a seat behind him, more of a passenger than the privileged copilot seat would have made me. He took us through the pink haze, flying low over the river and following one bend at a time. I touched him on the shoulder and pointed behind us in the direction of Dahl Creek, but he looked in my direction only briefly—and through me—then went back to his task of following the turns of the shrinking river. Through the smoke I could see the shapes of salmon in the clear water. I saw Daisy's fish camp and then Vera's. We were so low that Vera waved to us. My friend Gil was riding front right so I leaned up to him and told him where we were, now far upriver of where we wanted to be, and eventually he and I together convinced the pilot to turn around. To convince him, we each had to name names to prove he could trust us. The names of rivers and names of rivers that run into rivers are like collateral if you want to turn a plane around or tell a story. They say you can afford the risk. They say you know how to go somewhere.

The 402 bumps down again, this time at Hog River, to bring supplies to the miners at the dredge. I am glad to be on the milk run, glad to come into the country one little airfield at a time.

Dan Egan still runs this place, though I hear someone else bought out his Alaska Gold Company, and he is just keeping this operation going for them as only he can do, with a crew of fifteen men or so eating Spam and beans and barely maintaining the ancient noisy dredge. The dredge clatters and chews and digests the rocky ground in the creek bottom. Egan is one of the more famous misers of the Interior. No alcohol allowed, precious little variation in the food, and the minimum of tools and parts, a real baling-wire outfit is how the story goes. A Hog River camp foreman I once talked to said that if there was an ancient Ford Tri-Motor airplane still in one piece in the country, Egan would hire it to fly in Hog's food and mail and supplies.

To say "Hog River" is a little confusing. Hog River isn't really a river. It's a mining camp named after the Hogatza River, and calling it "Hog" is the result of the shortening and the laughing and claiming that people do, we do, to make the unfamiliar ours. The miners and traders made the shortened name, and knowing about it makes me an insider in a comfortable way. But the resulting confusion means that you will sometimes hear a young adventurer from the Lower 48 say that they want to "float the Hog River." This is dreadfully incorrect, and if there is an old-timer around, I have the right to catch her eye and share a nice camaraderie. But if you've been around a few years, it's okay to say, "I was in the Hog River country." There's a difference.

The layer of names and history that mines and miners live in is a different web of map over the Interior, attached at the points of little runways, old dredges, corrugated steel and new-but-castoff ATCO trailers bought cheap from dismantled Alaska pipeline construction camps. From the air, the ATCOs are little white bricks with yellow-and-black borders.

This particular universe is full of misers and the men who work for them and bitch about it. This is light years away from the Alaska of Prudhoe Bay, where there are recreation rooms and gleaming cafeterias serving ice cream and steak. This Hog River country is where everything you need to make, from furniture to lathes to stovepipes to pipelines, can be made from Blazo boxes, coffee cans, and fifty-five-gallon drums. This is the country of the hiss of the Coleman lantern. Mining is not an invisible enterprise from the air. There are mounds of yellow shat-out creek bottom wherever the dredges have been or still are, their factory-like forms rusted and rotted in squares and rectangles.

Before the dredges there were the little placer operations like the ones up Dahl Creek, where we still find iron nozzles. The mounds of gravel there are smaller, willowed over after more than a hundred years. A Swede named Johnson, the partners Ted Tromsted and Sig Goodwin, and Louis Lloyd were up there just before the turn into the twentieth century. All of them would go down the several miles to Kobuk to trader Harry Brown's place for Christmas—Louise Woods has old pictures of the miners and Kobuk villagers in their holiday clothes: white shirts and high lace collars. Harry Brown, a white man, was married to Mabel, an Inupiaq woman, and their daughter May still owns the store. Harry wanted to name the village of Kobuk "Long Beach," for a long sandbar that curved in front of the village, much longer than it is now. The story goes that the federal postal service headquarters said there already was a Long Beach, so he had to give it up. That story has the flavor of one that has grown out of a smaller story, perhaps just a joke or passing comment someone heard from Harry Brown long ago, but someone told me and so I tell it, like any good listener on a street corner or a sandbar.

Harry's grave is on the road to the boat landing, his own small hill of caribou moss and birch with a white picket fence around it. There is a real stone marker engraved with the entire Twenty-third Psalm. In the summer you can see green pasture and birch, still water and cotton grass on every side of him.

A new red Ford pickup comes out to meet the airplanes at Hog River and pick up the cases of supplies we've brought. This is a surprising indication of affluence for Hog. The old red truck must have met an irreparable death for Egan to consent to this newfangled thing. These miners will hook wheels up to the last moving part of a Model T or ancient Allis, making strange hybrid conveyances that never die, only change shapes. But life hasn't changed so much. Joe, a dredge mechanic who rode down to the runway with the cook, quickly looks through the boxes we brought and sees that he didn't get any cigarettes. "Damn Egan," he says.

When we leave Hog River, we skirt the left shoulder of Angutikada, which would be the right shoulder if you were looking southeast from Dahl Creek. All summer, it is the most prominent shape on our southern horizon. The radio repeater is there on top, not thrown down the mountain by a grizzly bear this year or torn apart by winter storms. Seeing its fiberglass box and antennas intact means our local "brown" radio frequency should work this summer, allowing us to talk to fire bosses and little camps up and down the Kobuk from our dispatch. Like a lot of the names on the map, Angutikada doesn't mean anything except the tin ear of a USGS employee, trying to transcribe the Inupiaq word for "Old Man Mountain," according to Beulah Commack. Beulah was our cook for the one summer they let us have a cook at Dahl Creek. On the slow days, she tried to teach us some upper Kobuk Inupiaq, sometimes the wrong word for the thing—for instance the word for "penis" when we meant to say "house"—so that we would get ourselves in trouble. Then there would be laughter, the real goal of communication. Beulah enjoyed it when I showed her USGS-attempted place name orthographies on the big dispatch map. "Oh, they were mixed up, I guess!" she laughed. "Have you got any more like that?"

I got in trouble with Beulah for jumping into the Kobuk River to fish out an empty Coke can she'd just tossed in while we stood talking on the bank. "Why do you do that?" she asked me, really angry. I had a precedent for this, having jumped out of a moving jeep to pick up the beer can my father had tossed into the desert. He, too, was furious at my self-righteous act. I say without irony that I didn't have the right to fetch either of those cans. And that I'd probably do it again. After a swirl or two passed, Beulah shrugged her face at me, resuming her characteristic patience with us interlopers.

We cross over the ridge into a swale where you can see the Selawik zigzagging off toward the coast at your nine o'clock. At your eleven o'clock you can see the Pick River looping one of its angles up to meet the Kobuk below Shungnak. At the top of the swale just below us is a hot springs, another place where Athabaskan people from the Koyukuk and Inupiat from the Kobuk used to come together to trade and fight, according to Louise. The Wheeler Creek side, behind us and south, coming up from the Koyukuk, she still calls "Indianside." The Kobuk River flows east to west through the valley. Sheep and caribou hides used to go down to the coast while seal oil and other sea plunder would come back up to these hills, she says. But now all that remains along that route is the habit of winter travel, of checking in with who you are as a person who can move around the country, easier and quicker now on a snogo than it was by foot or dog sled.

People still meet down at the hot springs in winter, driving fifty miles from either direction to get there, but the sense of nation meeting nation has diminished. The travelers are more likely to be just people who know each other.

On the map of a certain people at a certain time, these are the trails from story to story, along these creeks and rivers where the old people lived, different old people all the time, winter and summer back as far as you can listen, yet there aren't very many marks left from the old people that can be seen from the air. The Inupiaq trails are less visible than the miner's scratching with Allis-Chalmers in the 1920s and '30s or the gravel roads that struggle out from every modern village.

The trails that stand out most vividly below me now—coming up into the Kobuk Valley from the south to lace the woods and gravelly tops of hills—belong to the caribou's back and forth, not the humans'. From the air I can see that these trails do not go anywhere in the human way—to town or cabin. Still I trace them with my eyes with the expectation that they lead somewhere, just as I follow them with my feet when I am down in the woods. I feel that old excitement of being on any trail, of following, and the intention of making some discovery, finding some terminus. But the caribou trails are braided like rivers and don't go toward any warmth or any stopping place that is familiar to me. If I were high enough, higher than the geese fly, higher than any airplane can fly, could I see a pattern to follow? Or do rivers and caribou and all the mines and all the stories and all the maps make a kind of randomness I can never get outside of to find my way by their changing shapes?

When we disperse the last of the cargo and the mail in Ambler, I'm the only cargo left. Looking down on the rough rotten ice of first the Shungnak and then the Kobuk Rivers, we are west of Dahl Creek now and heading back to land there.

Later this spring the Shungnak, which means "jade," will run the color of jade—greener than the blue Ambler—its riffles from the air so exactly like the lovely imperfections in the rock it is named for, the rock you can pull from its banks. This is a strangeness unattributable to ancient astronauts, too funny and too metaphorical to be the work of the God I grew up with: that a river, from the air, looks like the rock it runs through. I think I'll save this idea as a joke to tell Ivan Stewart when he brings his crew up to Dahl Creek to cut jade boulders in July. He probably won't think it is funny, but he might. He tells me the same joke several times each summer, the one about how the environmentalist found the beautiful trout in the tailing pond. If I shared Ivan's ambivalence about the scientists and government people and outsiders that to him represent an intrusive new order, then I'd feel the jolliness of his joke too. What I can appreciate is how much he enjoys telling it to me.

One year the fire season was slow so I took off work to go with Ivan and several of his crew to the Shungnak River from Dahl Creek, twenty-seven miles overland at two miles an hour on a sled made of rough-sawn planks on log skids. We were pulled along by an Allis-Chalmers cat so old that Ivan's faithful "Blackie," Francis Black, was continually making parts for it and welding it when it broke, which it often did. The old tractor and its tracks were one big weld. On the trip, Ivan fed us rancid bear meat and the ends of loaves of bread and other things nobody had consumed at his Dahl Creek camp when there was anything better to eat. He did bring a plastic bottle of "jade juice," his special concoction of lime Kool-Aid mixed with water and Everclear. We stopped often to winch ourselves out of bogs, especially in the places on the old trail where earlier expeditions had exposed permafrost and turned swampy grass into muddy lakes. I picked handfuls of blueberries as we rattled along, or I walked alongside like some pioneer woman trailing her wagon.

Halfway to the Shungnak, we stopped overnight at a corrugated steel shack that the ubiquitous north-country pilot and miner Bill Munz—the Munz Air founder from Nome—had hauled to Cosmos Creek before Ivan bought mining claims from him. Being the only youngster and the only female, I got the privileged bunk—the upper one—with twelve or so inches between the thin mattress on the plywood bunk and the ceiling, so that once you wedged yourself onto the bunk you could not turn over onto your back. If you wanted to turn over, you had to get out of bed and get back in, and you could not do that because the floor was full of old men and you would step on them. They'd gotten a good fire going in the stove to warm us up, and it was pungent in there, with the old plywood and two-by-fours of the shack sweating off a summer's moisture and all of us sleeping in our sweaty long underwear.

Munz had hauled another cabin like that one to the Shungnak River, our destination, with more room in it for the top bunk. I noticed this potential roominess immediately when we got to the camp, but Ivan said there were fewer bears around the Shungnak so we should set up tents and sleep outside. He probably just wanted to save on firewood. We spent a week there, working across the Shungnak River on Promise Creek, a small tributary. I wasn't much help because they brought me along to cook, but there wasn't much fresh food. All that week, we winched pieces of jade out of the creek, even boulders the size of sofas. But there were two boulders so gigantic we could only look at them. They were beauties, in some places showing us their translucent greens through the water of the creek flowing over their slick sides. The creek had polished them until they looked like they were revealing the heart of the world, showing itself here for a few yards only, a secret interior made of wet, green glass. Ivan had prodded the hillside to determine the sizes of the boulders. He thought the biggest one would weigh about fifty thousand pounds. He wanted them badly, so conversations were all about hiring D-9 Caterpillars and heavy-lifting Chinook helicopters and how to bring them to the Shungnak. These were resources and complicated distances beyond hope, representing amounts of money unimaginable to a man accustomed to cobbling together or inventing every tool or machine he used.

We are flying over the hills of that old trip, approaching Dahl Creek from the Ambler side. When we fly over Cosmos Creek and its tiny tin shack, I can see the brown and white scratching of the Promise Creek trail running back to Dahl Creek ahead of us. The messy trail runs perpendicular to the mountain streams flowing down to the Kobuk. It cuts across those drainages as if it was a contour line from the paper map in front of me made real on the land. Finally, the warehouse, generator shack, and bunkhouses of Dahl Creek come into view and then the kitchen and shower house. The dispatch roof sprouts a scraggly bush of antennas and the bright red numbers I painted there several summers ago, announcing our air-to-ground radio frequency—127.45.

Scritch of wheels on gravel and the 402 is on the ground. Engines shut down and props slow to stillness. Now I can hear the *puh, puh, puh* of the Witte generator, our summer's heartbeat. Pretty soon, for the next few months, I'll belong here because I am hired to be here. Better yet, I won't be a stranger but a host: offering food, an emergency radio link, some ancient magazines, and an outstretched hand. If you misjudge the runway and your Super Cub flips over on its back, I'll help you find three long ropes, five or six guys, and we will dig a hole into the tundra for the nose of your plane to rest in for a moment as we turn it back over onto its wheels. That way, your prop won't get any more curly than it already is.

I'll visit Guy and Faith Moyer's house in Kobuk. Since Guy had eye surgery, his postmaster job has been taken over by his Inupiaq wife, Faith, whose other name is Tulagaq (raven). A desk in their cabin is devoted to the post office, with fifty or so little cubbyholes stacked above it for sorting letters. The parcels lean up alongside the desk, waiting to go to the airstrip or waiting to be claimed. Guy told us he came from Pennsylvania in the 1930s. He was headed for the Hogatza River and a prospecting venture when his plane, probably a Norseman or a Gull Wing Stinson, got lost in the fog and dropped him off at Norutak Lake instead. Norutak is about forty miles northeast of Kobuk. He spent the next fifty years in the Kobuk Valley as miner, trapper, storekeeper, postmaster. Now he is old and sits in his chair with one kid or another on his lap, perhaps the tiny Tulagaq, a granddaughter. He has a round white face and a shock of wild white hair. His skin is smooth and ruddy in the cheeks from long years in the weather, and his eyes glint narrowly above them, taking in everything. He has read widely, defied the latitude to raise verdant riverside gardens, welcomed countless strangers, raised a flock of children, put his Witte generator to use as the village's electric company. He's hauled tons of Ivan's burlap-encased jade rocks over the circuitous back paths to mail planes waiting on the little Kobuk airstrip. Worried about the D-2 land changes in the Brooks Range that would soon result in new national parks, Guy asked us to bring the visiting secretary of the interior, James Watt—known as an advocate of the mining companies and not the parks—down to the village so that he could have a word with him. Not accustomed to popular acclaim, Watt and his wife were wary and then pleased as Guy shook Watt's hand and told him "good job."

In the spring when we come down to Kobuk to visit him, Guy says, "Well look who's here." And in the fall he asks, "It's time for you to go, isn't it?" He would say something this matter-of-fact to a flock of cranes riding a thermal into the sky.

Before the fires start, we'll be invited down to the Kobuk school that's about to be let out for the summer. We'll eat goose foot soup. People will bring us their questions and puzzling pieces of correspondence from the government they've been saving for us all winter, because besides ourselves we are also a connection to that far-off officialdom, one that might help: "Your letter was sent when?" "Your father filed for this site when?" "I will find out who you can talk to." I will do what I say I will do, and there will be a bond between us to remember. Usefulness is a kind of belonging I cherish. Chameleon, starling, I start to resemble each role I am given, just as I answer each call from a passing airplane: "Oh, about fifteen hundred feet. I can see the top of Cosmos." "Nope, it was his sister who died. I have the phone number if you want to call." People in airplanes always need things from people on the ground, particular things like food or gas or what the weather is like on the way to the next stop. We'll see people from all the villages, berry pickers, hunters, pilots, miners. When the weather is bad outside, they will each set a story down with us like a pack leaned against the wall by the door. I am always eager to be the person there to listen, the person on the ground.

Turkey Gravy

In the East Coast family she belongs to, Karen said you have to strain out all the small pieces of skin and meat so that what remains are the cooked turkey juice and just the slightest rich glint of fat. Salt, cornstarch, and water, these are stirred in so the golden liquid thickens imperceptibly but remains clear. A pool of Karen's turkey gravy rises ever so slightly, held by surface tension, above the hollow made for it in your mashed potatoes. The butter drifts up through it like a yellow cloud through the sky.

My gravy, on the other hand, contains all the small chunks too ragged to be skewered on the end of a fork. Each little morsel on the tongue is a savory messenger from its source: gizzard, liver, neck. My textured gravy has plenty of the fat shining on top of it with a pancake-batter consistency of milk and flour poured in during cooking to make it thick. My gravy is likely to take twenty seconds, once it escapes the confines of your mashed potatoes, to reach the green salad next door.

Karen does not approve of my chunky opaque gravy, and I am suspicious of her elegant translucent gravy.

After an hourlong ride in a Cessna 206 to Anvik on the Yukon, during which slightly spilled portions of both gravies combine to blow grandmotherly smells up our noses and lull us to sleep under the aircraft's drone, Karen's beautiful gravy commiserates with my beautiful gravy at a college graduate's celebration dinner, while guest after guest spoons whole-kernel corn over mashed potatoes.

4
SHAPE OF AN EGG

Oh, who that ever lived and loved
Can look upon an egg unmoved?
—Clarence Day

Early morning in McGrath, Alaska. The sun has been up for hours, but I have only just untangled myself from the sleep-smelling warmth of my husband and daughter. I am looking for coffee and a book. Water on, I head for the big chair and crawl into it. I am looking for the place in this book I left days ago, as I hear a thump on the floor of the next room and the quick pad of feet. Vestigial peevishness flashes through me but is gone even before the face of my three-year-old daughter appears in the door. She smiles a closed-lip smile at me from under her brow, her head bent forward, her chin squeezed back against her chest. This is a very old game with us.

"Youuu," I say, and her teasing lips open in a grin as she hurries over to climb in my lap. As she does this she doesn't look at me, in the manner of someone shy who has been surprised. I fold her into my bare, crossed legs, little sleeper body with her knees bent up against her chest and my spread hands circling her shoulders. I brush my nose and lips across the top of her head for just a moment—not too long, because life is layered instead of long and because I am already more nest than womb. I lean my head back against the chair and let her fall asleep again, still safe in the shape she was made in.

When Jim gets up to rescue the boiling water into coffee, he smiles at us. I believe we have knowledge, if it is knowledge, of egg cup, womb, "life poured out for you." The Buddhists say the empty bowl has the promise of holding anything. A parent is a bowl full of the promise of absence, fullness and absence curled about each other like particle and wave, each one never quite true without the other. The body of my child in the bowl of my lap is round and smooth, nearly awake, made to be replaced, made irreplaceable.

I remember trying to write a letter to my oldest brother, Bill, an on-going discussion we have about abortion. Bill is a compassionate man. He was my favorite when I was very small, because of all my three brothers he had the most time for me and took me everywhere with him. I remember what the world looked like, riding on his shoulders. He set me up on the top rail of a fence that is long gone, down by the Snake River. I remember the smell of the frost, how it hung in the tamaracks over the dark dimpled water. Now, through the grownup distance between us, I've seen Bill struggle with the pain in his life. He and his wife, Teri, have a daughter, Erin, who lives her life at the mental age of two and with all the frustrated anger of a two-year-old, although she is as strong as an adult. For Erin, they have taken on whole professions' worth of learning and practicing of skills, skills mastered outside the regular jobs they've maintained and the other two children they've raised. There have been few vacations and no extra money.

Bill said to me long ago, "You know, this issue of abortion is just like slavery. Since the Civil War, we've never had such clear-cut lines between right and wrong." Knowing what he knows about accepting an injured gift had set him hard against the practice of abortion. I knew what he meant: if you draw your line at life or no life, how could you choose no life for anyone? But I was thinking of the Civil War too—the families split open by death, the beardless faces of boys in the Mathew Brady photographs. I wonder if my mom ever told Bill the story she has often told me, of our great-grandmother, a small child, watching Sherman's soldiers walk through her farm. They called out to her, "Hey, Sissie," so she thought they knew her. There is another family story of a woman in the North lighting a candle she would light every night for the rest of her life, for a son who never did come home. Arguing with Bill was like arguing with God, something I could do only with tears streaming down my face. I'd say to Bill, "It isn't that simple," meaning the choices other women make. But I wasn't able to say why it wasn't. Sometimes for me there are only pictures, little stories that peer into moments. Things that won't stand up in court.

It has something to do with what the old Eskimo woman we knew in Kobuk, Louise Woods, used to say of life: "It is danger." She told us all the men in her family had died, killed by a shaman's curse cast before they were born. But she was strong and silly and would smile at me while she "mowed" her lawn by rolling a fifty-five-gallon drum of gas around on it. "I laugh all the time," she'd say, "because life is sooo sad." I was younger and had no children, and I had so little an idea of what she was talking about that I saved it, like something odd I'd bring home in my pocket from a walk.

My daughter, Kari, is a fortuitous combination of chromosomes into sunlight. As deeply as I know this, I still struggle to allow each interruption of my own cloudier hemisphere. I have always hated waking up, and before Kari's birth I was usually ready to fight—or at least to temporarily despise—any agent of waking, be it mother or lover or alarm. The instant of total love that washed over me the first time I saw my daughter did not keep her night crying from stabbing me awake with indignant anger. I wanted to cry out, "Goddamit, why can't I just have some sleep?" and throw a few things around, maybe break something. But the time it took me to clench my rage and my body into obedience grew shorter and shorter, until my whole concession to Kari's blamelessness would occur below the surface of my sleep and I would find myself at her bedside without knowing how I got there. I would be patting her or picking her up, carrying her to our bed to let her pull the warm milk out of my breast. I would intend to carry her back to the crib when we were full and empty enough, so that Jim and I could not roll over on her and hurt her. But often I was drawn into sleep by the mesmeric, prickly, rhythmic pulling on my nipple.

When we woke up with her safe between us, I was always startled, before I remembered how she came to be there. Jim would shake his head slowly at me and grin. It had been our agreement that she would sleep in her own bed, but both of us knew my fury at being awakened had been transmuted to a mere unwillingness to sit in a cold chair with my cold feet on a cold floor. And there was the delight of waking up with all three of us together like the first surprise of seeing her—a new child where there had been no one—after she was born. We are people in whom rote form succumbs easily to delight, though it has to do this every day because of some pattern inside us, like the bees on their honeycomb paper.

Nap time was a time when I didn't need sleep and she did, when I wouldn't be nursing or at attention for harm or hunger for two or three hours. And I could read. There was plenty to read at our house, but the bookmobile came out one day, and I picked out a book, the only one I remember reading all that summer. It was *The West of the Imagination*, full of plates by Thomas Moran and George Catlin and the great lithographers. I would be bent so deep into it that I would jump like a heart-shot deer at the first noise from Kari downstairs. I would feel irritation, then shame.

That first July and August, Jim was gone sixteen to eighteen hours a day, seven days a week, working on forest fires. My mom and Jim's parents had gone home, so there were no extra arms around. For a time I thought I would go crazy, always nursing or holding or changing diapers or walking with Kari in my arms. She didn't sleep very much, never much more than we did except for her nap. I was used to going to work, being outside, arguing and making things, reading, and so I felt the loss of those activities almost as keenly as I felt love for this fresh baby. Every moment is always forever with me—lonely or ecstatic or tied down.

But I soon learned that Kari would not cry if I quickly put down my book and my interest in it and called out, "Who's that? Is that Kari?" If I hurried down the stairs and picked her up after her first sounds, I'd begin to get a smile in return, which turned into a peekaboo over the railing of the baby bed as soon as she was able to pull herself up and stand there, tottering and grinning.

What at first seemed like carving my own heart out, using the sharpened tools of pity for my hungry baby and anger at my own selfishness, somehow became something other than feigning joy—it *was* joy; it *is* joy. Waking up, hearing Kari call me from deep inside my attention to some other thing, is like stumbling up to answer the door with an eagerness, a hunger even, to let her in.

There is a song called "Shake These Bones" by Grey Larson and Malcomb Dalglish in which an unborn child calls to its parents from a doorway filled with morning light. When I'd play the song, after we brought Kari home, the tears would come squirting out of me—not because I had this child but because having this child was just what I had not been able to do: I could not be a mother of a child, and yet I *was* the mother. I took Kari to Oregon when she was several months old and a relative told me, "Well, you surprise me. I didn't think you could be a mother." So I knew the impossibility for me was not just something in my imagination.

It has to do with being the youngest, so that I had to be regarded as irresponsible, not grim enough. In reaction to this expectation, I have worked grimly at irresponsibility, to make irresponsibility work as a method. Inside, I am the grimmest person you ever met. Every good thing that happens to me brings me to my knees, crying praise. And in the next moment it will happen again. I can't believe these good things or own them, but so many happen to me that I am almost always on my knees, trying to embrace the open door.

I had a couple of miscarriages before I had Kari, so for months into carrying her I couldn't think of myself as a woman who was going to have a child. The first miscarriage had been truly terrifying. I was bleeding and crying and withering as they took me to an operating table to be "cleaned out" while my body was trying to perform the same function. The D and C procedure is carried out with you on your back, with someone looking into you and scraping you out as if you are a skinny-necked vase with the opening at the bottom, function and perception at odds with each other.

I couldn't tell if the pain was coming from the doctor cutting or the letting-go in the womb. I remember wondering which it was, trying not to move, but squirming away inside from the scraping tools.

Next time, the next year, I knocked the wind out of myself skating, hooked a tip while pretending to be Eric Heiden and went down so fast and flat I even bruised the front of my hips. I started to bleed the next day, and miscarried again. Since I had apparently knocked the fetus loose myself, I could feel that losing the baby was something I *did* rather than something I *was*, which is a kind of respite. I would not go back to the hospital but knelt by our bed over towels and bled the baby out. I say *baby* for the alliteration, not because it was a baby to me. It was just a failure, something I didn't finish. But this time I thought I knew what the fault was, what the mistake and the moment were.

I bled junk for days. I even saved some of it, and drew pictures of it, and asked the doctor (when I finally went to a doctor because I felt so low and rotten) what it was, what part of a baby it was. I think the doctor was appalled by the question and appalled by me. He gave me to understand that I was not to think of myself as a science project. But this was all I *could* do. I could set myself crying over not being able to have a child, whatever that meant, or I could try to piece together the evidence of my inadequacy, try to solve it so I could try harder next time. I had taken responsibility for this miscarriage—caused it myself, managed it myself, and not handed it over. The pain was never out of my control, or, even if out of control, it was still *my* pain. I had been trusted with this and it was mine.

There was one time I was hunting by myself and I killed an elk. I hadn't expected to kill one. Jim and I and our friend Brian had started walking long before daylight, at four in the morning. As soon as I could, I separated from them and found a thick spruce tree so huge that the ground underneath it was clear of snow. I lay down in the needles and slept until noon. When I woke up I started walking down the mountain, not up where the men had gone. The trail wrapped around the back side of a ridge and everything changed before I saw the elk, as if I were in another country. It was quiet as the air in church, and in the damp wallow at the bottom there were two elk standing, a spike and a larger bull. It took me two shots. The first bullet hit a tree that stood in the way of the headshot I'd wanted; the spike thundered off, up the far ridge, and the bull I'd shot at turned sideways to look at me, presenting his heart.

After I'd shot him, I waited a few minutes before I approached the place he'd crashed down. There was kicking, and I was wary of that. But there is also the room you give the death of an animal: a thickening of the air, a spasm where the particularity of this death moves to the generality of all death—and to my death. I had to bow to enter this act of mine.

I counted the tines. I dragged my fingers through the rough, piss-smelling belly hair, then stood with my hands cupped over my nose and mouth and breathed in for the shock of it. I fired into the air twice, our signal: "Come and help me." Then I slit him open, carefully, with the knife blade riding up between the index and middle fingers of my left hand so I wouldn't pierce the guts. I pulled the insides of him out onto the ground, cutting around inside the pelvis because I had nothing to split it with, digging into the neck for the windpipe so that the heat could pour out of him. When I was done I lay back alongside him, watching what I'd done, waiting for the others. But they hadn't heard me. I waited a couple of hours, in the greenest leaves and the reddest blood, then I took off with the heart and liver to find them, to show them.

I can't say what Jim thought about losing his potential children or the potential loss of his dubious prize, me. I can't say what he felt, and I can't remember what we said to each other. Probably "I'm so sorry" and "It's all right." The time that I came closest to knowing what Jim felt was when a dog we loved was run over by a pickup on the Richardson Highway. It was late at night. We were going up to Delta to camp and go hunting the next day. One minute we were half asleep in the back of our friends' van with Loki between us, then they were stopping to take a leak and the dog got out, not wanting to miss anything. We only half knew it, the half that should have held him by the collar, and then he was hit and lying in the road, instantly dead with the blood driven through his skin in wet patches.

You could say, well, a dead dog is nothing compared with miscarrying a child, but losing the dog hurt worse. A dog has been the dialogue between us when we've set our heels and slammed the doors, can't get back, with words, to the will to be together, which is below words. When I say, "Goddamit, I hate the way you do things," then it's a dog that follows me out to the woodpile which I am going to chop alltokindlingjustforspiteyoujustwatchme, and I put my arms around the dog and my face down in the stinky brown fur I like the smell of, and Jim watches me from the window and comes out and the dog wags his way between us, back and forth, spinning us closer until we can touch each other again. We are famous for being crazy about our dogs. One neighbor said that when he dies he wants to come back as a dog at our house. "No, I mean it," he said.

Here is something else to appall the doctor. I think when Loki got killed we grieved for the dog and the lost children all at once. For weeks we both cried ourselves to sleep every night. We'd hold on to each other or we'd just lie in bed, not touching, and shake with sobbing. Making love for ten years didn't do what crying for three weeks did, for being close. It was months before we could speak the dog's name without crying. In the morning, or at night before we turned the light out, I looked at the water stains on the boards and beams in the ceiling. The stains are there from the years before we put up the second story of logs and the real roof, and I intend to someday sand them off. Dick Tracy and Cat Woman are up there, and a random reproduction of God giving life to Adam.

When Loki got killed, I was pregnant, though I didn't know it yet. I am perpetrating a bit of family folklore when I say that I got pregnant on the moose hunting trip to Nickel Lake, where there weren't any moose and I had forgotten to bring both meat and coffee. It wasn't usual for me to forget anything on a trip, me with my lists and boxes. But at that time I was starting to relinquish my grim control of things, which I am still trying to relinquish. I do this by not trying to cook more and better than my mother, by sometimes saying I don't have an opinion (even though I always do) and by neglecting paperwork.

On this trip there was no fresh moose sign and what we had to eat was a lot of broccoli. We climbed a steep hill behind where we were camping and peered over the rocky faces to St. Anne's Lake and Tazlina Lake. There was sheep sign and some old moose sign up there, which tickled us because the moose were absent. We lay down in the moss and cranberry and kinnikinnick and slept until the heat of the sun woke us up. The breeze was upslope and a peregrine glided to a halt just a few feet away, anchoring herself to the air.

I am remembering this now for Kari, but soon after that trip everything was wiped out for a while by the death of the dog. When I found out I was pregnant it seemed like a trade I hadn't wanted to make. I remember saying to Jim, "This better be *some* kid if it's supposed to replace that dog."

Our friend Lloyd, an older man who nearly single-handedly destroyed himself with alcohol, would call me every day and tell me what to do to avoid miscarriage: "Don't you lift those logs," and "Don't reach over your head. I knew a woman who did that and when the baby was born the cord was wrapped eight times around its neck and it was dead." Still afraid to be moved by my pregnancy, I was moved by the tenderness of this tough and injured man, and I could accept becoming a lightning rod for the absurd and frightening folklore of giving birth. Needles hung on long threads over my belly swung either back and forth or in circles, indicating that I would have a boy or a girl—or maybe it meant the opposite. The slow, even heartbeat meant a boy, one nurse told me. She'd never seen it fail. Carrying the fetus high meant a girl, or a boy. I was amazed to find how many attempts are made to encompass or control this most visible of rites of passage, the appearance of a new human. Such attention made the invisible transformations of the continued life, like Lloyd reaching for the phone every day, seem neglected.

The ultrasound looked like a weather photo, and though it provided the only pre-birth opportunity to have legitimately queried the sex of the child to come, we didn't ask. We said we didn't care, but what we meant was that we couldn't imagine being parents of any gender of child, so "it doesn't matter" was more than insurance against disappointment.

There are few physiological reasons that giving birth should be harder the first time, but it almost always is. My mother told all of us so many well-meant lies to get us to come in out of the cold ("you'll die of pneumonia"), or brush our teeth ("they'll fall out"), or eat more ("I'll have to throw it away"—she never did) that none of us listened to the referential meaning of her words anymore, just the love or fear that spawned them. But on some level, I must have believed her when she said, "It never hurt to have my babies. I don't remember any pain even." Because at midnight before the day Kari was born—after I had been in labor on the 150 miles from Nelchina to Anchorage and then at the hospital, in varying states of discomfort for about twenty hours—I finally asked her, between contractions, if she had been lying to me. She then remembered that she had been forty-five hours in labor with my oldest brother Bill, thirty some with Clifford, twenty some with David, and a comfortable twelve or so with me. Twelve is about where most women start out.

The specificity of Mom's memory on this score was not comforting at the time. "You're a rotten liar," I grimaced at her. But I think now that these numbers were not any more reliable than her first revelations about labor. Memory itself, not just Mom's memory, always wants to justify or assuage some hurt in the present, and she was trying "to be with me."

I have always been a poor shot with a shotgun because of the speed with which one has to imagine the path of shot and grouse meeting in the air. I would get as far as imagining the gun to my shoulder and the necessary absence of other human beings or structures in front of the shotgun arc. Then I would not pull the trigger but would watch the loveliness of bird whir out of range and set its wings for another fence row. This was not an unwillingness to kill, but an inability to aim the process clear through the bird.

Likewise, when I want to chop a piece of wood, it doesn't help very much to think about how to hold the ax or even where the blade is going to enter the top of the block. I have to intend the ax down through the wood and into the chopping block. Even the hardest swing, if it is aimed for the top of the block, will make you think you are trying to split elm, or iron. You can hurt yourself this way, as the ax is left to its own devices after you get it to the top of the wood—it may end up in your shin.

This is how I needed to think about having a child, though I had never held one of my own. I needed to think of a child moving out of me, into the light, into my arms. What I was doing wrong was thinking about labor, breathing, surviving the next contraction in the way that I've survived any pain I've had in my life—by battening down the hatches, clinching and ducking into some dark ant farm where I have mandatory front-row seats for the pain that is nearly someone else's. But this is not the way to have a baby—strangling pain until it gives up. Something has to move, be allowed to change from a fetus being crushed down a tunnel in the body into a child looking for a breast, light, and the arms of its parents and grandparents. The miraculous stretching of tissues and moving of hipbones isn't really what makes a second birth easier, I suspect, but rather the knowledge of how it feels to hold the newborn child in your arms.

I have heard other women talk about the deep sleep you fall into between contractions after you have been laboring for many hours. It is a thirty-second deep sleep, twenty leagues under the sea, then surfacing with the bends for endless minutes and going back down again. Human voices are left behind on the surface. When they gave me an epidural—anesthetic injected into the lining of the spinal column—I fell almost immediately back into that sleep, far from any thought of having a baby. They woke me up after a couple of hours and said that they would take the baby by caesarean if my cervix had still not dilated. But the fist of my will had loosened while I was sleeping, and I was ready to push Kari out. Jim and the doctor talked about hunting and fishing, with my Mom hovering behind the head of the bed until the doctor invited her to join the crowd at the "action end." I felt the hard contractions not as pain but like rushes of emotion, a tide that receded and returned, coming in farther with each wave until there was a head, a child, and Jim was cutting the cord and they were wiping her off and laying her in my arms, and I was crying, and Kari's tiny mouth snuffled out my nipple to nurse.

We say, "Everybody came into the world this way," through some woman's body—as if the universal can take away the personal. And it can. Most of the women of my mother's generation were "knocked out" and didn't even get to see their children born. But we aren't just packaging for our children, something to keep the germs off till they grow skin. The individuality of our pain and joy, and our willingness to be a vessel for our very child—these belong to us. We own the miracle that having our own child is.

And the danger. The people, usually women themselves, who give shelter to battered women are often threatened by the husbands and boyfriends. People who give milk and eggs and cereal to pregnant women and new mothers and their babies are sometimes threatened by the fathers. It is not unusual, in that line of work, to find the message "I want to kill you" left on the recorder phone or to wonder about the unfamiliar car in the parking lot at night. Women and children are scared, pursued, and beaten to death every minute of every day.

Rage would stay simple if it would stay in the parking lot, but it seeps into us like a reprimand. I've heard Kari cry out in fear when I can't suppress the anger that sometimes pours out of my own misery and disbelief in myself, I who have everything. To imagine children's bones breaking, to imagine the kind of misery that kind of anger comes from, is to contemplate hell. What do I know about the woman who doesn't want to have a child?

When I think of my beautiful brother full of conviction and of my beautiful friends with their arms full of hurt women and babies, I can't choose between them. Couldn't we love the children we already have in the world, protect them from harm, prize the act of giving birth and the particular beauty of each child, value the acts of caring for children, grow some self-respect among women and men? Then, giving birth might be recognized as the sacrament and the miracle, the word becoming flesh, that it already is.

I know what "control of my own body" means, its political importance and how arrogant it sounds to people for whom God owns everything, or at least everybody else's thing. I know women need this slogan, but it isn't really viable. I don't want to "own" or "control" the birth of my child or to own my child. What I own is the loss of control that having a child is, this moving through me of something that does not belong to me. That experience, that stretch of the river, is mine.

I don't need those "owning" words, yet having a child made me more of a feminist than I ever was before. Accepting the loss of control over my body was like a prayer, like bowing. Taking responsibility for loving and protecting this child meant never accepting again what others thought I could or couldn't do, or ever being unhappy in a way I didn't choose to be, or doing meaningless work, or saying meaningless things. The world was not meaningless because I was part of a miracle, and I claimed it, and I could not be made to unbelieve that I can taste and touch and shape love into the air.

Many women experience this in childbirth, women who may have been afraid to connect with the intuitive, the self below thought. I would like to say that everything starts from here, from the belly of energy: strength and anger and love, every real thing. Many things also enter us from books, from the intellect, but we only own them when they dive deep into the bone locker that cages our hearts. When that baby comes out of you, there is a ribbon that is never cut, that you do not have to believe in to feel.

Something about life is denied by our denying of men's or women's intuition, as if we were not "smart" to feel love or to gather the electricity between people in a room into its shape, into the form that encourages retreat, or asks for tenderness, or twists a knife.

What is it that we know? I am thinking of Emily Ivanoff Brown, an Eskimo writer and teacher. She said,

> I was named after my mother's cousin. Her name was Emily—her Eskimo name was Ticasuk. And when I became older, my mother told me what it meant. That means a hollow in the ground. And I cried when I was a little girl. Big tears rolled down my cheeks because I was so disappointed. Everytime I saw a hollow in the ground, I would walk around it. I didn't want to walk into it because it was my name! And then my mother told me not to cry—that it was a beautiful name. You see, the four winds on this earth, when they blow from the north or south or east or west, they bring the wealth of the earth and they lodge into that hollow, and that's mine. Now I think it's a beautiful name.

What are we, that we flicker between particular and general on luminous lines, all our knowledge a convention imposed on the neither-wave-nor-particle movement of whatever this life is? Are we each just an illusion of separateness, a bump of desire experiencing a necessary loneliness for what it is made of? Or are we bowls, both men and women, little hollows in a landscape we don't even recognize as our own.

When my daughter tells the dogs to listen, that she is going to tell them a story, they sometimes do. "There was a moose, and we cut him. It was in trees, big trees." The dogs loll around, looking at their three-year-old grandmother. Jim and I catch eyes, then slip into the pantry where we can shake with the lid on our laughter, unseen. Joy at such times is a supernova, expanding and swallowing time. It has weight and force out of balance with the space of chronological time it covers.

Most moments we do not even feel, and grief can suck light out of time until the past is empty and we have no ingredients to make ourselves with. Dying, my father said, "You know what I mean, Mim," but I didn't. Yet his eyes looked blue in a way that the light in the room could not justify, and *that* is mine.

Time doesn't move us along a train track, but in a series of explosions and implosions that at any moment have the power to scramble us, turn us into something barely recognizable as ourselves.

Our experience of caring for children, of living every day with women and children and men, too, are such dangerously unprofitable and unclassifiable subjects that pieces of them fall everywhere, drift into the "women's section," the journalism of the catchall. Into this willing void, society pours knitting, giving birth, losing an arm, making Christmas ornaments from egg cartons, quitting a job to stand helpless by a parent's bed while he is dying with shame to be an infant again. This is where we learn to cook with I Can't Believe It's Not Butter and how to respond when we learn our child has leukemia, where we learn to crochet, to remove coffee stains with vinegar, find sex more satisfying, be a better mother, to die while our children are small, to stand up to the boss.

No society, no collective "we," can face this rag-and-bone yard that being born and having children and dying is. Do we put soap and dying on the same shelf so we can trivialize death, make it a "woman thing"? Or do women see the connection here, that you have to clean the sheet, remove the stain? *Somebody has to sleep in this bed tonight.*

The Fortune 500 and recreational vehicles vanish with just one heart attack, and then they are grist for *Good Housekeeping.* Suffer the little children and the ruined executives to come unto me.

It is danger.

In my arms is a shape I made and do not own, egglike, smooth as a tulip. It is my child breathing in her own thoughts, dreaming of birds and beds, stories, a bath. I don't know what she's dreaming. I don't know what I want for her, brightest star, little bowl. I lean back so the four winds can blow over us, bringing everything.

Creamed Salmon

Kari has always loved to eat it, and it is the reason that we preserve most of our salmon in jars every summer.

It was different when I had it the first time. White bread tasted like air with butter on it, a blank canvas for any taste you could spread there. Lucky for us, Aunt Anna's new life after marrying Uncle Pud included going to the Oregon Coast, an exotic thing to do, afterward bringing back cases of the salmon they'd caught and canned. Creamed salmon on toast, canned peaches, and sassafras tea was the meal she made for me whenever I was in self-exile from our house up the road. Eating with Aunt Anna restored my status to loved and lucky.

The other salmon aunt was Zola, living in Soldotna when I came to Alaska in 1977. We stayed up into the wee hours canning big silver salmon we'd danced in from the Kenai River. Aunt Zola was always laughing, as giddy as we were at the crowd of shining hot jars on her counter, our first time and her bazillionth.

Decades ago, Jim conceded that creamed salmon on toast was breakfast food. Empty a pint of canned salmon into a saucepan with soft butter and milk, with flour to thicken. Season with salt and pepper and ground nutmeg. Stir while it cooks, then serve over buttered toast. The flavor of the salmon will move over just enough for the flavor of good whole-wheat bread.

5

PEOPLE ON THE FERRY

I

In the morning, a few minutes before seven, I leave Jim and Kari asleep in the cabin and walk up to the cafeteria to sit and drink coffee and watch the sea and sky grow lighter. We are two days out of Prince Rupert, British Columbia, headed for the ferry terminal at Haines, Alaska, then back onto the highway toward our home in Nelchina. We have intentionally lengthened our journey to take this ferry; it is a break from solid ground that we decided to try. We could have driven all the way home through the crystal frozen interior, and we wouldn't have put any more miles on the truck, but we would have missed all of the west slope of the Canadian Rockies and the coastal range, the trees growing larger and the air moister until snow gives way to a shroud of rain and fog streaming on the windshield, hiding all but the toes of cedar and hemlock and white spruce with their hint of giants. Prince Rupert, at night when we arrived there, was a collection of smeary lights through rain. Entering the ocean this way, the uncertainty is mythic.

I can't tell what kind of weather is out there this morning, but I can feel that the boat is humming and traveling evenly through a calm. Because it is still dark, I can't know if it is a calm made by the mountains wrapped around us in a narrow channel of the inland passageway or if it is a more general calm, a calm sea everywhere on this northern coast.

We passed Wrangell in the night so there are new passengers on board, new faces already out in the narrow hallways of the cabin deck, shuffling up toward the daylight as I am doing. I am curious about them, why they are here. For a landlubber like me, merely riding on the sea is exotic, so it is hard to imagine that this is just another highway.

At the cafeteria, there is a woman sitting behind the counter reading a book. She is wearing the white shirt and dark blue slacks of the Alaska State Ferry system. A few yards away, an older Native woman stands, leaning on a cane. She looks at the woman seated by the cash register but does not come close enough to get in the woman's direct line of vision so the woman continues to read. With a slightly exasperated shrug, the Native woman turns and hobbles back toward the tables. She doesn't look at me, but I know the shrug was for me, for our customer solidarity against the impersonal officialdom of cafeterias and uniforms.

When I set my books down on a table near the window, the Native woman is at a table next to me. "I can't find out what time they open," she says.

"I'll find out," I say.

When I ask the woman at the cash register what time the cafeteria opens, she smiles at me and puts down her book. "Seven. If my usual crew was here, they'd be open now. But these guys go by the rules." She angles her face away from the food line before adding, "I'll be so glad when my own crew gets back."

"Well, may I get some coffee?" I ask her, since it is still two minutes to seven. "You sure can, honey," she says. The "honey" lets me know where I am. I am in a small-town diner, except that I'm on a boat, in the middle of the Inland Passage on the way to Alaska, and this is the hardened and wise and kind waitress, fifty or so, except the bleached hair is short, the cigarette is gone, the makeup is underdone. The odd stranger intimacy between women is here, however, and I thank her as I pay for the coffee and smile to let her know I hope she gets her own crew back soon.

To that woman at the cash register just now the Native woman was invisible and this invisibility is a curiosity to me. I noticed the Native woman as soon as I walked down the hallway into the cafeteria and I can feel her eyes on me as I move back to the table with the coffee. She is a large woman, not yet a very old woman—perhaps sixty, perhaps seventy. She has black and white hair, not gray. Her face is very broad, folded and smooth, darkening around the valleys of her large eyes. I want to help her, as I am a perpetual child who always wants to please older people, though most people in the world are now younger than I am. Also, I have seen that her failed claim on the cash register woman's attention poises her against the hidden motion of this boat, its unspoken rules.

"I want to have some breakfast," she says, "but I don't know what they have." Well, of course she had to walk past the big black sign with the white magnetic letters that tells what they offer on the menu. Later I will find out that she is no stranger to this ferry boat with its black and white magnetic signs. But she wants to *talk about* what they are serving for breakfast with someone, and this dialogue is not encouraged by the cafeteria system. Today I will be her human link to breakfast, and I am pleased.

"Shall I help you?" I ask her, and she says yes, and she heaves herself up from the bench and moves slowly out from between the steel-anchored tables with her cane. We look at the menu on the wall together. She orders oatmeal, and we go around the line putting this and that on the tray. I carry the tray for her, get the butter, put ice in the water. This is no different from helping any older person, and yet it is a little bit different from helping most older people. There are no effusive thanks, no apologies for having difficulty in walking and carrying a tray at the same time. Without much smiling, there is a comfortable formality between us that never moves to the friendliness that might require explanation and apology.

I sit and talk with Hallie for much of the day, between small adventures with my daughter. Kari has the kids' toy room located, down on the cabin deck, but the forward lounge is also a good place to play Barbies, so she drags Jim or me up and down the stairs. We alleged adults are a little dreamy here between foggy shorelines. Jim has a Tom Clancy novel shoved under one arm as he is relocated again and again by our enthusiastic daughter, and he would like nothing better than to find just one place to sit and read it. I am carrying a book and a tablet around too, like props, but off and on all day I return to the cafeteria where Hallie is waiting for me. I carry her food and learn the names of her children and grandchildren.

When Hallie sees I have a notebook, she assumes I will want to write down things about her. She says, "I can tell you some things you can write down," and she makes a little project of me. We draw pictures of how she cuts salmon, both for the strips and for the "newspaper style," where the fish is cut in layers but not all the way through, so that the cut fish is laid out in a big sheet, three times as wide as the uncut fish. I write down the recipe for the brine and how long the fish should stay in the brine. I write down "green hemlock" and "alder," though I will not be within two hundred miles of a hemlock when I smoke my fish, and I draw a picture of the smokehouse she describes, with Hallie correcting what I draw, making sure I get it right. I tell her I won't be able to cut the fish the way she does unless I have the knife in my hands and my hands learn the work, because that is how I learn things, but she shakes her head at me and says, "I know you understand this. I can tell by watching your eyes." Then, in the same tone of voice and with the same patience, she gives me a recipe for her baked chicken, which uses barbecue sauce—Lea and Perrins—as well as onion, green pepper, garlic, and cheese.

I tell Hallie how we smoke our fish from the Copper River in a hot smokehouse that kippers the fillets, and she tells me it is all wrong, not to do it that way anymore. She is very serious about this.

There is a tape, she tells me, of the Klawock dance group when she took them to the Fairbanks Native Arts Festival in 1978. Someone promised her a videotape of her group's performance, but she didn't ever get it. "Could you find that for me?" she asks, and I tell her I will try. She tells me about some people she knew in Fairbanks, but I only know a couple of them. She sends her greeting with me, to them, and I wonder why it is that this kind of greeting is so much better than the mail or the phone, this human relay which says "I have seen and touched this person who sends their greeting to you. They really exist, still."

We get hungry again, not surprising after all the talk of food, so we eat cheeseburgers together, and we still have fries and water on the table when the boat starts to ride big swells, tipping back and forth so that we catch the plates and glasses each time they reach the edge. We are entering Frederick Sound, and the swells are coming at us from the wide Pacific entrance. The wet brown rocks and feathery trees that were so close to us an hour ago and the little flags that marked our daylight way through the channel are gone. We are in a wide, gray ocean.

Hallie draws me a picture of Prince of Wales Island, with the roads to Craig, Hollis, and Hydaburg drawn out in thin strands from Klawock. When she adds on the little roads that go to logging camps, Klawock looks like the sun, sending out its rays over the wet, forested island.

A young waiter strolls past us, comically exaggerating trying to walk on a swaying boat, and he says, "I think we are lost," conspiratorially but loud, so that everyone can hear him. "If I was talking to another Tlingit woman," says Hallie, "I would say, 'He likes himself too much.'" I agree that this is so, happy to be invited to the underground of Tlingit women's commentary on young cocky waiters, however briefly.

I like being made aware of the unwritten system that Native people have, where you share what you get, and the younger people look to the older people for advice on the right way to live and the right way to make things, and they take care of the older people without really thinking about it, or perhaps the thinking about it is a part of the already accepted obligation, felt but permanent. The sharing between family households is part of my heritage, too, from rural eastern Oregon, but the constant identification of "self" as part of a "we," as in "we this community" or "we these women," is a gift from little towns along Alaska rivers. I recognize connections outside my family, or perhaps it is my family that has been extended. Somehow when the thinking goes, "This is what *we* are doing," instead of, "This is what *I* am doing," the thinking about taking care of other people, for example, is affirmed and not uprooted. To say that Native people affirm their connections is an idealistic and generalizing way to look at Natives, but it is also a real aspect of life in the communities where I have lived. I believe that it has helped me to appreciate being a female in my own family, being able to say, "This is what we do, we women," sharing food and talk and the right ways to make things. This is a gift I make use of. But there is more. There are gifts I can't make use of, can't melt down, things I must learn to *accept* in both senses.

I am on the Kobuk on a fall day, a colorful August day of bright yellow willows and red blueberry bushes, nippy and clear. Jim and I have been moose hunting and we are motoring home in Brian's boat, past the white wall tents and fish-drying racks of people we know from villages downriver. We have another woman with us, Debbie, a Park Service employee who has come to the Kobuk to learn about its people and how to plan the parks around them. And when Josephine Woods, a woman we know from Shungnak, comes down the beach to wave us in to her fish camp, Debbie says, "No, we mustn't. We can't disturb the people while they are engaged in their subsistence activities."

"She wants us to visit," I point out. "And she probably has something good to eat," Jim adds. Debbie is a friendly, reasonable person, but like all agency-indoctrinated people, she wants the upper Kobuk treated like a living museum. We are not supposed to eat and visit with the displays. We argue a bit, with Josephine standing on the bank, looking at us. Finally Debbie gives in, and we motor over.

"What's wrong, do you think I'm from NANA?" Josephine asks, then she laughs and we all laugh after her, a little nervously I think, because Josephine has nailed an issue directly. NANA is the regional Native corporation, and its stance is often political and anti-white in order to turn the hurtful tables. But of course the harsh words continue the hurting when they drift down to actual people. Upper Kobuk people have minds of their own, though, and Josephine was reminding us of that. To assume "they all think alike" is just as stupid and prejudicial as "they all look alike." What forms the "they"? Debbie is beginning to see that Eskimos on the Kobuk are not monolithic in their opinions and personalities, but this embryonic sense of the Kobuk country's complexity will later desert her as she writes for her NPS questionnaire the question, "Do white people bother you?"

Josephine feeds us half-dried salmon and lingonberries with seal oil and sugar. We soak up the warm food and the orange light of an angled sun through white canvas. Josephine's husband, Wesley, sings us a song in Inupiaq. We don't understand the words, or the dance he tells us about and explains. We have this in common with many Native people our age. I think it is very kind of him to give us this song, a little like pearls before swine or maybe more like one concentric ripple from the center of a story. If we come again, if we hear the song again, if we build the small circle around the little stove again and again, listening every time, then we will remember just a bit and the song will build into us, with the fish and the berries and the river. Then we'll know something about something, about the center of this culture where the ripple starts. We stay and talk until the sunlight goes behind Cosmos, and then we go out and get ribs and liver from the moose to leave with them and start the boat downriver for the boat landing.

The ferry will pull into Sitka at 6:00 p.m., and this is where Hallie will get off. Hallie tells us that her daughter will pick her up and take her to the hospital, where the doctors will look at Hallie's knee and check out some other troubles she's been having. When the loudspeaker tells us that Sitka passengers can disembark, Kari and I walk Hallie down the sloping metal ramp from the boat to the terminal building. I am putting a jar of my mom's peaches in Hallie's bag when the daughter clicks up in heels. She asks me what I'm doing, and I feel embarrassed. Here I am, some strange white person, rooting around in her mother's luggage. Hallie says, "She helped me, on the boat." I am still on the suspicion list of this well-dressed, curt daughter, who says, "Well, she better." But Hallie is smiling one of her first smiles at us, and it lifts most of the clouds off the moment. "Take care of yourself," I say. We say good-bye and Jim brings the dogs down off the boat to play fetch.

It's seven miles to town and we missed the only bus, so we'll see Sitka some other year. We run around in circles in the rain for nearly an hour, in someone's big equipment yard next to the ferry terminal.

II

Kari can't believe we have a room on a boat, with a whole bathroom in it and even a shower. We can hardly ever get her to take a shower at home, so we are amazed when she demands a shower right away on the boat and actually takes one after we get the water just the right temperature. She washes her hair and rinses it all by herself then reminds us that she has done it so that we congratulate her. Then the bath towels go up as stage curtains between our packs and the one chair, and we are treated to a most amazing puppet show featuring Barbie no. 1, Barbie no. 2, and the large plastic dinosaurs called, for the moment, "Tony" and "Lisha." Barbie no. 1 is eaten by Tony, but Lisha is a doctor dinosaur and she fixes the previously dead Barbie. Tony is eventually returned to kindness by the wise Lisha and all is well again in Barbie land. We are in this honeycomb cell of our own family, and around us are other travelers, stacked together for a few days, our destinations as similar as they ever can be.

We turn outward to the air and the ocean every few hours. I walk around the decks, staring at the other passengers, wondering why they are on this swaying ferry in the gray winter sea instead of eating a bag of peanuts on MarkAir or Alaska Airlines and arriving home in time for supper. One answer is that some of them are locals, like Hallie, and this is their highway. But no answer is ever quite as good as its question.

Outside and to the front of the boat in the early morning, I am in front of the main lounge and below the pilothouse. It's dark, and the air is cold and half sea itself, but there are lights from the shore, close to us now on either side. There are green lights on buoys to starboard and red lights to port. They mark the narrow channel. Once in a while a spotlight shines out from the pilot deck above me to illuminate the wet rocks of an island or a reef that would have been covered in high tide. I can barely stretch up on my toes to look up and behind to the upper deck and see the heads of one or two crewmembers moving in the pilothouse, watching the channel and talking. A man I presume to be the captain walks out onto the upper deck. He is portly and gray-bearded. I wonder if his appearance got him his position or if he adopted it afterward. This occupation is strongly in the traditions carried down from sailing, from steam. This is a ferry boat and not a triple-masted schooner, not an Alaska steamship. But the descendants of the mythic seafarers are here, and this is the real ocean, hiding the real reefs and rocks. Above me is a room full of radar and radios, legacy of navigational technology achieved during the Second World War, where mysterious signals vectoring with satellites now locate us precisely on the surface of the sea, between the hazards of this channel. But the power we give this crew—those of us against the rail in our little coats or inside the glass room in the lounge chairs or sleeping in the cabins—is as absolute as ever because the rocks are just as hard and we are just as fragile, riding inside this metal tub.

I don't see any women in the crew. There must be some women working as mates or other crew on these ferries, despite the old maritime folklore against their presence. But I have only seen women working in the cafeteria, women cleaning the rooms. I finger my own prejudices here and wonder if I would be comforted to see a woman's silhouette up in the pilothouse. There is Joe Hazelwood of the *Exxon Valdez* to consider and also the captain of the *Princess Sophia*, who went down with his ship in these waters in 1918. There were boats all around the *Princess Sophia* that could have rescued her passengers and crew, but the captain wanted the people to be taken off the reef-struck passenger liner by another ship of his company, the Canadian Pacific Railway. And then it was too late. Much of the early history of the territory went down with those four hundred passengers, among them the young man who was a close companion of Hudson Stuck, Walter Harper. Harper had been the first person to set his foot on the top of Denali, the great one. One hopes for captains less concerned about companies, about nationalities.

The silhouette I imagine to be the captain does not look down. I am attracted to this sturdy man shape, peering into the darkness beyond me. I am delighted by the primeval caretaking nature of his profession, the specificity of circumstances through which he guides this boat. I recognize how I am affected by the cap, by the beard, how I wish his wisdom to extend beyond the depth of this channel, how I wish for him to be a wise *man*, now that I have trusted him with my life. I wonder about my willingness to hand myself over to this guy in a cap; I feel the sexualness of this idea, and even a tinge of the troublesome dependence that can follow sexual attraction, which is somehow very like the wish for captains to be wise. Is this an ingredient of how hard it is for my culture to hand over authority, even very specific authority, to women? Of young men's fear of older women who are immune to dependence upon them? Of this deep identification of control with male sexuality? And I wonder what convolution of self it may require for a woman to wear that cap.

III

Kari and Jim and I walk into the carpeted main lounge, where the big windows wrap clear around the front of the boat. The lights are dimmed here and big reclining chairs are bolted to the floor in rows. A few sleeping bags are still laid out between the chairs, though most of the people in the lounge are by the windows, watching the gray water and the islands slowly change shape. A few minutes ago Kari and Jim saw four killer whales leaping along next to the ferry. Kari's eyes are still bright with the black-and-white flashing memory of them.

Near the window, there is a round woman in a Russian-style sealskin hat. Head back and eyes closed, she's singing quietly. She has headphones on, and the headphones are connected to some kind of instrument she is playing on the table in front of her. It looks like a Ouija board more than a keyboard, but it has some keys on it, and many other symbols and knobs. The woman in the sealskin hat scrambles her short fingers over the board as she sings and never opens her eyes. She is remarkable in that room full of passengers for her seeming isolation.

"Mom, what is that lady doing?" Kari asks me, not softly. Several people turn to look at Kari, recognizing a four-year-old's loud curiosity and its potential to stun and embarrass her parents. Their glances seem to ask, Oh, what odd family prejudice or practice is about to be revealed now? But I head off any such entertaining revelation at the pass. I say, "Shhhh. She's singing. That's her instrument." That seems to satisfy Kari, causing her attention to fall on the strange instrument and not on the strangeness of the women in her rapt solitude. We settle our books and Barbies across from the woman.

There is a man next to the woman in the sealskin hat. He is smaller and slender, with short gray hair and a beard and mustache. I think he is a perfect French trapper type, with his thick wool shirt, his neat small face and black eyes. He has one arm around the singing woman busy in her own world; he holds on to her as if to anchor her to the big chairs in the lounge inside the blue-and-white boat. He smiles at Kari and nods his head at us in acknowledgment of our proximity and then goes on with his job of hanging on to the large musician woman. In the dearth of conversation from the pair, I imagine that it has been a lonely winter of trapping for him and that he is bringing a sweetheart back to his cabin in the woods. Perhaps she is his cousin, and it is a marriage of convenience. She used to be an opera singer, and still dreams of chesty soprano parts. These speculations entertain me, even while I know they are not nearly as interesting as the real people. The couple's silence invites the legendary and stereotypic from my personal store of Alaskana: He will teach her to make biscuits and fry salmon and moose. He will have to buy a generator so she can play the Ouija keyboard. She is learning to love him.

When we see them later in the cafeteria, his arm is still around her and he is grinning a gap-toothed smile at us. Now they are both wearing fur hats. Kari is happy to see them again and goes right over to ask the woman about her "instermint." We find out the woman is Tlingit, from Klukwan, and she and her husband live with her mother's family. Sometimes she brings all her sound equipment on the ferry, and her friends do too, and then they make rock and roll music all day, wherever they are going. Very slowly, and with a heavy accent, the man tells us, "My wife is a composer." He gives her shoulder an extra squeeze, and she squeezes him back, giggling. "He's Italian," she says. And adds, "My mother made his hat." The hat is sealskin, like hers, but with a broad, fastened-up brim that announces his name, "Jesus," in sequins. I think she already loves him.

IV

There is an old man I've seen every day since we started from Prince Rupert. He's usually smoking outside on the deck or just standing behind a door or stairway where he can get out of the wind, or he's sitting in one of the lounges by himself. He's thin and nearly transparent, with longish white hair and a straggly beard that emerges unevenly from all around his face. He wears a big red plaid wool jacket and looks straight ahead, even when people are pushed up against him talking and eating. I've seen this look before, on my own father. This was the look my father wore when he was sitting in the back room of our family grocery store, thinking, thinking about being someplace else or living in some other time, and he was annoyed with those of us in his real surroundings, or he just wanted to be alone and couldn't figure out any other way to get there. It's probably the vestigial urge to annoy my father that makes me want to say hello to the man in the red wool jacket.

When I finally do say hello, the greeting misses him by a mile, hitting the people at the next table who stop their conversation to turn to look at me. It makes me wonder if the man is senile, or deaf, or very determined not to respond. I decide to leave him alone.

But a few hours later I am walking by a lounge and the old man catches my eye for just a second, then unhinges his gaze again, so it seems there is someone in there who might want to talk. I sit myself down next to him, in the row of lounge chairs facing the empty row of lounge chairs on the other side of the room. The chairs are bolted to the floor; there is no way to sit down and face the man without being twenty feet away from him. And although I am now very close to him,

I am not in the way of his gaze, which is blankly forward again. I say hello anyway and I comment on the snow line, considerably farther down the slopes here in the Lynn Canal than it was at Petersburg. The snow makes the mountains look like they have long petticoats on, but I don't mention this. There is a long silence. I am a pest, I think, and I look around the room, hoping that a graceful exit behavior will now occur to me.

"Well," says Leonard, which turns out to be the old man's name—Leonard Joseph—"it's colder here than it is in Ketchikan. Ketchikan is a good place to winter."

I'm looking at Leonard's bedroll, on the floor against the metal wall, the only wall without chairs bolted against it. He has a full-length Therm-a-Rest mattress and a Woods bag, that wool-lined, down-filled, and canvas-covered bag famous among old-time Alaska outdoorsmen for sturdiness and warmth. You can sleep outside in even an Alaska winter if you have a "four-star" Woods bag—and a dog team or snow-machine to carry it for you. It's a heavy bag and most backpackers have never heard of it. There is a large worn frame pack next to the bedroll and a pair of scuffed up Redwing boots with the tops laid over next to the pack. The bedroll and pack and boots form a neat line against the wall. On his feet, Leonard wears a pair of Romeos, those slip-on leather shoes with the little triangle of elastic between the toe and the heel but below the ankle, and some not-quite-white socks.

Romeos are old person shoes, and everyone seems to know this, though the shoes are much too comfortable not to be shared with younger generations. I was swinging Kari in a Fairbanks playground one time when a neighbor girl about eight years old came over to visit with us. She sang us the songs she was learning from the other kids at her school, jump rope rhymes and "Glory Hallelujah, teacher hit me with the ruler," songs remarkably like the ones I learned thirty years before, three thousand miles away. Then she asked me if I was Kari's grandmother. Taking a breath, I said no, I was Kari's mother, and why did she think I was her grandmother? "You have old *shoes*," the girl said. I was wearing my Romeos.

Leonard tells me he was a civil engineer for the U.S. Army during the Second World War and after. He worked on communications stations and spent most of his time out in small stations in western Alaska around Bristol Bay and up as far as Unalakleet. "I spent some time here in Haines too," he said, "but it's too cold. I like Ketchikan in the winter because it doesn't take much to keep warm." I look at the bedroll again. It doesn't look like Leonard is getting off here. "Going to Haines?" I ask him. "No, I just like to ride around," he says. It occurs to me that Leonard might be a very familiar face on this loop, the long way around that goes out to Sitka, up to Haines and Skagway, and back down the channel openings to Ketchikan, a journey of just over a week. Senior citizens ride free.

Trying not to talk too much, but wanting to, I say the chili wasn't too bad in the cafeteria. "Bah!" Leonard says. "This food is no good. They don't care what they serve here." He had pancakes and the middles were runny, he says. He adds, "I make the best pancakes in the world." This is said without any self-irony, as he turns to me in the first direct, head-on gaze we've had, and his eyes are very blue, with little slices of black circles in the irises. "I had one of those griddles, and one of those pans, too, with the coating on them, they call it 'Silverstone,' and I left them at the dumpster." When Leonard says "Silverstone," he squeezes the word out of his mouth distastefully. I don't think the cook crew on the ferry is using Silverstone, but I get what he means, about shortcuts, about mistreating the food and not caring.

Jim and Kari come up and, surprisingly, Leonard introduces himself, leaning on the arm of the chair in Jim's direction. Kari looks at Leonard and at the sleeping bag and gear against the wall. I feel a question coming, maybe one I would ask too, but she keeps it to herself and crawls into the chair beside me, content to watch the green water and the forest slide away from us. Later she will tell me that Leonard lives on the ferry and I trust her knowledge of this. Jim and Leonard talk about cast iron and cookstoves. Jim wants to talk about trapping out west, but Leonard drags the conversation back to cooking. "No, there's another kind of fry pan I mean. Not cast iron. Not this new stuff. Do you remember those steel pans, those thick ones with the long handles they used to make?" Jim does; I don't. "Well, I found one in a pawn shop. And I knew the fellow didn't know what it was worth. And I gave the guy two bucks for it. And so I have a pan like that and a griddle made out of the same stuff. It curves up at both ends and it never sticks, never does." Well, doesn't it warp, I ask, if it isn't cast iron and the fire cools down on one side?

"Nope, never does. It's thick, thick steel."

Leonard bakes bread too—somewhere. I don't quite get where this cabin is that he's talking about—in Ketchikan, or Haines, or somewhere out on the Bering Sea coast, and I can't tell if this is Leonard's present time or his memory. "Friends come down to see me and I cook. That's what I like to do, is cook."

The smell of Leonard and his stuff is all around us now. Not unwashed, exactly, but a kind of cabin smell, out of place with the metal and plastic and diesel of the humming boat. It reminds me of visiting the little houses of old men we know, full of smoke and coffee and the sweaty sweetness of a bedroll slept in night after night. Now Leonard is showing Jim the curve of the griddle, thumb and two fingers held stiffly out, stained yellow to the first joints, describing the curve with his whole arm from the elbow. In this motion, he is dignified and spare and eloquent.

My father would do this, too—talk to strangers, come out of isolation to hold court on a favorite subject such as a fishing lure for bass or how to pick a ripe cantaloupe. That is when I would hear my father as the knowledgeable, expressive man he could be when you caught him unawares, no axes to grind, no children to correct. I used to be jealous of strangers, that my father would talk to them as if they were all good people already and did not need to be improved, as if we could all share what we know and take the other knowledge home, reciprocally. There would be a lot more swearing when my father talked, of course, mostly "helluvas" and his favorite exclamation, "Hell's bells!" I'd love to be able to squeeze that one in sometimes, but not now. I am a female, so for Leonard that strange, excluding chivalry of old men is probably in effect. I can rest here in it for a time. I wonder if Leonard has any family. But I don't feel like asking; he has already gone out of his way to care about us.

"You know what I'm talking about, you people," Leonard says, to us as if few other people could know about having a good cookstove. He says this with a near-smile, then, "Well, I need to get a cigarette," and he's up on those pin legs, walking out of the lounge very slowly but straight, with the kind of inward attention that I was mistaken about, that made me think he might be mentally ill or sick when I first saw him. Still, it is hard to say how deep the silence is that he crossed to talk to us.

Haines is our stop. We will be in Haines Junction on the Alaska Highway by ten o'clock tonight and we'll be in Nelchina by tomorrow afternoon. I think the universe is going to seem a little scattered and less contained for the next few days, perhaps more dangerous. I have grown accustomed to this boat, where I have the boat in common with the other travelers. It is a foothold, a foothold on the sea.

When we get off the ferry I look around for Leonard, to say good-bye, and I find him in the lounge with the tiny tables, playing solitaire. When he sees me he raises his hand, "Have a good trip, now," he says.

Canned Peaches

Patsy says get the ripe fruit from the tree right before you start. The peaches should be a little firm, she says—not green and not too ripe either. She and Cliff like the variety called "Improved Elbertas," a freestone peach. In eastern Oregon, these are ready in early September. A bushel, in a basket if you are lucky enough to see one anymore, will produce twenty to twenty-five finished quarts of peaches. The amount depends, Patsy says, on how tightly you pack the peach halves into the jars.

She writes, "You need clean, hot quart jars. Wide-mouth jars make the work much easier. Jar lids and rings, sugar, water, a big water canner, canning tongs and funnel.

"You have some choice to make about how sweet you want your canned peaches. We like a light syrup, which is two cups of sugar to every four cups of water.

"Start by washing the fruit under hot water, which helps when you start to peel the skin away. Peel the peach, cut it in half, and remove the pit, and put it in the jar with the inside of the peach facing downward. Repeat until the jar is full. Tap the full jar on a folded cloth or hot pad until some of the peaches slide farther down the jar, making room for more peaches. Continue until the jar is full up to the neck of the jar. At this point you can add the hot syrup to the peaches, leaving a little room for expansion at the top. Apply a hot lid (put lids and caps in hot water in a pan on the stove when you start peeling so they will be ready for this stage). Cap each jar snug with a ring, and repeat until you have all the jars that will fit in your canner.

"Your canner should have a wire divider to keep the jars from directly contacting the bottom of the kettle. Pour hot water over the packed jars in the canner until the water is above the lids. Cover the kettle, turn up the heat and bring to a boil. Then adjust the heat to a steady boil for thirty minutes, twenty-five minutes if you are doing pints instead of quarts.

"Using the tongs, carefully remove the hot jars of peaches, placing each on a counter with towels under and on top, out of a draft. Wait for the jars of peaches to seal and cool—you will hear each jar lid pop down and seal as it cools.

"When the jars are cool, check to make sure they are sealed, and then wash any stickiness off the outside with soap and water. Remove the now-unnecessary rings if you wish. Date the jars and store them in a cool dark place until you need them. They will keep two to three years on the shelf.

"Repeat this process until you are happy with the final quantity and/or you are out of fruit.

"Cliff and I have great memories of growing and picking the fresh fruit and then having a canning party with our moms and aunts and friends helping with the process. The largest number I remember canning on one day was 125 quarts with the help of Ruth, Alta, Aunt Anna, and Mable Piercy. We had a lot of laughs, ate tacos and cantaloupe for lunch, and Cliff kept bringing in more beautiful fruit, which brought smiles to the oldsters, groans to the younger ones, and more sticky to the floors and counters."

6
SEEING THE RIVER

All the rivers run into the sea; yet the sea is not full;
unto the place from whence the rivers come, thither they return again.
—Ecclesiastes 1:7

My mortgage says I'll never die, just pay hundreds of dollars a month forever. Television advertising suggests that if we just solve the bladder and joint and bowel problems of this generation of old people, there aren't going to be any more old people. Especially not me. But as soon as I open a history book on the level of nations or movements that span more than one generation, I have to face the knowledge my ego won't allow—I'm just a passing thing.

Looking at history from the standpoint of messy generation after messy generation made the writer of Ecclesiastes a pessimist: "The thing that hath been is that which shall be; and that which is done is that which shall be done; and there is no new thing under the sun." Weariness and vanity. Early Jewish scholars are reputed to have argued about whether this unique text should stay in the Old Testament or not, but the rumor persisted that Solomon himself had written the piece. It stayed, thus preserving some of the loveliest thought owned by our culture. Much of the beauty comes from the overview itself. The way rivers are beautiful from the air, the way earth is beautiful from space.

Human activity viewed from such a distant platform is a swiftly revolving door—birth and death over and over again. It is a perspective without detail and without voice but with its own discouraging poetic: "A time to be born, and a time to die" and "The race is not to the swift nor the battle to the strong." But I forgive this writer who finds women even "more bitter than death" because he admits he's not sure that dogs won't go to heaven. "They are all one breath," he says of men and beasts.

I think I understand why he's in such a bad mood.

I feel this way every morning from about 3:00 to 4:30 a.m. That's the time of generalities, when sleep has removed me to an outer space from where nothing is visible but aging and loss, far from the particular joys of hugging my kid or eating a sandwich. Between 3:00 and 4:30, if I get up to pee, that's particular enough and I'm OK again. Another way I enter the doldrums is when my mom sends me one of those big epic historical novels with the man and woman embracing in torn-up clothes on the cover, the kind of book that covers four generations and buries three of them—in which characters drop like flies. Reading one of those puts me in a dust-to-dust mood for days. It is a crazy-making virtual reality of hard closure where all loose ends are tacked down before the final page and lives are spent like nickels. This kind of long view is breathtaking in two senses: it is vast, and it is a thief of detail.

I prefer a particular kind of history whose very unimportance is profound, which examines even a day or a conversation and is not consumed by its flowing backdrop. Dorothy Stone, an old woman in McGrath, uses a ski pole for a cane. Winter and summer she walks the road and when you meet her, she starts right in the middle of the story: "We had foxes. Way up the river. My son and daughter-in-law are up there now." She doesn't remember me, though a few times each summer we have coffee and cake at my house. I see her walking by and go out to get her. She says, "I had a good husband. Politician. I used to know the people who lived in this house." She is looking at my house. "They had a little girl." My daughter, the current little girl, will come out to see the rocks Dorothy has in her pockets today, because Dorothy always picks up tiny stones that look like they have noses and eyes and mouths and shows them to anyone who stops to talk to her. After three or four rocks, Kari loses interest and wanders off, but Dorothy shows me several more. "Look, here's a cute little fellow. See him? He's laughing at us! I used to be a schoolteacher. You have to show children, or they won't learn." I say yes. And I offer her coffee because one time she told me that everyone thinks old people drink only tea. She accepts, and when we are inside the house I put out canned milk, even though she told me the miners drink it because they ran away from their mothers too soon. She pours a little milk in her coffee today and takes a teaspoon of sugar.

Dorothy doesn't remember who we are, but she likes us. If I bring out one of the local historical calendars, she'll page through it and tell me stories about the people in the pictures, half of whom she is related to. Her stepfather, Charles Koenig, drove a mail team through Ophir to Flat, the end of the line from Fairbanks. Her mother, Helen, came from a family of reindeer herders near Bethel. Dorothy was schooled at the Catholic mission at Holy Cross and went to Chicago for the Eucharistic Convention of 1926. "It was a biiiiiiig town. I held on to Father's skirt. I was so scared he would leave me!"

There is little continuity in what I know about Dorothy, only pictures and pieces, and I am a stranger each time I greet her. But the frame itself provides continuity: the stories she tells to introduce herself, the familiar offering of coffee, the river town where we like to talk to each other. People pass by on the river and we invite them in, one by one, detail by detail.

Alaska rivers provide a point of view on history, one that does not deaden and discourage the watcher. In Alaska, rivers are still a serviceable metaphor for history because there are few roads, and despite the all-important coming of airplanes and airstrips, the river serves as road, stage, human journey. Especially before the advent of bush television in 1980, river villagers pulled out couches and chairs and left them on the bank for years. It was all the news: Who's on the river? Who's coming to visit? It was and is an attention to the river itself: Is it rising and getting dirty or falling and clearing up? Did the ice move? Is the channel open?

For those looking for a quintessential Alaskan thing, my vote is not for the cute little face made from the caribou anus, but for the couches that sit up above the freeway at Eklutna. I saw them twenty years ago, with people on them, and the people were just sitting there watching the cars go by. Last Thursday the couches were still there, maybe the same ones, but without the people. Twenty below and several inches of snow on the cushions should explain the absence of life. But those couches are *prima facie* evidence that rivers and travelers on rivers have been of singular importance to Alaskans, such importance that a road's mere similarity to a river is enough to make a person drag out a couch and sit down to examine the wayfarers. God knows if the sparrow falls, but the folks at Eklutna know that I've been to the dentist, to the grocery store, to pick up my mother at the airport. The fact that eighty bazillion people Eklutnians don't know are going back and forth on the highway hasn't discouraged their attention in at least twenty years. So I hope it was the cold and the snow that emptied the couches, and not that looking down at car after car full of strangers on errand after errand made the watchers feel their observations were futile and in vain.

For many towns in the Alaska bush, the river is a road to be tended to winter and summer, with short, dangerous interruptions at freeze-up and breakup time. When you live with maintained roads that connect all across the country, it seems that rivers are untrustworthy and full of danger, if they are anything at all to us, but in the interior of Alaska the rivers stretch farther, join more communities, carry more freight still. They are as reliably treacherous and changeable as the weather. People live with them, on them, with knowledge and skills gone from roaded landscapes. The barge captains who make their way up from Kotzebue on the Kobuk, from St. Mary's on the Yukon, from Bethel on the Kuskokwim, all know what each riffle hides, what each cutbank tells about the location of the channel, what the wind will do to the boat when they come around the next finger of silt and spruce. The river they travel is not just one river, but rivers within rivers, rich with episodes and dangers and prescriptions.

There was a Yukon River pilot who could not read to pass his Coast Guard examination, but he drew the officials a map of the entire route he would run, every cutbank, every sandbar and eddy in such detail that they gave him his license. The story is surprising to me: the kindness of the officials and the confident will of the pilot.

It is difficult—without listening to their voices, indeed without living their lives—to imagine what a former generation of Alaskans hoped the rivers would bring. Spending time where rivers—not roads—are primary, river people drag you into the texture of history. The roads around McGrath are bad, dusty, and rough, and many people use all-terrain "wheelers" instead of passenger vehicles. This shifts the concept of traveling in a car or truck to novelty, even luxury. After a summer of bicycles and wheelers and boats, my five-year-old daughter begged to ride in her father's work truck. A few weeks later, she glowed with pride when our friend Barb toured us around town in the old Chevy she had Northern Air Cargo fly out from Kenai. It is a pleasure when our habits are rearranged so that we can see them. One laughing moment in my job as a forest fire dispatcher was toppling an Anchorage dispatcher's belief that he would be trucking fire supplies out to McGrath. His refusal to understand that there were no roads through the Alaska Range prolonged and sweetened the discussion for several minutes. Not being able to get here by road is an exotic idea for an American in the early part of the twenty-first century. And the exotic is charming, which hides its importance.

I do not know more than five bends of the river at McGrath, but this small knowledge helps to pry open the primacy of river that is new to me and old to the world, to make me aware of the barges and the older steamboats, parts and pieces that stick up through the surface at low water. Walking slowly leaning on sticks, quiet in their houses, the aging practitioners of the river life are seldom visible in this small town. When the river comes up in the spring, plugged with ice downstream or swelled to the top of the bank with August rains, then I see Einer or Tex for the first time, hobbling down to the bank or riding a wheeler. A government program built them a line of houses, which they themselves have named "death row," but I've heard this black humor only secondhand.

In fact, everything I haven't directly heard the old people say about themselves separates me from them: how many miles one traveled on a dog sled to dance all night in Ophir, the clunky old troop carrier another sailed single-handedly from Seattle to Bethel, the kids another taught to read in a shack on a willow bank. Mostly they don't spare a glance for the townspeople who haven't sought them out; their attention is for the river. What will it do? Over the banks or not?

This attention to the river is compelling and can teach us younger ones to look too. Even the very young. In a world of Nintendo and malls and motorcycles, eleven-year-old Aaron took a look at the big McGrath flood of 1991 and announced gravely, "Now I've seen everything."

Ethnographers everywhere are noticing a curious phenomenon: after dutifully announcing year after year that a particular generation of old people are the last to hold on to a story, a song, a point of view, another generation of old people suddenly pops up that knows the words. To everything there is a season: "a time to keep silence, and a time to speak."

River-watching is preserved here as attitude long after the particularity of river travel and the knowledge of old travelers is gone. Bush airports gather storefronts and houses as rivers used to, but rivers and their functions are not yet completely gone, and houses and storefronts do not just turn themselves around. When we were in the village of Kobuk and an airplane came in, we'd follow the small crowd's circuitous route to greet it. And when it was us arriving at the airstrip, we'd follow the mail and packages back through town, walking up behind the school and through dog lots and caches to the postmaster's house. I always had a sense that I was sneaking up the back way, as if the town's attention was turned in another direction—toward the river.

There's a lot of scorn from some visitors about the way Alaska villages and towns look, all spread out and "junky," disorganized. But when you come in from the airstrip, the way most visitors come, you're coming from the dog-lot side. Unless it's a town built around an airstrip, such as a mining town up in the mountains or an Air Force station, the buildings aren't looking at you when you come in on an airplane. They are tending the water, where the boats and fish and visitors came from historically. The water flows in the direction of Kotzebue, Seattle, San Francisco, the rest of the world. The barge will land here with gas, fuel, oil, Sheetrock, and metal roofing. "When will my new truck get here?" "I'm gonna run out of gas if the barge doesn't get here by Tuesday." To build your house away from the water is like sitting in a room with your back to the light.

Alaskans are reluctant to abandon their homes and places of business on the side of the river, even when the river threatens them with flooding each spring and in many rainy Augusts. The Bureau of Indian Affairs built Galena a "new town" in the 1970s, but for years people would move back to the bank of the Yukon, to the little line of cabins and shacks outside the big nine-mile circle of dike that held the air force station and runway. There were three towns in town: the Air Force, the "old town," and the neat little BIA subdivisions with the houses looking at each other in rows. Twice in recent decades, six feet of water and ice have flowed through old-town houses for a week. Many of their owners camped out on the dike, played cards, built campfires, and waited patiently for the river to leave their living rooms. No wonder the rivers towns need to watch the river. It's like waiting for the mail: bad news, good news.

When I come back to a river town at the end of a day of eddies and cutbanks and gravel bars and moose in the willows, I feel like the town has been watching for me, watching from storefronts or the chair on the bank. A neighbor may see me come in and walk down and grab the line at the bow of the boat to pull it up the bank and tie it up in its place—my place. I believe the people on the couches above the freeway, even with a chain-link fence between them and the seventy-mile-an-hour traffic below, still hold a kind of vestigial voyeurism and faithfulness to neighbors.

Many present-day Americans from roaded areas can grasp some universal concept of river but not specific ones. To a city person, a wild caribou becomes abstract; it stands for nature but without the specific qualities of the caribou you hunt and eat—without the round circles chiseled on top of each other in the beaten snow of the trail or the hollow clicking sound of caribou ankles moving through the brush in front of you, like a handful of sixth graders popping their index fingers out of their cheeks.

Where I grew up, the river is beautiful and dirty and in the way. It is the famous Snake River, and it divides the landscape like a wall. I have felt drawn to the riverside as to a blank thing ready for meaning—a void left over from an old usefulness of rivers. When I'm standing by the Snake, I often have the curious experience of not being able to recognize whose house is on the other side unless I am close to where the bridge crosses. I will look across at Joe Witte's square fields sloping up from the river's far side and not recognize them. His farm could be the moon, so far removed from the possibility of going there. I can't recognize the place across the river because I can't go across the river at that place.

Standing in Joe Witte's cornfield down in "the Bend," that little chunk of Oregon nestled inside a curve of the Snake, I can gaze at the other side of the river, that picturesque but foreign place, and recognize, with surprise, that I am looking at my friend Carol's house. No one I know thinks of crossing the Snake River with a boat to get to the other side, though it is a broad, smooth river. There are no boats tied up along the bank. Not being able to get there from here becomes not being able to think about that from here. The white house with its fence and flowers, a stone's throw away if you have an arm like George Washington, is to my mind's map about seventeen miles away, all on roads.

Other than interdictions like "Don't go near it," nobody paid the Snake River much attention when I lived there. Even now the new houses built along the river in the town where I grew up face away from it, toward Main Street and the highway a half mile away. If you were a traveler on the river (and you wouldn't be) you'd climb up the bank and be greeted by all the backyards of town, the junk cars and weed patches, and you'd think, "What a neglected, scraggly little town." All the new little trees along main street and the one-hole outhouse labeled "city hall," a wry comment on government, would be lost on you.

There were different ideas about the Snake River at the town of Adrian when people traveled on it and before bridges when you had to come across on the ferry. There's one building left on the Snake that looks at the river across from Adrian. It was a store and ferry boat station, and it is very old—nothing left of it but a silvery-gray shell of planks. But it is obvious from the opposite bank, where the town sits, that the building tended the river and not the road. It looks too close, unwisely close, to the bank. From its own side of the river, coming up behind it on the little highway from Roswell, you see its back like the back of a man standing off to the side, turning away from you so he can take a leak.

There are few square fields in Alaska to draw attention away from the sweep and suck of rivers—their dangerous, necessary utility. Here, you are never far from the knowledge that the valley was carved by the river, the valley serves the river, and the river can take it back. The evidence is in the shapes of sloughs and in the meadows left by old sloughs, like the tracks left by some monstrous procession of caribou at the beginning of time, sloughs like the front curves of hooves separated by trees like green stacks of eyebrows. The old Yup'ik people say yes, raising their eyebrows. The land raises its eyebrows in the old bends of rivers, says yes to river, winter, ice, change.

Heraclitus is at home here, telling us we cannot dip into the same river twice, that *we* itself is a convention, whether vanity or bravery. The river cannot flow around the same *us* twice, still we wish to hang a name on ourselves that will hide our movement, limit and contain the daily and seasonal changes and the shifting of channels over a continuum. There are the changes of weather: rise and fall and "Better check the boat—it'll take four of us to get it down the bank and in the river again," or "Better go bail it out and tie it up high." And there are seasons: rainy season or low water or the ice coming, bringing the river to a stop, boats long stored away for the winter and then the whole land filling up like a sponge in springtime until even the river comes up, up nearly over the bank, thousands of square miles saturated with melting snow coming down and the rivers still plugged up, oatmeal in the drain, clotted with rotten ice.

And there are the changes that official deeds and appraisals and surveys deny: we drive out on the one road to look at the place where the river wants to come through above the town, trying to make us an island, trying to make the river in front of us a slough. A woman in California writes the city of McGrath a letter asking about her property, but her property is gone, the last of it sifting into the Kuskokwim five years ago. We cannot administer properties that dissolve, literally, and so we joke that we all will have riverfront houses if we can only wait a few years. Still, we call it the same river, and we call ourselves the same people.

You have to go fishing, gather plants, look closely along the sides of rivers to see that what seems static is only moving a little slower that the river itself. Berry-picking is good around the old horseshoe sloughs left by rivers. We found most of our blueberries around the margins of old sloughs this summer, on the old riverbanks, and not so much back in the woods. I think it was too rainy for the tree-sheltered bushes to produce fruit—maybe that's what happened, or it was something else? Too many variables make the overview difficult, so many details that there are only details, wonderful in profusion. Only when I've been out a few times does the shape of where the berries are this year come to me. They are looking for sun, clinging to the drier ground, hanging out over the open grass of ancient rivers.

Often when I am looking for berries, I can't see them. I walk around in the berry patch for minutes, unsatisfied with the berries I see, unwilling to stop walking for just a few berries, then all of a sudden I can see enough berries, and I know they've been there all the time. It's putting my back to the sun so the colors of bush and berries pull apart, but it's something else too, something secretive about berries that won't let you see them until you deserve it, until you've settled down, out of the future or past you've been thinking of and into the present moment where the berries are.

And when I close my eyes for a moment at the end of a day of picking berries, I see berries on bushes, lots of them and big. I never close my eyes and see berries in buckets or bags, ready for the freezer. It's always berries still on bushes, etched with desire on my eye, and I relive finding and wanting them. They are like story cycles—their details fade with time, eventually leaving only forms and frames: emptiness and vanity, if you will. Berries are a gift of a moment when detail cannot be hidden in abstraction. In their moment I am privileged to be among them, their small dark roundness in my hand one at a time, or a lucky handful in the right season.

Stories are hidden in the river, as in they are in history, yet the parts are greater than the whole. They do not deaden, discourage, despair. They come into view and pass out of view, usually unfinished, and their details offer a vertical dimension to the flow. If I don't look for names, search out the memory of particular people who have lived where I live, the forward movement of time erases definition and specifics, all the evidence of the deep vertical axis of my life. To avoid despair in the strong current of generations, I must uncover names, moments, old jokes I don't understand. We have always been new things under the sun, each of us.

McGrath has been built at least three times. The first time, just after 1900, it was called McGrath after Peter McGrath, a U.S. Marshal, and it was up at the Forks, so called because that's where the Nixon Fork runs into the Takotna River. That place was the farthest that boats from downriver could reliably travel toward the mining districts on the upper Takotna and the trailhead to Ophir on the Innoko River side. There was a warehouse at the Forks, owned by Archie Higgins from Takotna Village, and he had a gas boat that shoved a little barge up the Takotna River, but he had to wait until it rained so he could get his boat up over the shallow riffles.

After a few years, though, the boats that came upriver got bigger and the town had to move down to deeper water where the Takotna runs into the Kuskokwim. That's where it was in 1917 when David Alvinza Ray, the wireless operator for the Army Corps of Engineers, fell off the tall wireless pole where he'd been repairing something and was killed. My friend Margaret, who has lived in one McGrath or another since 1929, told me about this wireless operator several times. When she arrived in McGrath, the story was polished but still fresh, told by many and connected in many directions across Alaska. Now she is its only storyteller, and in the version I heard her tell recently, the wireless operator had no name, only "the wireless operator who got killed." The life of that story is nearly over, an empty frame.

But I know the wireless operator's name because she used to know it and tell it and because the water was high enough this spring for us to get our riverboat over into Old Town Slough. The cabins have mostly been eaten up by mushrooms and rot and roses, but there's an outhouse made from half of a round-hulled boat, green paint still clinging to it in patches, and David Alvinza Ray's grave, with a small granite headstone. The grave still has a neat picket fence, though the white paint is all gone. This is about the only thing left of the second McGrath.

What would have been obvious about McGrath in the twenties and thirties would not have been David Ray or the outhouse made from half a boat but the big Northern Commercial Company warehouse and shipyard on the upstream side of where the Takotna ran into the Kusko. Margaret says there was a dog barn for travelers and mail carriers, big enough that you could drive your sled right through the middle of it. If you were the mail carrier, Carl Seseui coming in from Telida, you'd leave your sled in the barn all night and bed your twenty or so dogs down in the stalls on either side of the sled run. Every mail stop had a dog barn. You drove right up off the river and into it, Margaret said.

Old man Dan Sprague was a buffalo hunter from Montana who was a feature of the second McGrath. He had a homestead across the river, where the town is now, and he'd come over to what was then McGrath in the daytime with an unlit lantern so he could light his way home in the dark after an evening of poker. But the game would stretch into night and back into the short winter day before he'd whiskey-weave across the snow and back across the river to his home, lantern still unlit. In the summer, his farm was literally a one-horse operation. He'd borrow Vanderpool's old white horse so he could plow his field. Vanderpool, the magistrate, lived one bend up the Kuskokwim, a mile and a half away, so they'd bring that horse up and down in a boat. Sometimes it wandered down through the woods on its own to be around people. When Margaret tells me about Dan Sprague, she often points to where his cabin used to be, a square of absent land off the end of the crosswind runway, long washed away by the shifting Kuskokwim. She said he was "a nice old man with long white whiskers" when she knew him in 1929.

The NC Company had to move their warehouse and store across to Sprague's homestead in 1935, after the Takotna ate through its bank and into the Kuskokwim one bend above its old mouth, which silted in the very same summer and became too shallow for the steamboats. The rest of the town followed gradually, buying up lots from the NC Company. Now what you see when you look across the Kuskokwim from the boat slip is cutbank all the same height, but where the Takotna used to come out, the willows are a touch shorter, maybe thirty feet instead of thirty-five, and that's how you know the river has hidden the channel and has hidden the town where the channel used to go. Rivers shift, and then towns drag their heels to new banks and wait to be washed away again.

Margaret has lived on both sides of the river because she came up to McGrath on the steamboat *Tana* in 1929. She saw the second town go down and the third one rise up. People and events flow through her talk so you can watch them, coming and going. We drink tea, couch and chair angled toward each other, and are surrounded by the hardware and mementos of a wilderness life, a river life. Nameplates from steamships, log tongs, lanterns. I am amazed by Margaret's varied enterprises—her trapping, freighting, and cooking for mining crews—and by her stories of her father, the steamship captain. She knows a trick that turns canned milk into a caramel-tasting flavoring, but you have to use a stove with plates, not burners. I like the big garden she still grows in the deep river dirt of Dan Sprague's old homestead and the delphiniums as big as blue trees above us when we sit outside in the summer. Margaret can't remember if she or Dorothy Stone brought the first delphinium seeds to McGrath, but now they're in every yard, and sometimes a stalk or two leans up out of the wild grasses and bed-straw along the road, invisible until it blooms.

Margaret helps me to resist the temptation to view my own life as a solid thing, just one kind of thing, or to get too far away from it, trying to see it. My mother would say, "It's an angry river," because in the experiences of her life, rivers do not have any specific dimension except for danger. If it is a flat, shiny river like the Snake, it's hiding something. If it is swift and silty like the Kuskokwim, it's angry. Its character, like its mood, seems to her an immutable fact. It's easier to think about rivers and even whole people and whole lives in this way, never looking any closer, as if we all are just one thing, one kind of person, one kind of life. This kind of looking is a shorthand for being conscious, and I practice it incessantly. Although people are kind or cruel or smart or dumb one right after another, it seems like I know each of them, and myself, to be just one thing. When I think this way, there is no "give" to the way I treat others, no idea that we all could break through into another channel anytime, out the other end of even this moment, leaving expectations behind like a vestigial circle of slough.

I met Ted and Margaret in 1991 when an ice jam downriver brought the Kuskokwim out of its banks and through the town. We were renting one of the few houses that didn't flood, though we had water over our top step, and we sat with our feet in it and handed out coffee and cake to people who were driving up and down the streets in their motorboats. Across the street, Margaret and Ted brought everything they could up out of their cellar and off the floor of their house and stored it in old barge containers up on blocks that looked to me like railroad cars. Then the two of them waded around in rising water, tying empty barrels together as a breakwater to keep all of the lumber and boxes and boats in their own yard—fifty years of stuff to try and keep from floating away. We hadn't collected anything that needed saving, so I watched Ted and Margaret and the other neighbors struggle, wanting to help but not knowing how to grab ahold of anything.

All day, kids got canoes stuck in willow thickets. There was a break-up party at the Alaska Commercial Company boat slip in the afternoon. The ice was gone by then, even if the river wasn't. We cooked hot dogs and hamburgers and drank beer and pop, standing in icy water and trying not to make waves that would wash over the top of our breakup boots. In the morning, when the water was going down, I took some hot biscuit cake out to the barge container where Ted and Margaret had found a dry place to sleep. The flood made us friends. I've been thankful, as I listen and grow close to them, as their lives open in stories I hope will last the winter.

After the water went down, people went into their houses and scraped out the inches of mud, peeled the carpets off the floors so the boards wouldn't rot, and moved back in. Most of the kids were disappointed that the water went down so fast. They looked at their old town in a new way for a while because it had done something surprising.

Sometimes when you come down to McGrath, across the Kuskokwim from the Takotna mouth, it is a smooth mirror, and you see the little pointed tops of the AC store and warehouse reflected in the water. At the moment, the storefronts are dark green with big white signs and red letters. They peer at you across the runway because there were already airplanes landing at McGrath in 1935 when the town moved and the old NC Company built a runway in front of its store. Main Street runs alongside this old runway. The buildings along Main Street—the stores, the electric company, the café, the radio station, the FAA—all have to squint to see the river, but they do it. They are still curious to see who is coming across.

Details of our lives cross the flowing length everywhere. Each lived moment divides the current and makes the river new. Each story ties us up for a moment to another life and opens—briefly and out of time—a view of what we are to each other and to the earth. When I look across the glassy mouths of rivers, seams invisible, I want to go close to the bank so I can see who's coming and who's passing.

Draw up a chair with me on a nice day.

Potluck

It's better when you don't have to sign up. Wild chance and how different we all are anyway brings main dishes and vegetables and noodles and breads and desserts. Someone has brought just moose ribs, cooked for hours, with only the magic of boiling water to separate and suspend the textures and flavors of muscle and sweet fat. In that pot, nearly empty already with half the line of people still eager to dip into it, vegetables would have been an unwelcome distraction. All the cartilage between the bones is cooked to delicious jelly. Don't leave those ribs in the woods. Don't waste: ribs are the best part.

How good it is to eat what other people bring: food I could not think of, food I don't have any left of in the freezer, food from another culture. *Agutuk* (Ah-goo'-tuk) is usually there on the long table. It is never exactly the same, even from the same house and hands. The berries are different this year, or there is no seal oil, or it is a different white fish. Sometimes it's made with what people here often call salmonberries. These are not the salmonberries from down around the coast but the quiet ones hard to find and farther inland, just one on each little stem. The Scandinavians call them *moltebaer*, and in plant books they are cloudberry.

Most often, agutuk is made with blueberries, my favorite, especially when they are mixed with white fish—cooked and pulled apart then smushed to a latticed texture on your tongue—and with seal oil if the cook has it, brought by some cousin nearer the coast.

Sometimes the cook uses Crisco instead of kidney fat or that lace from around a moose or caribou gut. Crisco, fluffy and white and odd, but an old friend in the villages—a canned and stable fat, a familiar, and if you think about it, no weirder than the white stuff on wedding cakes. Always sugar though, that old treasure.

We call agutuk by its Inupiaq name, even though an Athabaskan grandmother brought it. She knows how to call it in her language, but this is easier and everyone who loves this place loves to say it. "Eskimo ice cream" is for people who might start looking for eskimaux. Ordinary and precious, agutuk is there in the middle of the table with the ribs and meatballs, hardly ever with the cakes and cookies at the end. It is not a dessert but a hope and a surprise so it defies categories. Someone is generous with her berries and her idea of who we all are. There's a big spoonful in each paper cup, just enough cups to go around.

7

SOUND OF A MEADOWLARK

My daughter was six years old and we were spending the winter in Nelchina when I sent the new CD-ROM-equipped computer back to the company. She sobbed as I packed it. The thing was still under warranty, and I had been in line on the toll-free technical support number for hours trying to find out why it stranded itself mid-program, abducted by aliens, lost mid-thought, an ugly gray error message on its face. No one but a recording talked to me on the phone, so I boxed up the parts and pieces and sent them back, promising Kari another computer someday soon. But I understood her tears. She clicked on the word *wolf* and out popped a howling picture. She clicked *snake* and the thing gave us a list of options: do we want to see snake eggs or hear a rattlesnake rattle? There was suddenly in our very house access to latitudes and habitats past the end of roads, an instant hot desert or green forest inside the hundreds of frozen pastel miles of our December.

This computer, when it worked, took us to objects and animals we could see, hear, even dimly touch in the virtual skittering of the mouse. Beam me down, Scotty. But encountering this genie-in-a-box for the first time, I could only think of one experience I wanted it to visit for me. Could it play the song of a meadowlark? There was *find* and there was *play*, and then here was the little yellow-and-brown-speckled bird, a photo, and here came those seven or eight notes with their impossible intervals, competently recorded but lacking the life of the meadowlark. This is why I did not cry.

My lack of knowledge about meadowlarks is pretty appalling, given my hunger to hear one. The sound of a meadowlark is a very early memory from eastern Oregon where I grew up. For me, the meadowlark's song is associated with the smell of freshly cut hay, that warm exhalation of breath from the earth. The birdsong has the hot sun and the green smell in it, but somewhere since the childhood moments that formed this memory, the song's parts have failed to add up, to make sense. Now I hold on to the meadowlark in the hayfield as a moment that made me: my own creation myth. But the meadowlark didn't come that way, packed with the importance that distance and separation from family and farms and even the dreadful hot days would slowly give it. As with some canonized family story told until memory will no longer support it, I begin to question. The first hay cutting in Oregon is not made until after Memorial Day, and I am not sure if meadowlarks are singing then.

Curious about this once I got the idea of meadowlark back in my head, I called Althea Hughes, who lives up at Gakona and knows a lot about birds. She told me what I thought I knew, that there aren't any meadowlarks around here, and that they've only stumbled into southeast Alaska, far south of us, a few times by mistake. Early in the twentieth century, one was spotted near Craig. As was the custom in those days, the bird enthusiast "took it" the next day to prove to the world he had seen it. A meadowlark's song, says Althea, is supposed to be more dramatic in the western species than the eastern and is probably associated with their mating and nesting season in the spring, though she hadn't been able to find any literature that said it was, or that limited the occasions for meadowlark singing.

I'd like to know more about meadowlarks, almost as much as I'd like to hear one. I believe I should know a lot about the things I love, but I often don't, and sometimes I'm not even sure how I come to love them. Perhaps my first memory of a meadowlark was just sound, then I learned it was a bird singing, then I learned the bird's name, and so on, detail by detail. Was it luck to be able to say the meadowlark was what I wanted to know about and not the hayfield, to be able to separate them? And was the longing to hear meadowlarks already an ingredient of the first meadowlark song I heard, or does every loved moment grow with loss, as in summer, as in childhood, as in how eastern Oregon was when I heard meadowlarks, as in every story about meadowlarks, all mixing into and appending this longing? Will this kind of desire for lost moments accrete in my daughter around the nervous clicking of a hard drive as it searches for a picture of snake eggs?

I like to think a meadowlark is more "other" than a computer, more unlike me, so that loving its sound is less narcissistic than loving a computer, which is the corporeal form of a human idea. Put grossly, the distinction is between art and nature, art being a human order or vision imposed between what is and the observer of what is. Mathematics, which allows the binary movement to express itself through all the circuitry and logical arrangements I do not understand and which enabled this interactive encyclopedia that so entrances my child, is also an interpretation of our experience with the world and so by this definition is also art. Nature, in this broad dichotomy, is what comes to us without human filter, though there is a sticky little philosophical problem involved: that sensory perception of any kind is *already* a filter. We can't get to the world from here, with our Midas touch of mind, so perhaps nature is what doesn't come to us at all, even though we are nature, too. Perhaps we have to wistfully but resolutely accept nature's separation from ourselves, as celebrated in the Bashō poem whose first line Robert Bly borrows as the title for a book:

> The Morning Glory—
> another thing
> that will never be my friend.

But most of us have faith that what we touch and see and smell is truly out there, and most people would agree that a meadowlark is nature and a computer is not. None of us can satisfactorily know what nature *is*, just that most of us must have it in our lives and want our children to have it. I believe I have to go *to* nature to see a meadowlark, but I am not sure what I have to do to hear one.

One July my firefighting job sent me to western Colorado. On a day off I chased a meadowlark from fence post to fence post for several hundred yards on a deserted ranch road without hearing so much as a peep out of him. At least I thought it was a him—I don't know much about meadowlarks. A meadowlark pursued by a panting middle-aged woman may not feel like singing no matter what the season, or perhaps the birds don't sing past springtime, and the summer hayfields have only been tumbled into their song by my untrustworthy KitchenAid bread hook of a memory.

I can't remember when I last heard a meadowlark, and that is part of the problem. I live where meadowlarks are merely accidental and I go Outside to the Lower 48 infrequently and usually in the winter. So although it seems that I heard a meadowlark with my father in 1987—the last spring he was alive, when he could still drive the van and we went up the Owyhee River to go swimming—I am not sure. I thought I heard one when I visited with Carol Shultz at her ranch the same spring, when the snow was still around her high-pasture fences. Two years before, I went to Idaho in midsummer and worked at the fire center in Boise. I got off shift at three in the morning, so buzzed up from the work that I had to walk around for a while before I could go to sleep. There were hayfields, the smell of them rising with the sun. The meadowlark song is there, tangled with my senses, but its sweetness cuts through these memories, making them unreliable. I am sure I heard a meadowlark by a big globe willow tree on the road between Greenleaf and Wilder, west of Boise, but I cannot imagine why I would have stopped a vehicle on that narrow little highway. Decades past childhood, birdsong stitches me together like a quilt; I do not know fabric from thread.

The sound of a meadowlark, for those who have not heard it, is like whistled lace. It is sweet and sour and piquant on the tongue. Each time I hear one is like the first time I heard human voices in harmony— the joy of it so in the moment that it made a physical hurt in my chest.

We, as human things, can and must go to art to see and hear what we have made of meadowlarks. And art then earns some kind of credit or ownership for bringing our attention to birdsong, which is so un- owned as to break our hearts. Art must try to get at the bird, to bring it out from behind the camera or brush or violin or eyes or ears. I believe we should be able to do this part by part—a meadowlark's song is music, as mathematical as any computer. In some technically perfect future, we may reproduce the meadowlark's song so perfectly that, like some music, it will return in my mind at unexpected intervals, so beneath thought that I will not remember the moment of its source and will be bowed again by its otherness, beauty, and distance from me. But the computer and the television, even the marvelous nature documentary, cannot at present do this because the sound of the meadowlark only lives in whole moments, sewn into the fabric of walked-through landscapes. The song is inextricable from the story it inevitably becomes in memory. And whatever part of direct experience survives in this memory makes it so superior to any entertainment or education we have planned for ourselves that we are compensated for not being able to hear the bird itself apart from us. What we may make of this birdsong, even longing, is the art that drives us back to nature, that not-art, that *thou art.*

The Peterson and Singer bird identification books—illustrated by paintings—are superior to the modern Audubon field guides, with their color photographs, because identification clues are stressed in the brushstrokes, analogous to the way literature teaches us to recognize our lives through focusing on details and themes. Paintings of birds teach our eyes to discern the differences among species, genders, and phases, leading us back through the bird in the hand to the bird in the bush. Where we will again be reminded of why we wanted to know.

And that is our nature in nature—to have to try to see what we cannot perfectly see because the definition of seeing is the fabrication of understanding from unorganized possibilities. Art is how we attempt to see, and how we try to get at what we have seen and heard and touched in nature. Art is universal, doomed by definition, and meant to be cherished—not for itself but as the only tool we have to touch the world. I am not puzzled when art turns to art or language turns to language for their subjects; I am only puzzled when I'm told there is no escape from this tail-eating discourse. If I walk outside, the slightest flower that blows reassures me—not that I won't die, but that I am not the center, and therefore my powerful, wonderful, dangerous eyes will not destroy or encompass the mysterious nature that sustains me.

And then I see the computer as a valiant mimetic tool, useful in the still life of its description and only wrongheaded when I make it the object of my desire to contain the ever-changing meadowlark and its ever-changing idea within me. I cannot *have* the meadowlark.

Barry Lopez retells a Nez Perce story of how Coyote loses his wife and accidentally ensures dead people will stay dead so that we can never have them back again. Coyote is about to bring his dead wife back, past the dead country's threshold, but he breaks the rules by looking at her and touching her too soon. He cannot bear not to look at her. He cannot bear not to touch her. Sometimes Coyote is so much like us that I forgive him, though he is the reason that every moment I live is the last time I have that moment. He touches her; she disappears, and the country of the dead disappears, its old friends and flickering fires. Morning comes in this world, and Coyote hears a meadowlark.

For this American Orpheus, memory and a momentary experience intersect on the invisible vertical axis that is our true life—deep rather than long, lyric rather than epic. Though we seem to go only forward and in a line, we live deep and surprising moments at these intersections that are not at our beck and call. I wish to be a servant to such moments, the last one and the next.

In recent years, out in the mixed deciduous and spruce forests of the Alaska interior and so far only in the spring, the varied thrush has helped to heal the absence of meadowlarks in my life, if not the absence of hayfields. A cousin of the meadowlark, the thrush has a throaty, tangled call that keeps you awake in the never-dark of late May. Camping last spring in a small birch grove up the Nixon Fork River with our neighbors and mesmerized by the campfire and the amazing sleepless goofiness of my daughter and two friends, we stumbled off to our sleeping bags at 2:00 a.m., only to be serenaded for hours by our local thrush, directly above the tent, and its answering partner, some hundred yards away. The impact of each close blast of thrush music stunned me half awake. Mysterious cup full, I thought of meadowlarks grown ephemeral and stylized for me in their long silence. With gratitude I relinquished them to the woven story that begins with thrush song and wants to return.

I cannot say what sights and sounds of this world will rive my daughter past what she can know, bring her to faith past all the silly schematics of belief, but I hope that childhood midnight of dying fire and singing bird might be one such moment—remembered but not within mere reach, not even from the perfect digital throat of the future, so that she will have to come outside again and again, drawn through all the made moments she can summon, to the banks of this deep and unruly life.

Pumpkin Pie

I've been making a pumpkin pie. As usual not measuring, I ended up with too much crust, and as usual I rolled those remainders out and baked them with sugar and cinnamon on top. Pieces of this in a bowl on our table will provide an unhealthy snack for days. My teenage daughter, Kari, is off with friends today and I feel a little lonely doing this without her. She has helped me make pies since she was small, as I helped my mother make pies. Early on with my mother, my grand-mother Mary was there too, peeling the apples or washing the bowls and knives as soon as we used them. Those are good memories, because in this family most of our kids arrive late in our lives, with one grand generation about to tip over by the time the little guys are old enough to lick the bowl.

I had to try and remember what went into a pumpkin pie. I am making the pie from the nose and eye and grinning mouth pieces of this year's jack-o'-lantern. Even though I cut those holes extra big, I was surprised to see the pieces—the delicious negative spaces—cook down to enough for a pie. I'm pretty sure I remembered the rest of the ingredients: evaporated milk, white and brown sugar to taste, two eggs, then cinnamon, ginger, salt, and cloves in descending amounts. Twenty years ago I stood beside my mother as her still-quick hands put all these ingredients together and smoothed them to sweet velvet with an eggbeater, then poured the spicy orange deliciousness into the waiting crusts. In spite of all the Thanksgivings and Christmases of watching her, I still asked about the ingredients every time I made the pies in my own house. "It's on the back of the Libby's can," she'd tell me. "You don't have to remember it."

Now without the Libby's can or my mother, I think I've got it pretty close. What I'd really like is to have my mom and my daughter making pie together, with a few of the aunts there too, so that I could listen to those long-ago people get to know Kari as a young adult as we cook and joke around together before some big family dinner. I'd like to hear the pot lid rattle on the boiling potatoes. And just before the potatoes are done, it will be time to put the peas on. We'll use a little of the potato water we're pouring off to mix with the cream and the flour for the peas. The rolls will be "up enough" to stick in the oven so they'll come out at the same time we are ready to sit down at the table. We can make the gravy now.

8

MY LIFE IN THE SERVICE OF DOG

The free animal
has its decline in back of it, forever,
and God in front, and when it moves, it moves
already in eternity, like a fountain.

—Rainer Maria Rilke, *Eighth Duino Elegy*

Our old Labrador retriever, Pika, had a big seizure. At sixteen and three-quarters years old, we'd wondered which day would be the beginning of her end. Before the seizure, she followed us and the other dogs down to the lake, taking her exploratory and limping time to get there except for the last fifty yards at a gallop—when she saw the other dogs were already playing fetch in the water. She snarled at the pug we are dog sitting, waded into the lake, and swam like a slow beaver after the water toy. Her straining body rode low in the water with her shiny black head leading the wake. As we held the other barking mutts, she brought back the precious object and laid it at Jim's feet. For months now, we have called her "Pika the Great."

Minutes afterward, while our attention was on the other dogs, she fell down thrashing in the mud and tall grass at the water's edge. When we got to her, it looked like she was trying to regurgitate the inside of her body. Her eyes were rolling, then unfocused. After that, she became still and we could not feel her breathing. Jim gently lifted her out of the wet and up the shore onto the dry gravel. With my hand on her warm chest under a front leg, I could feel her heart pound, then stop for seconds, then pound again. I talked to her, knowing she is deaf, and I felt her hear me. As real as anyone's out-of-body experience, she hovered around us and decided we couldn't make it on our own, not yet. After a while we could see her breathing again and her little heart took up its familiar beat. Jim brought down the pickup, with a soft dog bed to carry her home. After a few hours on a rug in the entryway of our house, her head came up and her brown eyes looked for us. The next day she was eating, drinking water, walking around, showing the pug a snarly tooth.

We live near Glennallen, where it says "PREPARE TO MEET THY GOD" on the old sign that used to decorate the parking lot of some church displaced in the frothy revisionism of local denominations. Whoever rehung the sign made it inescapably close to the road, another kind of speed limit. I am the person who wants to make a sign that says "DOG" and hang it over the word "GOD," but I am not yet acquainted with the new magistrate. Jeanie Wilkinson has retired and moved away, taking her stress-lined face that hid so much mercy for the kids and drunks who appeared before her. Anyway, I don't know what to do with the other side of the sign that says, "Your Sin Will Find You Out." So cowardice wins over my annoyance with the self-righteously saved who desperately need the rest of us to remain despicable. Mark Twain wants me to go ahead and change the sign, but I think I'll wait a hundred years until it is safe.

Enter this moment with me. On a January morning, I'm sitting in a chair by the woodstove, lightly tickling the cheek of a sled dog in a manner I learned from my mother, who used this method to keep me quiet in church. I stroke his fur so lightly that he has to concentrate on the sensation to know that it is there. Although I am now nailed to this chair, it is not a bad place to be on a cold day in winter. The dog's sighing, his pacing around the house and his meaningful stares have subsided. His head is lowered almost to his front paws. His panting, at first like a woman in the last stages of childbirth, eventually slows and quiets until what remains is the long mesmerized rise and fall of his chest as he relaxes to the floor. When I think he's asleep I take my hand away, but he immediately raises his head and looks concerned, so we resume my tickling and his suspended animation.

This isn't just any dog, and it's not my dog. Dweezil belongs to musher Monica Zappa. He nearly died of some mysterious neurological disorder when he was a youngster while Monica was away running the Iditarod Sled Dog Race from Anchorage to Nome. When she and her partner, Tim Osmar, returned, Dweezil was a limp and gangly invalid who could not even stand up. Monica nursed him back to health in her arms then gave him the freedom of the dog lot because the invisible chain between Monica and Dweezil was now stronger than any of the real chains holding the other dogs. Now he is the charismatic ambassador between dog and human species, weirdly communicating Monica's wishes to the rest of the huskies. She says he is a peacemaker who stands between belligerent dogs until their growling at each other subsides. He is a trickster, stealing sticks and bowls, and for a short time was a lover, siring two litters of puppies before a trip to the vet ended his romantic career. He has his favorite playmate, his friend Picante, and every dog enjoys his youthful overtures as he roams their territory at will. He takes responsibility for the similarly unbound puppies, taking them for short jaunts around their Caribou Hills home to see the world before their working careers begin. So far, everyone has come back safe.

Dweezil's own career has been a subject for speculation. By breeding he's a sled dog all the way, from his naturally bobbed Lime Village dog tail with the little hook at the end of it, through his rangy, powerful form inherited from a Susan Butcher lead dog, past the vivid Alaska Husky mask that starts around his intelligent eyes and runs clear down the long cream and brindle nose that I am tickling. Rather than single or double occupancy in the dog box, though, he prefers the view from up front in the truck cab, sitting between Tim and Monica as they drive highways to practices and races. And he's a picky eater. A sled dog has to eat a lot in a hurry and drink enough before his water dish freezes shut. A sled dog learns to poop on the run, occasionally a problem for the person standing on the back of the sled. Everything is on the run or about the run. Tim told Monica she could have her choice between a sled dog and a pet, that Dweezil could not be both.

But somehow because she wants him to, he loves to pull with the other dogs. He strains mightily in whatever harness position Monica tries him at, and his big ears twitch around like satellite dishes scanning the air for her wishes. He's still too young, but she thinks he may become the next leader for her team.

Tim was running Dweezil in his practice team two days ago when he noticed Dweezil changed from a trot to a lope at a different speed than usual. A musher is attuned to any indication of illness or injury in the dog team and knows the moving rhythm and style of each dog intimately. Pushing gently on the front of Dweezil's left hip, Monica found a strand of muscle that made him swing his big head around and look at her when she touched it. So today he rests with me, restlessly, while his dearest dear runs a nearby trail with his teammates for fifty or so miles in the thirty-below-zero winter day. "She will be back," I tell him.

If the snow is slow in coming to the Caribou Hills or Valdez, we might have dog team visitors in our more northerly yard for a few days each winter. We aren't dog mushers, though we watch that all-consuming lifestyle with interest and feel our similarities. Like mushers, we are cabin people, plank floor and five-gallon bucket people, conversant with Costco and other elegant places to dine quickly on a Polish sausage before hurrying home 150 miles with the groceries. We are always partly turned toward the roadless Alaska where we once learned to live. We have never lived anywhere that was not a good place for a dog to visit or call home, or had a couch too nice for a dog to use for its nap. In general, people do not think of us without also thinking of whichever dogs currently live with us.

Our first dogs had to chill at the end of chains during our workdays, but gradually we were the ones tied, like the errant pencil running obliquely from John Donne's faithful compass point. If you draw back at Donne's love poem being refitted to a dog, consider a point of view in which the universe is not at our service, in which the connections between us and what sustains us are visible.

I know that dogs are not humans. A dog is not thinking what I say she is thinking, yet Jim and I put words in the dogs' mouths as easily as we converse with each other. I accept that I cannot express what is probably crystal clear to the dog, but I'll take a stab at it anyway, confusing whoever else is in the room: "Sweet toy. Needs a squeaker, though." Perhaps when the physicists identify gravity's earliest ancestor, they will find a particle for our partnership with dogs. They will be able to tell what neurons dogs pull to claim us and reshape our attentions, and how our rotations slow to meet their faces. We may learn something about the mother of gravity that will cause us to reexamine our ideas about who owns who.

In the meantime, we view our dogs through ten thousand years of ineffable connection and, in the culture I call home, a hundred years of schmaltz. The clichés about our friend the dog are a boarded-up mine shaft leading to unknown depths. There's real substance below, but we can't see beyond the entrance. My email inbox is full of beginner-level dog appreciation; my friends know better than to send me hateful political glurge, but I'm an uncritical consumer of photos of dogs with tennis balls, dogs upside down doing the Macarena, dogs in sunglasses. I sometimes produce these cute dog photos myself, and you are liable to receive some if you are my friend. If there is another person in the house, I will frequently call his attention to the cleverness or beauty of a dog.

What we say about our dogs or the words we put into their mouths are never accurate; our chatter is just a placeholder for significant connections on both sides. There is always mystery in how dogs and people need each other. One dog-generation ago, our old yellow Lab Nilla had a stroke in my arms. I sat on the floor and he clung to me with his eyes and leaned hard into me with his body. His communication with me was a live open circuit between us. I felt it in my gut.

We take our connected moments with dogs for granted because we can't explain them, and because those moments stand for all of our misunderstandings about who we are in relation to other living things.

Our inability to comprehend our connections with animals doesn't prevent us from exploiting those connections. In books, movies and TV, blogs and tweets and photos, we love imagined stories of animals who care for humans or act like humans. Narcissism are us—who can resist creatures whose apparent regard for us is like a mirror reflecting our own best features? It's easy to confuse dogs with their images, with the digital ephemera that mimics our lives, anticipates and amplifies our wants. Real dogs show us our lives from a perspective outside our-selves, change what we want, amplify our ability to love—but which ones are the real dogs, the real animals? I tossed the Bambi book and the Bambi movie out of the house long ago because I thought they turned animals into humans and humans into demons with no place in the natural world. Now that I am older and more uncertain, Disney lives here again. Who knows—maybe children thinking about imag-inary animals full of smart comedic dialogue will somehow absorb a better regard for the diminishing nature beyond the cities. Nothing else has worked and besides, the graphics are getting better and better.

It is easy to react against personification, anthropomorphism—those things other people do. Backlash is a complicated cynicism: blaming women for their emotional connections with animals—trivi-al ribbons and silly haircuts, doggy treats that look like little ice cream cones. We blame children for their empathy and naïveté toward ani-mals—regarding as "childish" the same trusting behavior and mallea-ble features we "select for" in our young animals, thus perpetrating our long-standing evolutionary connection with them—the very practice of neoteny. And of course we blame the dog, whose name can be a sort of insult. An ugly car or ugly girl is a "dog." A "cowering dog" is vulnerable, dependent, transparent, and despicable in his fear—of us.

But some part of personification is a necessary tool for understand-ing a dog because we don't have any other tools. Personification and faith—faith as in accepting the "what is" we will never be able to know. Even science must be conducted from our side of the wall.

Here is another. Anny is stretching herself awake, getting ready for another meal or a squirrel hunt, and Pika is watching us for our next move. I'm about to be yipped at and asked to play and driven mad and reminded that "there is always a door between a dog and where it wants to be." I ask for and facilitate that relationship.

The dogs ride with us and go to work and on trips with us. We try to find hotels where dogs are welcome, or we might sleep with them in the back of the truck. I am not too old for this. I want the dog where I can reach my hand down to touch her. I am stubborn, and I don't like stuffing dogs in airline kennels. As a result, we are reduced to local and drivable adventure. We have not visited New Zealand. On the upside, we are dragged on walks along beaches and through berry patches. We would be even fatter if we did not own dogs.

When the dogs have to stay home without us, I worry about a house fire, not because I'd lose my stuff, but because thinking of causing a dog's suffering hurts me. If someone else is taking care of the dogs, I worry about porcupines. I leave a needle-nosed pliers next to the bowls and the vet's number on a sticky note. For the dogs' sake, I despise porcupines.

At my house, dogs are the electrons popping in and out of their orbits around the humans while also taking us for granted. A dog may or may not seem to return my affection at the moment I am offering it, but that doesn't matter. Our indenture to one another is a contract I have written for me. I choose to exhibit loyalty to my dogs. This is in part a physical bond, driven by oxytocin, the same touch hormone that locks parents and children together. This is in part a disaffection with the larger society and its relentless artificial trends. Commercial messages on the TV or radio make me long for a big, noisy hailstorm that shuts down the power, a time-out issued by the sky, leaving only the book in my hand and the dog beside me.

If Jim is away, I'm not lonely if I have the dogs. If I am the one who is gone, part of the empty space next to me is the shape of a dog. I spend time contemplating the shortness of dogs' lives, and I grieve each dog before she dies. I mourn each loss of playfulness, of agility, of sight and hearing as the years pass. While I prematurely mourn, some dog is dragging me out of that silly funk into the now. And after decades of living with dogs around our feet all day and dogs sleeping on the bed with us at night, I know that I am a little strange for the world. Except for the small appropriation of physical space in the bed, in front of the fire, or in any doorway I am trying to walk through without tripping over the dog, I know the dog is not an interruption but an amplifier of our life together: a boy and a girl, a boy and a girl and a dog. You can feel it.

Humans in the service of dogs are not uncommon. Besides mushers there are hobos and other people on the margin, Mr. Bojangles of the Jerry Jeff Walker song grieving twenty years for his dog companion. We knew an old woman hoarder who had a house full of nothing of value and no place to sit because her beloved dog had just given birth to puppies in the only chair. Over the years, the category of people who partner reciprocally with their dogs has included many people that I admire. It gathers in a handful of women cowboys with their Blue Heelers and collies and mutts. A legendary Athabaskan Copper River fire crew boss, Lemmie Charley, told me several times in recent years, "my whole life was horses and dogs."

Dogs commonly serve people. Dogs make themselves available and useful, for kibbles or for the more mysterious bonds we think of as loyalty and love. Their willingness to be of service to us has helped to give us our outsized opinion of ourselves as masters of the universe.

A young friend of our family teaches dogs American Sign Language so that their deaf owners can communicate with them. She teaches mostly border collies, a breed with an estimated average vocabulary of 250 words. She teaches other smart and eager-to-please breeds, too, such as retrievers. She taught a golden retriever to push its paralyzed owner back into the sitting position where he can breathe when he falls too far over in his chair. I read about a dog who chewed a rotten diabetic toe off of its owner when the owner was in a coma, saving the owner's life.

Our dogs are service dogs too; we just never know which of their services we are going to call on. Nellie, a golden retriever, had a limitless affection for people. But when a belligerent drunk fellow broke into a house we were renting and stumbled toward the room where our baby was sleeping, Nellie showed teeth we'd never seen before. By the time we got down the stairs, she had the intruder flattened against the door trying to get away from her. Less tangible services provided by our dogs include stretching out on the floor between us when we play music and pretending to understand what we are talking about. As we grow older, the nuanced services expand in value.

We like the big bird dogs because the world they care about is the world we care about. Out of all the unknowns that a relationship with a dog presents, narrowed by the thousands of years humans and dogs have been shaping each other, one strand of human yearning has selected traits in retrievers that suit the way we like to live or how they have taught us to live. Some interesting research has been done on the fact that no other primates hunt or socialize in just the way humans do—more like dogs than apes. Who taught us to do those things?

Our marriage is into approximately its fifth generation of dogs. Up through the fourth generation the dogs went to fields or wetlands with Jim to hunt birds. Hunting dogs' human-refined instinct to hunt doesn't just go away if a dog doesn't use it. Pika remembers her hunting days and measures the worth of birds and squirrels on a sliding scale of can she catch it or will Jim shoot it for her. While you watch her, you can see her make a quick decision about which thing is most likely to happen, then she will pursue or wait. When she was younger, she made an amazing aerial catch of an unlucky spruce grouse that glanced off our house. She had it in her mouth and brought it to us before we registered what was happening. We thanked her for our dinner.

Somewhere back in the Labrador lineage were pointers. Although it is unusual for a modern Lab to point, Anny can get stuck halfway through our front doorway if she suddenly spies a grouse in the yard. The tail goes straight, the front foot comes up, the body stiffens, and

Anny's eyes lock onto the bird in an icy, unbreakable stare. As precious warm air escapes from the house, we try to pry the dog in or out.

Our present dogs have transferred most of their instincts to saving us from red squirrels. The sound of a chattering red squirrel about to wreak havoc on the shop's ceiling insulation can wake Anny from a dead sleep on a bed inside the house, two outside walls plus eighty feet away from the offending rodent.

We seldom hunt now, but retrievers hunt the world for its details whenever they are not sleeping or eating. They bring motion, scent, and sound to our attention. Our dogs warn us when there are bears around. They have an inherent dignity and their attention to us is not subservient. Pika runs back to check on us like a parent checks on a young child. She knows our understandings are imperfect and we might screw up at any time.

I'm grateful for everything dogs do for people, but I am wary that stories of dog service appeal most to humans who see their lives and the society in terms of our primacy. I think of my father who kept our bird dogs in a pen until the start of the fall bird hunting season. He did this for decades, explaining to me that random, unfocused affection and peripatetic commands from children would ruin the dogs for hunting. But I watched him grow inseparable from his last hunting dog at the end of both their lives, their mutual unfocused affection a profound last exploration of the world together.

My mother taught me that I should love children and want to give birth to a few of them, hopefully redheads. But it was a dog who taught me to feel how another being loves and trusts me and depends on me and how not to betray that trust. Dogs taught me how to slow down to the speed of joy. In the moments I've actually learned something I wasn't already capable of learning, it was often a dog showing me how to be kind, shaming my cruelty, teaching me what I would need to know to live with other people.

It's out there in the culture that we make fun of old women and their poodles with haircuts and bows, but I wonder which services are really gratuitous. I feel the raw edge of a societal jab at females, who are not regarded to have "real" uses for dogs. It's great to have a delicious pheasant fried with biscuits and gravy, but it is also so good to have a dog sleeping by your feet while you read. We have a friend who taught his Lab to stand on its hind legs and raise one front paw in a salute. I never asked if this was meant to be ironic. It was never quite cute, never quite cruel. Bringing back a stick or a bird or herding a sheep is fun or useful and more natural to the dog, depending on the breed as amended by us. So what I must object to in that salute merely addresses who I do not want to be in relation to the dog. Training is a good thing that enables us to live with our chosen animals, but I want to leave open the matter of who is actually being trained and what the training is for.

I was a first grader when the cocker spaniel Rocky waited for me by the front gate every day when I came home from school, something no one taught him. He picked up the wild yard kittens when he thought they were straying too far, then delivered them back to the mother in his mouth. Was he thinking in terms of service or obedience to humans or obedience to cats? The latter, according to our idea of a dog's ideas about cats, would be like the Pharisee's opinion of Jesus allowing his feet to be washed by a prostitute. Are there dog saints?

The theme of "dog waits for owner" is omnipresent in our society, handily bundling the dog's sweet loyalty to us with her self-sacrifice, characteristics we admire in our saints but don't much practice ourselves. Dogs wait for their masters by the village well, by gates, by roads, outside buildings, on graves. If we need to feel what it means for a policeman or a soldier to be killed and never come home, we don't show photos of their weeping children. What makes us weep is that no one can explain the death to the dog. It is the very stuff of tragedy. Capitan, Masha, Woody, Hachiko: there are waiting dog stories in every culture.

Here's my family's most important waiting dog story. The next day after a niece and nephew were severely injured in a car accident near Salcha, Alaska, we drove past the accident location on our way to the hospital. There was our brother's Chesapeake Bay retriever, Yadu ("yes You," in Norsk), sitting by the side of the road near pieces of broken glass and plastic. We had forgotten that the kids had the dog with them. We opened the pickup door and called to him and he leaped into the front seat with us, frantic to be with someone he knew. We stopped in at the next door business and they told us they'd seen the dog and tried to get him to come to them, but he would not leave the patch of asphalt where the crash happened. He was uninjured, but trembled all the way to Fairbanks. His presence took away a numbness that had set in with us after the accident, knowing that something had happened that would change our families forever but not being able to feel it. Yadu's loyalty made it raw and real and we cried.

Loyal animal stories are put on the children's rack at the bookstore, which keeps others from properly regarding them, but the stories of animals who give their lives for us or who suffer at our hands are too horrific to read or view by anyone—unless they have been painted over by some overwhelming human aggrandizement. Beyond *Old Yeller* are the war dogs with prosthetic limbs. It wasn't their idea to be there. What part of us are animals serving when we calculate to spend their loyalty to us? What is a legitimate spending of an animal's pain or life on a human project?

My husband's grandfather, Christ Odden, logged white pine in Wisconsin with teams of horses. One winter around 1900 he was crossing Horseshoe Lake with a load of logs, and the ice gave way beneath the four-horse team. The huge skid of logs behind them pulled the horses down in their harnesses and he could not save them. Jim's father remembered that his father was unable to tell the story without weeping.

When the suffering of an animal is the result of a human choice, or a human's bad aim or ignorance, it becomes a horror story. I heard a dog wail after it had been shot in McGrath. The owners were moving and couldn't take the dog with them, so after they left town and the dog was still tied to its house, they asked neighbor boys to shoot it. The shooting was botched and the dog's hollow cry filled our end of the small town. I'd never heard a sound like that before; it was pure surprised betrayal. I can still hear it. I bring that sound to the surface sometimes when I am looking at news service photos of human pain, in order to be able to understand what pain is. The most horrific animal pain is, like child abuse, about betrayal of trust. It is well documented that people who hurt animals are also willing to hurt children. Animals are our canary in the mine shaft—of course an animal. We read, "No animal was harmed in the making of this movie." We do not read, "No human persons were harmed in the making of this movie." It's not that animals are being elevated over human importance. It is that only the pain of animals, with their pure dependence on us, is able to make us feel what we should feel.

Do dogs love us?

Dogs are everything I wanted horses to be when I was nine years old and dreamed that my uncle Pud the government trapper would bring back a wild white horse just for me from the Oregon desert. My family eventually had horses, including a sweet pony I loved who tolerated kids crawling all over him, but I learned that most horses are just interested in other horses. That sweet nickering was for the oats.

Our dogs are towering examples of food-motivated self-interest, but their insistent proximity is more than that. The most convoluted explanation of dogs' apparent love for humans I have heard is that dogs are parasites on human affection—that they push their way in between lovers or between parents and children to soak up the sweet attention and cuddle hormones available there, or into the lonely space of an adult longing for a child or a human friend. As that story line goes, the dog thus becomes indispensable to the human and gets itself fed and cared for, thus serving the intentions of its selfish genes.

If I start down the road of blaming the dog and her evolutionary biology for stealing my precious affection, then I have to accuse my own selfish reasons for creating the dog in the first place. I, in cahoots with my ancestors, have spent all the time since the Pleistocene shortening her head, choosing her great expressive mammal eyes, adopting and caring for her cute or obedient or affectionate or useful ancestors and sending the rest of them to the bottom of the river in a rock-weighted gunny sack.

I'm looking at the pug's poor face. Sorry pug lovers, but this little guy can hardly breathe through his pushed-back nose. Remnants of the wolf are difficult to see; human desire for a helpless, baby-faced lap dog is alarmingly apparent. Our ability to get what we want has never been adequately tempered by the question: what should we want?

Last night I read a magazine article about our new human ability to edit DNA. Technicians can now do this as easily as I can use my word-processing program to move this sentence to a different part of the page. If you have a big enough microscope and the right tools and know-how, you can order a kit that costs approximately $130, cheaper than the latest version of Microsoft Word, to change the inheritable traits of any organism you want—animal or vegetable. Instead of selectively breeding generations to deliver a tame animal, or a monster, you locate the characteristics you want in the DNA strands and plug them in or snip them out. You are constrained only by your idea of what you should do: by what your preacher, your professor, your instruction book, or your mother has taught you. Law has precious little to say about this new tool, and little anticipated control over it.

After learning this, I was stunned and sad in that helpless state where I cannot sleep, cannot say to hell with it and get myself out of bed. If we humans can have whatever we want—certainly longer lives and freedom from illnesses but also zucchini that tastes like prime rib and things we don't even know how to want yet—then we no longer have to accept the world as it is given to us. We've never accepted it anyway, but we've never had instant gratification either. Our sciences and our wills have been slow partners, never quite keeping up with our ignorance of what is out there. Now we will cure sick children and make children sick. The tool of my kindness is the same tool of my anger. I can do better than you. You can do better than me.

In the stark night, I am certain that my best expression of faith is the acceptance of gifts I may not understand, to say, "Yes, we are the striving imperfect animals who must witness the world as it is." When the proselytizers bombard me with miracle tales and the vending machine where you pay in prayer and magic words so that eternal life comes out the flap at the bottom, I'm thinking about how hard it is to talk with the injured and the insane, even visit the sick and feed the hungry. I'm thinking how impossible it is to love someone who would want to cut my head off. Being good is not a simple transaction when the other's face is as inscrutable as the intentions of a swan or the hatred in a marketplace bomber. But now it will be harder still, as we can change ourselves before ever learning what we are. If we weren't doomed before, we've done it now, and the prayers to love the others as ourselves are all blown up. The unknowable "others," given to us, will all disappear as the world is remade in the image of our desires.

It's lonely here. I do not want to be the only witness, the only responsible party.

If you feel our misunderstanding of what is outside of us, then enjoying nature and mourning the losses in nature are conjoined. Walking to the lake when each spring is warmer than the last, I worry about the morass of assumptions that keep us from acknowledging our common fate with these trees, these birds. I care whose fault the warming world is, but to figure it out don't we have to acknowledge that we are not the only important life here?

Let's be emotional, act like a girl. We need to feel it and not let it be numbed. I want to hurt if I need to hurt to be human. I also know that I may not know what I'm asking for when I ask for that.

Jim had a beloved uncle who could not bear the suffering he believed he had caused as a military pilot in the Korean War. Sometimes he would fall through the margins of his full life and remember the details of a mission decades before. He would say, "I have killed so many people." His awareness of suffering and his culpability—against the demands of his "ordinary" life—often incapacitated him. For the rest of his life, his empathy for innocent people and animals was profound. Stories of animals suffering at the hands of people threw him into despair.

What we can feel is limited to what we can identify with. Most of us are not Jains or Bishnoi who sweep their walks and strain their water to avoid causing harm to any living thing including insects. I reflexively squish a spider that crawls on me, unconcerned except I might hope superstitiously for rain. Charismatic megafauna, the animals with big eyes, are the creatures that can make us acknowledge our complicity in creature pain, allow us to feel fear for the loss of the natural world. Plants, insects, fish, and ugly animals don't get much respect unless their survival can be shown to support the survival of a tiger or a panda.

Those animals with eyes are doorways to our own souls too. I am eager to touch the "otherness" of dogs and whales. I want the "miracle story" of the humpback who thanked the divers who freed her from the fishing nets to be true. I want the kindness of the divers to be real, and I want the thanks they saw in the eyes of the freed whale to be true, while the whale nudged them gently one by one and then disappeared into her depths.

The space between the divers and the whale, full of their thoughts about each other while they are interacting, is not empty. Empty space has never been empty. Because the whale and its universe are so strange, the miracle of its seeming affection for the men responding to it is so much greater. In the divers' description of the whale's gaze, I feel the distance the whale had to cross. I feel the distance even more because the harm of the net is a human harm.

A wonderful teacher at the University of Alaska Fairbanks, Walt Benesch, liked to talk about a theory of language that gives communication its own living realm. There is me and there is you, but what transpires between us when we talk is neither of us but an additional entity, a third something we have created that has its own power.

This is a place of hope, if there is a corporeal life of language that happens between me and you, between us and dogs. There may be a goodness curled up, like another universe, waiting for us to acknowledge it and learn at last what we should want. We may have to follow a dog's gaze to find it.

Pika is still here, still my shadow. We take her for a ride in the boat where she stands up with her feet on the bow, ears flapping back like banners. She sleeps more each day, but if I leave her side some clue of my absence seeps into her sleep and rouses her to find me. She is deaf and she does not see very well, but her toenails click on the wooden floor as she searches room to room. When she finds me she will heave her stiff body down beside me.

A dog leads me here, putting up with the piece of cheese I've balanced on her nose. Or she's sliding down the snowy hill on her back, making me delighted to be alive too. Dogs are my midwives to the mysterious something between me and nature that reduces my isolation. Whatever is there, they see it—but it has a different look, a different smell.

My miracle stories are inside ordinary moments, probably sleeping. Dogs bark them awake and give me access, like the doorway in the back of the wardrobe, to the country of between. Just a degree less foreign to me than the rest of the universe, dogs are my friends in a big strange room where I don't know the host. Here are their names: Duffy, Rocky, Mike, Jill, Lady, Ginger, Cookie, Gabie, Rip, Nellie, Loki, Tigger, Nilla, Pika, Anny.

Here's a shining day. In August, after a bad fire year in Alaska's interior, the smoke is finally gone and the world is a rain-washed jewel. The dull, diffused pink light of many recent days has lifted and the clean air and excited dogs drag me outside. Don't I know there are rabbits everywhere? Can't I smell that rascal fox? The lynx was here, too, and left fresh rabbit parts to chew.

I understand that what I see when I walk out my door is always skewed and incomplete. A dog is a separate lens, an interpreter, a necessary crutch. I try to triangulate what I see through my self-interest-tinged view with what I have come to believe the dog sees through her self-interest-tinged view.

The dogs want to go to the lake and never mind breakfast. I don't mind, because I've noticed this summer that the swans hang out on our side of the lake only in the early morning, moving to the far side or clear to the other end all day, away from human activity and noise.

The swan pair has four cygnets, still alive despite a nearby eagle family and the foxes and the egg-stealing mink. Maybe the hordes of easy rabbits have something to do with these swan babies growing and gliding with their parents, turning lighter now as the fireweed loses the last of its blooms.

Sure enough, when we get past the crest of the road going down to the lake I can see them just on the other side of the lily pads, two graceful white adults with gray stems waving between them. Without my glasses as usual, I strain to count the stems. I know it's the nature of nature to thin the swans, and eventually to thin me, but I still cheer for them fervently.

Cob and pen are apparently so curious about us that when we come down to the lake they swim closer, until we can see their beaks, their eyes, and we can truly take in how big these trumpeters are—with wingspans up to seven feet and hefts over twenty-five pounds, their bulk doubled by reflections in the still water. We gaze at each other across genus and species, my nose pressed against one side of the impermeable glass and the swans, well, the swans.

They start moving away as we come down the hill toward them, the resolute Pika leading the way at a trot, a nucleus ringed by the bounding, thrashing valance of the younger white dog.

As soon as we get to the edge of the water, Pika begins one of her favorite activities, dredging impossibly large rocks from underwater to shore. In her youth she once carried a five-pound rock up the hill and back to the house.

Anny, already swimming, tunes her Labrador frequency onto my attention to the swans and I think for a second that she is going to swim after them. Instead, she comes out of the water, shakes herself, and sits down beside me to watch. The swans are mid-lake now and one of them is honking softly. On a one-to-ten scale of swan trumpeting volume, this is a one.

You can never really tell when a swan changes direction because just as when your first-grade teacher showed you how to walk with a book on your head to improve your posture, your attention is on that long vertical neck and the stillness of balance. So with some surprise I see a slight V of wake behind the male like an arrow pointed back at us. All propelling motion beneath the surface, he seems to just drift in our direction, leaving his family behind at the lake's center.

I don't move and the white dog doesn't move. We watch the swan, and the black dog splashes in the shallows. With all the habits of human, I think about the swan. Diplomat? Lone general who crosses the waiting field of battle to the opposing side? A gesture of friendship, warning, curiosity, sacrifice? These human words made into things. Science might be able to tell me what this swan is doing, but not why I want to stand with this handful of keys, never knowing which ones fit the lock between me and what is out there.

The swan stops at the lily pad reef tens of feet away from us and it is clear that whatever his mission, it is because of us. That would make us a "we," I think with happiness, and after a minute of that I call my mismatched little family back up the hill so the swan can return to his.

Pika is gone now. The spaces she recently occupied on the rug, in the bed, by the lake are empty, but she will live there for a while in our expectations. Along with her dark shape, we expect her intelligence and her watching. She wanted things, and she wanted us to be who we are. She knew, more than we know, who we are. And, as with our dogs before her, we will miss her forever.

Lefse

Life on the farms meant eating a lot of potatoes, and Jim's grandfather Christ Odden made lefse early every morning out of the last night's supper potatoes. Many Scandinavian-Americans, farmers or not, still eat a lot of lefse during the holidays. For the last decade or so in Nelchina, we've made stacks of lefse on the day after Thanksgiving with every relative and friend who wants to be a part of the production and the noisy fun. Each family takes a stack of lefse home to eat at Christmas.

Lefse is a kind of Scandinavian tortilla made with riced potatoes, flour, butter, and lard, all seasoned slightly with sugar and salt. You roll each lefse out flat and round on a floured cloth until you can see the writing on the red-and-white rolling cloth through the thin dough. Then you pick up the delicate thing with a flat stick and transport it to a 400°F lefse griddle or the top of a wood cookstove. The rounds are delicate, so moving them is a kind of dance, with the lefse-rolling person moving aside so that the lefse-carrying person can waltz in.

Dogs are appreciative of tender, uncooked lefse that regularly breaks and falls off the stick on its way across the kitchen to the griddle. Dogs are the beneficiaries of husbands or wives who admonish the lefse rollers that they are not making the lefse thin enough. Little Lutheran church ladies, now in heaven, are also present and looking squinty-eyed down at the poor lefse rollers, whispering "larger," "rounder," "thinner," and "I can't read the writing, dear." Why we do not carry the rolling board over closer to the cooking surface is a question the dogs believe is best left unasked.

Lefse is one of the most colorful foods in the Scandinavian culinary pantheon, which means it is not entirely white.

Despite the stressful pressure on lefse rollers, everyone wants to try rolling. A kid starts with a little roller and makes a too-thick but recognizable lefse that is eaten right after cooking with lots of butter while praising the kid. Everyone who makes lefse is soon covered with flour. No one who ever makes lefse forgets about it.

God's way of eating lefse, according to my husband's family, is to roll it up with warm pork sparerib meat or lutefisk, seasoned only with salt and pepper and butter. Or you are sometimes allowed to butter the hot lefse, sprinkle sugar on it and eat it that way. No other foods belong in a piece of lefse, but this rule is occasionally, secretly broken by people who have married into the family.

9
ST. ANNE'S REEL

A1: TO THE CENTER AND BACK

I once heard Peter Yarrow of Peter, Paul, and Mary say that he was a young child riding in a car when his father started singing harmony to a song on the radio. Yarrow said he had never heard harmony before, and he regarded that as the first moment he was alive.

Patsy Hodge, even before she was my older brother's wife, made me her friend forever when she taught me to sing harmony to "Today While the Blossoms" and "The Cruel War," both popular culture folk anthems of the mid-1960s. There was a cruel war raging, but I didn't know anything about it yet. Listening to the commercial versions of those songs now, I can hear they are bland and overproduced, not traditional but merely borrowing some of tradition's winnowed power. But the words and tunes were from the mysterious adult domains of desire and tragedy, so I signed up then and there. Such songs would drag a generation of us toward authentic roots music. These moments told me I could get the news about the world from songs. They made me want to tell the truth, though they didn't tell me how.

With unspoken small-town interdictions around us like unpleasant weather, my best friend Carol Burroughs and I used to ride around in her old Studebaker station wagon and sing harmonies without words. It isn't something we agreed to do, or thought of, or ever started with a spoken invitation. Out of silence, one of us would start humming or nonsense-singing a musical phrase, known or unknown to us, bom bompa bom bom, bom bom bom, just enough for the other to hang on a harmony or counterpoint, then we were off on several minutes of barely controlled invention. Sometimes the music we made was as lively and marchy as John Phillip Sousa, and sometimes it was dark and slow, expressing things a teenager barely knows how to feel.

When the fiddle is in tune with itself, you can sound two strings together and octaves above it the empathetic harmonic chime is faintly audible. In voices, that laser-fine pleasure of being in tune is more like a ghost you reach for, a perfection you remember.

Families do it best, brother and sister harmonies. Those of us with unrelated throats have to search for the sweet spot. In the light, you can watch each other's mouths form the syllables. Singing in the dark at an annual Trail River gathering with Robin Hopper and other fine Alaskan singers, the harmonies just flow into tune beyond our bodies. Harmony is generous and selfless and has no owner or star performer. Richard Wise gathered us into the layered fold of "Angel Band" on the grass of the ball field at McGrath. For years after that we followed him to the Anchorage Folk Festival, until it felt like he would always be there, nodding his kind welcome to join in.

Jim and I took a trip out to Lake Minchumina in our little airplane, Rags, to sing in Walt and Molly Maakestad's cabin. Our pals Ken and Barb Deardorff were over there working on a powerhouse project with Walt. All afternoon and into the evening we ran through the *Rise up Singing* book and an old hymnbook Walt dug out of his stacks. Jim sang bass, Ken tenor, and Walt was a towering baritone weaving the distance between them. Barb, Molly, and I filled in the spaces with alto and soprano. Walt's voice has so much power that it could ring out above the windows in a cathedral. In their crowded cabin kitchen, all of us around the table, even the logs and iron pans sang with us. The old hymn "Farther Along" transcended its context of a Christian whining about other Christians and became an elemental song of a cappella beauty. Later on that summer, still under the spell of that harmony, I couldn't resist making more cheerful words for that old song; "The Homebuilder's Hymn" is the complaint of an Alaskan builder living with blue tarps while his neighbor's house seems to build itself without effort. Try it to the tune of "Farther Along."

Building our houses, we often wonder
Why every project takes oh so long
When there are neighbors hanging their pictures
No lumber piles stacked on their lawns.

When Sheetrock's come and covered our loved ones
Piles of fine dust in our lungs and our food
Then we do wonder where's the contractor
Who knows how to tape and sand this stuff smooth.

Often I wonder why I put dormers
Into a roof so slippery and steep.
Must have been crazy to buy that skylight
Botched the installing and it still leaks.

"Save lots of cash," said the Do-It-Yourself book
Just a few years of weekends and nights
We're pretty good now at pounding nails
Too bad our house still needs plumbing and lights.

Farther along we'll know all about it
Farther along, we'll understand why
Cheer up homebuilders living in sawdust
We'll understand it all by and by.

On the flight home from Minchumina to McGrath it was getting dark. Little puffs of clouds hanging over the twisted creeks below us gathered into a cottony fabric. We made it to the ground through the obscuring sky at midnight, still full of echoes from the singing.

In McGrath, Ken and Barb and Jim and I often sang "Diamonds in the Rough," a John Prine song made in four-square harmony. Like people who know each other so well that they only need to tell a few words of a joke before they all start laughing, we'd naturally form a square at the end of any evening together. Ken would hum his first low note to start us. He'd put a hand over one of his ears, as serious unaccompanied singers often do to be able to match their own voice against the others, and the rest of us would eagerly join in to the old hymn-sounding piece. When our voices were clear and tuned, the harmonies of the song flowed together like the sighing of a pipe organ. But sometimes at the doorway, getting ready to sing, Ken caught us in the middle of taking a big breath before the first note. One hand over his one ear and the master of an evil deadpan face, he put his other hand over his other ear and we dissolved into giggles.

A2: FIND YOUR PARTNER

For a week or two before the annual contra dance at the Kenny Lake Fair, we practice our tunes like crazy. During the rest of the year we want to organize more dances to play for, but it is hard to find a caller and the tradition of community dances wavers here. We would like to play for dancers more often. A folklorist would say we were caught between survival and revival: dancing to the old music on a Friday or Saturday night was something done by the parents of our now middle-aged generation. Most of the younger people who grew up here have not caught on to the extreme coolness of spending their time in the resurrection of contra and square dances, a vast improvement over "hanging out." Native communities in our valley have a stronger tradition of dancing, both Native dance and swinging each other to old time country songs from the forties and fifties. These traditions mix slightly, as do our families. Some of the popularity of Athabaskan fiddle dances also emanates outward from the Fairbanks festivals and shines into us.

Lucky for us, in Kenny Lake this afternoon there are twenty or thirty dancers of all ages and sizes who have agreed that this is the place to be.

Dance caller Lynn Basham will soon ask us for "four potatoes" to start the music. Why do they call them potatoes? Four strong beats from the hammered dulcimer or galloped hard across the fiddle strings are the early warning system for the start of the dance. Iditareds, German Butterballs, Yukon Golds, Finlanders' Boots. My mind goes sideways like this, waiting to begin.

Lynn came four hundred miles for this dance always held the night before the Kenny Lake Fair. He is a sturdy grandfather full of grinning optimism and awful puns. I have never seen his beard and wavy mop of hair anything but white, though we have all done this evening together for I don't know how many years. Lynn brings ties and bandanas to keep "ones" distinct from "twos," or to distribute genders equally in the dances where such things matter. He calls the ties his "gender disambiguation devices." His corny comments inspire the best efforts of the young and the new to dancing, both of these at this moment standing in a puzzling and unintended formation, unable to move. "Congratulations," says Lynn, "you are a pretzel." Laughter rings out of the hall above the music as he unwinds the knotted and bent-backward arms so that lumpy human lines are finally able to step and turn. When we start each song, though, there's a wrinkle of concern on his forehead. He has to be as ready as a shortstop to catch our wayward notes and put them down on the floor for his dancers' feet. In the break, he asks us through the microphone for our band name. Sometimes we are "The G Strings," or "Home Brew," but today we are "Ibu and the Profens." People on the dance floor have heard these jokes before, but they laugh anyway. They are breathless and grinning.

"Soldier's Joy" is a great old-timey tune. It was the first fiddle tune I learned, but I learned a version with half as many notes. The noises I made caused friends and family members to scatter to quieter places as I squawked it out sans teacher. Now everyone in the band knows this standard and we play it fast, so fast that Lynn raises his eyebrows at us when a swing with his dance partner turns his face in our direction. I pass the meaningful look on to Nigel and Skip and Jim and Diane and Jenny, coupled with an exaggerated slowing of the fiddle bow and my stomping foot. Just as well: if we speed on "Soldier's Joy"—about morphine, if we sang the Civil War words—it is going to kill us when we switch over to "St. Anne's Reel" for the rest of the dance. "St. Anne's" is an even busier tune for fiddle fingers. For each dance, we put two or three tunes together to switch it up for ourselves and the dancers, though the dancers mostly don't know that they've noticed. We also do it because a few hundred years of fiddlers and whistlers and pipers have done it this way. You can follow it back into the mist.

This is my favorite moment, when we've been around the tune half a dozen times and even the youngest dancer knows the moves. The dance will go around another six or ten times before we are done. Awkward teens and unsure elders have joined into the dance together, passing through each other's arms in blooming swirls of colored fabric and smiles. Our tunes are whipping up this roiling sea of happiness; we are the wind.

B1: PROMENADE TO THE END OF THE LINE

I have an early memory of an eastern Oregon dance tune played in an old Grange hall. It was variously called "Little Foot Waltz," or "Put Your Little Foot." In obstinate resistance to the modern age, women in aprons and farmers in flat-brimmed hats came out to the Oregon Trail Grange Hall for these dances, bringing backward grandchildren who went to my school though I'd never noticed them before. The songs tended toward country and western standards, Hank and Hank, with preference toward the danceable. Nostalgia might drag a fiddle into the words now and then, but there was no actual fiddle in sight. The melody might even have been played on an electric guitar. There was an actual fiddle renaissance underway less than fifty miles away at Weiser, Idaho, but its rising tide hadn't yet leaked out onto our back roads.

"Little Foot Waltz" stayed in the back of my head for the plainness of its tune and also its rhythm, because the "A" part has a skip in it, giving the dancers a little flourish before the high gliding of the "B" comes around. The waltz shares a space in my memory with another old dance from the grange hall—the schottische—where the dancers promenade and skip. A schottische didn't come up very often, probably because it takes some know-how on the part of the dancers, so its practitioners fade with the tradition of the weekly or monthly country dances. I'd be surprised and delighted to meet it again later, in places where the continually refreshed supply of old people was still dancing.

I had thought that "Little Foot" was uniquely mine—a souvenir. But what I know now about souvenirs is that they aren't made just for me, and might not even be from around here. Decades after I'd first heard the song, I got a cassette tape of dance music from a Scandinavian band and the "Little Foot" was there—I recognized the tune—but they called it "Varso Vienna," which I mistakenly decided meant "Viennese Waltz." Looking into that later, though, I found that the "varso" comes from Polish for "Warsaw" and the dance originated in the mid-1900s in Poland. It was matched up with the "Put Your Little Foot" tune in America in the same time period, where it has been a favorite in old-timey dances ever since. Maybe those Vikings had ripped a sweet waltz off of the Poles and somehow, like the Kensington Runestone but a little farther west, had dropped it off in Malheur County, Oregon.

B2: LEFT-HAND STAR

Traveling music is generous and fervent and you will not be sued by its creator for singing it. The back of a Woody Guthrie songbook used to say something like this: "Anybody who wants to sing these songs is a good old pal of mine because that's why I wrote them." A musician who hears a good song will pick up a guitar and extend a song's life into the future. More often, songs flicker into and out of existence like fireflies. Like us.

Left-handed itinerant folksinger Bill Staines is playing his guitar upside down and backward. I know he won't mind if I learn "Red Bird's Wings," his beautiful anthem about flying in Denali Park, but I will have to stand on my head to figure out his fingers on the chords. People like Bill still crisscross the nation in ones and twos, showing up in libraries, coffee shops, and bars. When elder minstrels fall away, another generation of Woody's children buys old cars and drives out West and out East and down South to take their place. Some of their songs hang in the wind, à la Bill, or catch on the culture of protest. Some of them adopt the twang of Nashville and make it onto the radio or at least the Internet.

At its best, a song can tell the truth, slipping into the heart between the long rib and the short, like the long, thin knife of a jealous lover in a hundred folk songs.

Traveling singers sing everything we need to hear. It's hard to get the news from poems, William Carlos Williams said, but what he didn't mention is that it's easy to get the news from songs. Utah Phillips, who died in 2008, had a worker's perspective on the world. He chronicled every rural profession that could get its hands dirty and wrote social commentary wherever he saw injustice or the hubris of privilege. Bruce Phillips jokingly called himself "U. Utah Phillips, the Golden Voice of the Great Southwest." He called love songs "entry-level material" with all entendre intended and gave away the only bitter love song he ever wrote, "Rock Salt and Nails," to his friend Rosalie Sorrels the moment after he wrote it. But his simple "I Think of You" is a love song profound with understatement, like the spare wording on a husband and wife's double gravestone.

The bulk of Phillips's story songs portray unions, mines, immigrants, trains, the cowboys of the West. With Phillips, you meet the people and you care about them. "Enola Gay," in which Hiroshima's children's eyes turn to ashes, is set to a simple child's tune. The horrific mismatch between story and tune tears your heart open so that Phillips's anger and sadness can pour into you.

Songs go deeper when you are in the same room with the singer. Once you've had that happen, sitting at the front table in a dim club or in someone's living room, you've become kin to the singer and the stories he or she tells. Traveling singer Bob Bovee impressed us mightily when he showed us the hole in his hat where Utah Phillips had whimsically taken a bite out of it at the Spokane World's Fair in 1974.

Bovee, along with traveling brothers Bodie and Pop Wagner, introduced me to Phillips's music. I'd also heard about him from folklorist Barre Toelken, a friend of my favorite professor from college the first time around, Louie Attebery. Toelken admired Phillips for the accurate detail in his songs. He saw Phillips as one of those great creative voices who not only usefully chronicle the times they live in but are likely to live on in tradition with a tune or two—songs that might go on being sung beyond knowledge of the author's name. Louie didn't see things that way. To Louie, the hairy, cowboy-hatted travelers were emissaries of the unwashed hippie throng. Louie had grown up in the real West on a ranch. He loved the old cowboy songs of the early twentieth century but preferred to take a close look at traditional materials after decades, if not ages, had sorted and distilled their truths.

The Wagners and Bovee, like Phillips, looked and sounded like old men. Phillips had served in Korea, but the others were younger, probably in their late twenties when I met them. Being old wasn't a function of their physiology yet, but it was an agreement with the old songs they sang. And the new songs about old things—love, greed, war, and the forever unfair distribution of privilege and luck. After the Wagners and other individual traveling singers and ensembles had shown up in my college town a few times, I encouraged Louie to come listen to the amazing histories and points of view they opened up for listeners. But he dug in his heels, avoided the campus coffee shop and our living rooms, and so missed hearing Bodie Wagner sing "The Ballad of California Joe" in the wee hours at the house on Dearborn Street designated by its sign as "Looney Springs." The sign bearing my maiden name, stolen from a Forest Service road by my friends, signified an outlaw moment in my life. The local police would scare the hell out of me about that sign only to then hang it on their wall, a prize to laugh about.

There were five or six of us and not enough chairs at the house that I shared with my friend Penny Young, so people perched on pillows and rugs. All the shorter songs anybody knew had already been sung that night when Bodie brought out "California Joe," a jewel saved for earnest listeners. This long story-song, twenty-three verses in the version Bodie sang for us, is about a friend of famous mountain man Jim Bridger who rescues a young girl from the group of Indians who killed her family. The ballad is long enough to chronicle a decade of events: Joe is the girl's savior and stand-in father, then gives her up to an ailing uncle, then years later is nearly shot by the now-young woman at their accidental reunion. This event is followed by a fervent and ambiguous blessing on the now-lovers from the uncle on his deathbed. It is, ignoring the case that could be made for statutory rape charges in most

states, one of the only pieces of Victorian hyper-sentimental prosody I
ever heard where the story shines so brightly through the rhymed verse.
Here are Captain Jack's original song lyrics:

> Well, mates, I don't like stories, nor am I going to act
> A part around this camp-fire that ain't a truthful fact.
> So fill your pipes and listen, I'll tell you—let me see,
> I think it was in fifty, from that till sixty-three.

> You've all heard tell of Bridger, I used to run with Jim,
> And many a hard day's scouting I've done 'longside of him.
> Well, once, near old Fort Reno, a trapper used to dwell;
> We called him old Pap Reynolds—The scouts all knew him well.

> One night the Spring of fifty we camped on Powder river,
> We killed a calf of buffalo, and cooked a slice of liver:
> While eating, quite contented, we heard three shots or four
> Put out the fire and listened, then heard a dozen more.

> We knew that old man Reynolds had moved his traps up here;
> So, picking up our rifles and fixing on our gear,
> We mounted quick as lightnin', to save was our desire.
> Too late; the painted heathens had set the house on fire.

> We tied our horses quickly, and waded up the stream;
> While close beside the water I heard a muffled scream.
> And there among the bushes a little girl did lie.
> I picked her up and whispered: "I'll save you, or I'll die!"

> Lord, what a ride! old Bridger, he covered my retreat.
> Sometimes the child would whisper, in voice so low and sweet:
> "Poor papa, God will take him to mamma up above;
> There's no one left to love me—There's no one left to love."

> The little one was thirteen, and I was twenty-two.
> Said I: "I'll be your father, And love you just as true.
> She nestled to my bosom, her hazel eyes, so bright,
> Looked up and made me happy, though close pursued that night.

A month had passed, and Maggie (We called her Hazel Eye),
In truth, was going to leave me—was going to say "good-bye."
Her uncle, mad Jack Reynolds—reported long since dead—
Had come to claim my angel, his brother's child, he said.

What could I say? We parted. Mad Jack was growing old;
I handed him a bank-note and all I had in gold.
They rode away at sunrise, I went a mile or two,
And, parting, said: "We'll meet again—May God watch over you."

Beside a laughing, dancing brook, a little cabin stood,
As weary with a long day's scout, I spied it in the wood.
A pretty valley stretched beyond, the mountains towered above,
While near the willow bank I heard the cooing of a dove.

'Twas one grand panorama, the brook was plainly seen,
Like a long thread of silver in a cloth of lovely green.
The laughter of the waters, the cooing of the dove,
Was like some painted picture—Some well-told tale of love.

While drinking in the grandeur, and resting in my saddle,
I heard a gentle ripple like the dipping of a paddle.
I turned toward the eddy a strange sight met my view:
A maiden, with her rifle, In a little bark canoe.

She stood up in the center, the rifle to her eye;
I thought (just for a second) my time had come to die.
I doffed my hat and told her (if it was all the same)
To drop her little shooter, for I was not her game.

She dropped the deadly weapon, and leaped from the canoe.
Said she: "I beg your pardon, I thought you were a Sioux;
Your long hair and your buckskin looked warrior-like and rough;
My bead was spoiled by sunshine, or I'd killed you, sure enough."

"Perhaps it had been better you dropped me then," said I;
"For surely such an angel would bear me to the sky."
She blushed and dropped her eyelids, her cheeks were crimson red;
One half-shy glance she gave me, and then hung down her head.

I took her little hand in mine—She wondered what I meant,
And yet she drew it not away, but rather seemed content.
We sat upon the mossy bank her eyes began to fill
The brook was rippling at our feet, the dove was cooing still.

I smoothed her golden tresses, her eyes looked up in mine,
She seemed in doubt then whispered "'Tis such a long, long time
Strong arms were thrown around me I'll save you, or I'll die."
I clasped her to my bosom my long-lost Hazel Eye.

The rapture of that moment was almost heaven to me.
I kissed her 'mid her tear-drops, her innocence and glee.
Her heart near mine was beating, while sobbingly she said:
"My dear, my brave preserver, they told me you were dead.

"But, oh! those parting words, Joe, have never left my mind.
You said: We'll meet again, Mag, then rode off like the wind.
And, oh! how I have prayed, Joe, for you, who saved my life,
That God would send an angel to guard you through all strife.

"And he who claimed me from you, my uncle, good and true—
Now sick in yonder cabin has talked so much of you.
If Joe were living, darling, he said to me last night,
He would care for Maggie when God puts out my light."

We found the old man sleeping. "Hush! Maggie, let him rest."
The sun was slowly sinking in the far-off glowing west;
And, though we talked in whispers, he opened wide his eyes.
"A dream—a dream!" he murmured, "Alas! a dream of lies!"

She drifted like a shadow To where the old man lay.
"You had a dream, dear uncle another dream to-day?"
"Oh, yes; I saw an angel, as pure as mountain snow,
And near her, at my bed-side, stood California Joe."

"I'm sure I'm not an angel, dear uncle, that you know;
These arms are brown, my hands, too, my face is not like snow.
Now, listen, while I tell you, for I have news to cheer,
And Hazel Eye is happy, for Joe is truly here."

And when, a few days after, the old man said to me:
Joe, boy, she ar' a angel, an' good as angels be.
For three long months she's hunted an' trapped an' nursed me, too;
God bless ye, boy! I believe it— She's safe along wi' you."

The sun was slowly sinking When Mag (my wife) and I
Came riding through the valley, the tear-drops in her eye.
"One year ago to-day, Joe—I see the mossy grave—
We laid him 'neath the daisies, My uncle, good and brave."

And, comrades, every spring-time was sure to find me there—
A something in that valley was always fresh and fair.
Our loves were newly kindled while sitting by the stream,
Where two hearts were united in love's sweet, happy dream.

Bodie sang all the verses by heart, his yellow curly hair falling out under his cowboy hat, letting the words form images slow and vivid. It felt like the best moment of my life.

Years later I was digging around the Internet searching for the words to "California Joe" and found hours of reading, connections that would certainly have gotten Louie's attention, had either of us known about them. Captain Jack Crawford, the "California Joe" author, was born in Donegal County, Ireland, because his father had been kicked out of Scotland for preaching revolution. He immigrated to America in the ugly Irish years of the potato famine. He learned to read while being nursed back to health from the Civil War wounds he got at Spotsylvania and Petersburg, just before Lee's surrender. Crawford then read too many dime novels, he said, which drew him west, where he worked as a newspaper correspondent in gold camps. For a time, he was chief of the Black Hills Rangers, escorting settlers through the dangerous Indian country. After Custer's defeat in 1876, Crawford was inspired to join General George Crook's Fifth Calvary as a scout. General Crook had gotten orders to punish the Sioux for Little Big Horn. The Sioux Wars and his part in the Battle of Slim Buttes gave Crawford fame and sickened him for the rest of his life.

Reading about Crawford, it is clear that between the stage performances and caricatures of the Old West he did not forget the horror:
Chief American Horse stoically holding his intestines in at his surrender, the bullet-ruined women and children, the scalping. Crawford,
who penned the "painted heathens" line in "California Joe," was also
reported by his biographer Darlis Miller to have admonished a reporter: "Don't you suppose that mother has the same feeling in her breast
for her young as your mother had for you?"

Crawford was a great friend of Buffalo Bill Cody's and, like Cody,
took turns living the life of the frontier and popularizing it. Captain
Jack once shot himself in the groin during a performance with a
drunken Buffalo Bill. Crawford was a teetotaler himself, keeping a
promise to his mother, and purportedly once brought Cody a bottle
of rye whiskey three hundred miles—the entire distance unopened—
another celebrated feat. He was a famous storyteller and wrote books
of poetry, short stories, and plays. In the 1890s he worked for the
federal government and battled alcoholism and corruption on Indian
reservations, and in 1898 he went north to spend two goldless years
as part of the Klondike Gold Rush.

Crawford said the "California Joe and the Trapper Girl" poem was
a true story, though it features every compelling frontier and classical
motif he could sew into it, enough to keep a folklorist busy for months.

Captain Jack was also a close friend of Robert Edmund Strahorn,
a fellow veteran of the Fifth Calvary and the Sioux Wars, a *New York
Times*, *Chicago Times*, and *Rocky Mountain News* correspondent, and
in his later years a fellow promoter of the American West. Strahorn's
cohort, Reuben Briggs Davenport, was the *New York Herald* correspondent who commissioned Crawford to race the news of the Slim
Buttes victory several hundred miles to the telegraph at Fort Laramie.
This stunt killed several horses, earned Captain Jack immortal fame,
and got him kicked out of the army.

Strahorn reportedly shared his friend's painful silence over details
of the Sioux campaigns, but he was a personal force in the western
expansion. He worked on power and utility projects throughout the

Northwest, was a publicist for the Union Pacific Railroad, and would go on to promote and build the Oregon Short Line Railroad. That project spawned small cities all around eastern Oregon and western Idaho, one of them my college town. Strahorn had a house in Caldwell, Idaho, and gave his name to the academic hall where I listened to Louie and other legendary College of Idaho teachers. We called our literary magazine *The Short Line* because of the handy and appropriate name of Strahorn's railroad; details of his life and details of his friend Captain Jack's life were all unknown to us.

All of that was standing with its old hat in its hand, behind the song.

A1: DO SI DO

Two young men greeted each other on a street in Dingle, Ireland. After a brotherly embrace, before any word was exchanged, each man pulled a tin whistle from a hind pocket and together they launched a tune. When that tune was done, there was another—to a foreign ear, nearly the same as the first.

At a tavern in the west of Ireland we saw a man sitting at a table by himself throw his head back and sing a song to no one and everyone. In Killybegs, Donegal, we'd just walked inside when the pub man told us, "Fiddle's there on the wall if you want to play it." The fiddle's location was clearly as important as the water closet's.

Tunes are "chunes" as our friend Nigel pronounces it, and not all of them are for dancers. Some of the tunes lilt in and between the musicians and are for us. There are extra beats and notes. There are wordless words. We play after supper if Nigel is over with his "box."

Nigel, who spent his young adulthood playing tunes in the Irish pubs of Manchester, England, speeds his fingers over the concertina buttons. He doesn't have to reach over the top of a loitering fiddle string to get from a low E to a high one, as I remind him when I'm trying to learn a melody he is playing that's racing by so fast I can't grab it. The structure of most of the tunes is AA BB over and over, and it is my old joke to say, "eh eh, bay—bee" while raising an eyebrow—whenever I'm trying to explain the musical architecture to a newcomer. The old

American dance tunes like "Liberty" and "Over the Waterfall" have the same structure as those from the British Isles, because Celtic tunes are their ancestors and because these similarly structured tunes were dance tunes too.

Minus dancers, as we play the dance tunes in each other's living rooms and at parties, listeners are obviously divided between enjoyment and boredom. Some people say they can't tell the difference between one tune and another, a difficulty that seems to increase in proportion to the distance between the location of the listener's childhood and the birthplace of the tune. Like a Quaker service joined by attention to spirit, Irish or old-timey musicians lean together in a spiky knot of instruments and tapping feet. Some bluegrass players say they can't understand the introverted old-timey session over in the other corner of the hall, with all its participants sitting in chairs dragged together, their heads hung down over fiddles and banjos, playing some old Appalachian tune in apparent unison—AA BB over and over. For non-practitioners, an Irish session is even more inscrutable.

One of our jam-session companions delighted Nigel when he told him that after a few years of listening to Irish tunes when we showed up at the American Legion jam on Wednesday nights, he'd finally realized that the "chunes" were not just a bunch of random notes. He could finally hear the separate melodies.

I can marginally read dense black notes printed or scribbled on a page but I most enjoy catching old-timey and Irish tunes through exposure, like catching a cold—I tell people that to drag them past the formality of learning a tune and to make them smile—and I like the nuanced changes as the tunes come around again and again. I don't mind just listening, if Jennie's nimble flute and Nigel's concertina buttons take off on a whirl of songs I don't know. The names make me grin: "Push That Hog's Foot a Little Further in the Fire" and "I'll Get Married in My Old Clothes." And in my imagination, that dramatic B part change in the old American tune "Cattle in the Cane" is turning a room full of colorful dancers in a new direction each time it comes around.

Because my fiddle mostly languishes under the living room table while I do other things, my fingers have only a fair ability with most of the music. I practice when inspired by a new tune or a recent get-together. That's enough, though, to be nearly everything I need. The players are my family and the tunes conspire with my aspiration to live in peace. The repetition in the tunes and scattered evenings echoes the repeated themes in our neighborly lives: gardens, snows, mornings, loves.

A2: FIND YOUR NEW PARTNER

Before I wanted a fiddle, I wanted a set of Uilleann pipes, Irish traditional pipes, softer and sweeter than the war pipes of the Scots. But then an actual piper told me that twenty-seven years is the life of a piper: nine to learn, nine to practice, nine to play. Fiddles' voices have taken over many of the pipers' tunes, and fiddles sing through the southern mountain songs. So when our neighbor Dan wanted to give me a violin, I took it. He'd been trying to learn, but when he picked the thing up to practice, his young son said it gave him a stomachache.

My great-grandfather Aaron Henderson was a naturopath and a fiddle-maker in Silver City, Idaho, where his cheating partners divested him of ownership in the Morning Star mine before the turn of that other century. That's one of the few stories we have about him, other than that he'd shot two fingers off his left hand during a mishap with his rifle in the Bannock Wars, circa 1870. That was the end of his fiddle playing but not making. There were two fiddles he'd built that my mother knew about, but she'd lost touch with the cousins who owned them.

A fiddle's voice can cut through time itself, but before that it just makes the dog run upstairs. My playing was a test of our little group's patience and several people didn't pass. If you ask them today they might tell you that I haven't moved far beyond that determined screeching and I agree. The dogs, however, have settled down, and thanks to my remaining friends, many fine old tunes are entwined in my arm and fingers and around my heart. There's a plethora of styles for playing fiddle music on violins, but if you want to hear what I hear in the back of my mind, listen to old-time Virginia fiddlers J. P. and Anadene Fraley play "Wild Rose of the Mountain." In that tune, you can hear the Scots-Irish climbing up into the Appalachian Mountains after fighting the British in the American Revolution, carving out their little farms on land grants promised to them by General Washington.

That first violin was a "serviceable student instrument," said Petr of the famous Violin Shop in Anchorage, and he immediately tried to sell me a fancier one. But I couldn't tell the difference myself, so I knew it wasn't the right time. Several years later I could finally make a better note on a better instrument, so I bought a dark red violin made in Romania. It had a wide-grained spruce top and a resonant deep voice when my fingering was firm and my strokes on the bow were long. It inspired me to take a few lessons, where I learned to cherish hearing my instructor play Massenet's "Meditation from Thais." This was completely worth the cost of a half-hour lesson. I didn't improve much myself, but now there were more lovely sounds to imagine I might be able to draw out of the instrument.

About the same time, a friend offered to sell me a violin given to her father by the late Eskimo violin maker Frank Hobson. I eagerly agreed. Frank Hobson was already a notable person to me because of a dulcimer.

Our friend Sam—who grew up in the mountains of southwestern Virginia and had introduced me to the music of the Fraleys and so many other old-time musicians—had a handmade dulcimer that could not correctly sound an interval between the notes in a song. A mountain dulcimer is a simple fretted board upon which at least one of the three strings sounds a neutral drone at any given time, so we knew that something grievous was wrong with the instrument. Like the parents of a sick child, when we reached that conclusion on a winter evening, we immediately felt that we had to take the dulcimer to the only local music emergency room we knew of: Frank Hobson's house. We drove the forty-five miles from Nelchina down to Hobson's house by the

Tazlina River, south of Glennallen. Though it was late, he graciously received us in his shop, turning the dulcimer around and around in his hands. He'd never seen one before, but the problem was clear to him—the frets had been placed carelessly. He handed the sick instrument back to Sam and then told us how he became a fiddle-maker.

The story he told, same as the one he told many reporters and admirers over the years, was about how he'd asked his father for an accordion. He was sixteen years old and it would have been around 1917. The family lived in a remote mining camp on the Seward Peninsula, south of Kotzebue, where Isaac Hobson, of England and more recently of Oregon, had come in 1897, early in the Alaska gold rush. There he met Frank's Inupiaq mother, Molly. Molly played the accordion and Frank had saved up fifteen dollars for his own accordion—quite an amount for that time and place. Alas, either there wasn't an accordion for sale or the shopkeeper talked Frank's father out of buying one—because he came home with a fiddle instead. Frank told us he was angry but there wasn't anything to do about it, so he taught himself to play the fiddle. Years later, as a fiddle he'd played at parties and dances was falling apart from use, he looked at the pieces and decided he could make a fiddle for himself.

It took him two years. More than fifty violins in the Stradivarius style followed that first one he finished in about 1948, plus cellos and violas and mandolins and guitars. Hobson was written up in local and national papers and by the Smithsonian. The scattered accounts tell a personal history that parallels Alaska's own history. He got a job as a tie-tamper on the Alaska Railroad in 1919; that railroad project was completed from Seward in 1923 and gave the Richardson road its first real competition for moving people and goods to the interior of Alaska. Frank also worked as a heavy equipment operator building the Glenn Highway that was completed in 1943, just one year after the Alcan Highway was built through Canada during World War II to support the lend-lease airlifts to Russia. The Glenn Highway met up with the Richardson at the road camp that would become Glennallen, and the new highway would quickly give Anchorage its undeserved prominence in the state. Hobson married Walya Billum, daughter of Doug Billum, an important Athabaskan leader from Chitina, where the great gray Copper and Chitina Rivers join muscles for the push through coastal mountains. It's where the Copper River and Northwestern Railroad used to chug Kennicott copper down to the then-chief port of entry of our state, Cordova. Frank worked as an operator and mechanic for the Alaska Road Commission on the Glenn and Richardson and then went over to the state highway department after statehood. He was there for another decade, retiring in 1969. To trace the paths and workplaces of Frank's life is to watch a bright thread being woven through the Alaskan fabric.

In his spare time Frank made fiddles with maple from Outside—how Alaskans used to refer to the rest of the United States—or birch from Fairbanks, topping most of them with mellifluous Alaskan white spruce. A 1971 article describes him with a near-mystical connection to his materials: "A block of wood has a tone to it," he told the reporter. "I rub my hands over it after it is cured to see if the wood is alive. If it isn't, there's no point in going further with it." If the piece of wood was alive, it would get a chance at an additional life. He'd carve and shave and bend the pieces around heated brass. Then if a mostly made fiddle didn't sound right when he played "On Top of Old Smokey" or "Swanee River" or some other standard, he'd discard it. The fiddles he liked got a bright finish and made their way out into the world through Alaska music stores and friends and family. Frank Hobson died in 1984, about a year after he met our dulcimer.

Petr, known to be a picky judge, says Hobson was an excellent violin maker, though his instruments are not all standard-sized and they vary in voice and tone, as other fine singers do. Petr points me to a reddish-colored Hobson hanging on his wall waiting for restoration. Now I have met several siblings of my Hobson.

The Hobson fiddle has a warm golden color and stays in tune, though it loves to unravel A strings under the callus on my index finger, so I keep an extra string handy. Early on when I had two fiddles, I alternated playing them until I realized I only wanted to hear the Hobson's sweet voice. It has every note inside it, even the high wavering ones. It learns the tunes before I learn them and tries to teach them to me.

B1: ALLEMANDE RIGHT

Welcome to the rural: non-soluble hippies solving electricity and plumbing conundrums and raising rosy-cheeked children, homesteaders in their Little House on the Prairie garb, evangelical missionaries, Vietnam vet grumps whipped up by pundits and preachers, whites and Natives at odds over land or privileges, neighbors of all pigments at odds over children or dogs, dog-musher folks smelling of wool and salmon scraps, earnest government and grant workers eyed with suspicion by the others, and the dratted environmentalists. It's easy to regard each of the groups as monolithic, but that's just silly from up close. Kenny Lake homesteader Bill Sutton would show up on our doorstep once in a while, usually with a CD or DVD from his cousin Perry in his hand. Sutton, who could make even Tea Party sympathizers squirm uncomfortably when he'd cuss the government blue or offer to shoot certain people and their pets, would turn from dreadful to droll if he liked you, and we liked each other.

I heard plenty of bad stories about Bill Sutton before I met him, mostly from people he'd disagreed with. But I met him in person when I was admiring a photo he'd brought to a library meeting. It was of his grandfather in Idaho in the 1920s with several other men on a grain threshing machine pulled by thirty-two horses and mules: five rows of six horses with two leading in front, with long reins threaded back from the leaders to a driver standing on the front of the machine. Unbelievable, except that you can see the swath of cut grain following behind them on the hill. Bill told us he'd grown up on a farm in Midvale, Idaho. My eastern Oregon high school had played that school in basketball. I had ranch relatives who undoubtedly knew Bill's relatives. Everything about the way he talked and the neat plain way he dressed reminded me of the old farm people of my growing up.

I soon learned that Bill enjoyed baiting whoever he was talking to. Sometime after we'd met at the library, he was sitting at our table drinking tea and looked over at our dog and said, "If you ever need someone to shoot that dog, I'd be glad to."

Instead of reacting to the raw edge of that suggestion, I asked him, "Did you know that when you are fibbing to someone your cheek twitches a little bit?" Not missing a beat he said, "I am going to go home and practice in front of the mirror so that it won't do that anymore."

I used to know a lot of farmers who worked sunrise to sunset at their farms like Bill did, but who also knew how to stop in and loiter a bit at the café if they had the excuse of an item to pick up in town. Bill liked tea and he liked pie, so he'd stop at our house on his way to Anchorage. He'd drop "the dirt" on people who were annoying him—he could be a terrible gossip—plus he had come up with innovative ways to shock his small audiences. He'd built a three-foot-high model of a guillotine for executing chickens and set it out by his front door where everyone could see his wry handiwork. But if you bothered to challenge him on one of his sour notes, he'd laugh and drop back and punt. For instance if you let him run down the state highway department and local Natives and the environmentalists who had ruined everything—and you did not interrupt him until he got to say that he wanted to shoot all of them and their dogs for good measure—you'd eventually learn that he had a wide and unprejudiced admiration for people, even some self-deprecating stories of kindness. We learned that he'd taken on the settling of a neighbor's estate, a huge nation-crossing, lawyer-negotiating, time-consuming task with no benefit to Bill. The neighbor had no children or close relatives and it was a deathbed request. With humor characteristically aimed at himself, Bill said, "If I'd known how much trouble it was going to be, I'd have killed him before he asked me."

My favorite Bill story was his account of driving a neighboring farmer up to the local courthouse on several different occasions to pay the $300 fine for killing a moose out of season. The moose were always eating hard-won hay from Kenny Lake farmers' haystacks, and this neighbor felt it was his right to shoot one now and again to get even. But he also believed it was his responsibility to turn himself in and pay the fine after he did so. Bill was impressed by these perverse displays of honesty, and one day he stepped up and paid the neighbor's fine for him. "I never told him why I did that," Bill told us, "but I had a moose in my freezer too."

Jim and I loved old-time fiddle tunes and so did Bill, so it was after he'd seen me trying to saw on a fiddle in Kenny Lake that he started to visit us at our house, about eighty miles from his farm. His love of music had boundaries delineated by Bill. He said, "The instrument I hate worst is the violin. And the one I like best is the fiddle. They look kind of similar. But the fiddle is the best music I've ever heard and the violin is the worst music I've ever heard." As with most of Bill's ultimatums, you didn't have to dig far for a contradiction: he'd heard young local virtuoso Wesley Voley playing difficult classical pieces on the piano and told me in admiration, "Wesley could teach me to like that music."

Bill was especially proud of his cousin Perry back in Midvale who played guitar and fiddle and Perry's brothers Roger and Larry who played bass and fiddle. Unlike most people who show up with a CD for you to listen to, Bill wanted to listen to it with you right then and there, and he'd shush anybody who tried to talk while the music was playing. Whatever you were doing, when he came to the door with a disk or cassette in his hand you dropped your task and everyone went to gather around the music machine. Bill would make sure we knew the name of the song that was playing. He'd tell us who was playing what instrument but other than that we just listened to the whole recording until it was over.

Bill started visiting us in about 2006. He was increasingly fearful about losing his memory, and early in 2009, very much in character, he had a story to tell on himself to illustrate his dilemma. He'd been working on a berm pile in a distant field he was clearing so that he could grow more hay, and he needed to pull a log from the tangled pile of cut brush and branches. He drove his wheeler all the way back to his shed and picked up a chain to do the job. Back at the pile, he'd hooked up the log with the chain and was looking for a good solid place to hook the chain to the wheeler when he saw that his wheeler had a winch on it. "I forgot there was a winch on that machine," he said and he looked at each of us in turn, trying to find out if he'd just told us a joke or if he'd said it because it scared the bejesus out of him. This kind of thing was happening to him all the time.

Visits became infrequent and also more silent. One time when I wasn't home Bill came around and Jim invited him upstairs for tea. Bill sat down at the table to wait, then after a few minutes disappeared wordlessly while Jim was busy at the stove. At the fair that fall, I was sitting in the audience when Bill, already isolated by his silence, walked through the crowd. He caught my eye and pointed to the stage where Jim was playing bass, letting me know he knew who we were, but he didn't say anything. Several times that afternoon he walked past me and just held my gaze for a few seconds. Each time, it was like an embrace.

Bill's last visit to us was in late summer. He came to the door with a DVD in his hand and we invited him up. The usual signals weren't there, so after a mostly wordless cup of tea I asked him if he wanted to watch the DVD. He could not even nod in reply, but he blinked a yes and the three of us watched a slide show made by Perry's family after Perry's death. Family photos of farms and fiddle dances, some with Bill in them, lingered on the screen, backed by Perry's old-time music. During the thirty minutes or so, spoken words came from Bill in ones or twos, often just "Perry." Here's what we knew about Bill: he loved his family and he loved sharing his music. When the DVD was done playing we walked Bill to the door of our house and he turned to look at us, the last time we saw him, those light blue eyes with him lonely at the bottom of them.

B2: FOUR JOIN HANDS
Oh for this love let rocks and hills their lasting silence break
—from "Africa," a shape-note hymn by William Billings

When I was a child in church I listened to the hymns I liked and played with the pencils and programs while people talked, mostly missing the points of dogma that distract Christians from that impossible home-work assignment: to love ourselves and our enemies interchangeably. Each Sunday I waited impatiently for the music to start and took away the wordless message subsumed in the harmonies: we are all one. In this view there's a light at the center and the choices are toward it or away from it in a 360-degree myriad of dissonant directions. There is no one emperor of darkness.

My aunt Anna told me, "Of course you are an alto." Our province was the intervals of thirds, which is what happens when you hold your thumb and middle finger about an inch apart and play the first and the third whole notes anywhere on a piano. The pianist or organist kept us there, oblivious of the absolving loveliness of the fourth, the soaring view from the fifth. We sang "Onward Christian Soldiers" and "Joyful, Joyful, We Adore Thee." I ignored cruel God passages awful enough to make Jonathan Edwards cringe, waiting my turn to sing:

> For the beauty of the earth
> for the glory of the skies
> for the love which from our birth
> over and around us lies.

For the sake of that song, I didn't mind being a flower of earth, rooted in its warmth, and just a mere bud for heaven.

Because of singing in harmony and the enfolding images of mercy and beauty, faith for me became a placeholder for something so import-ant and beyond my understanding that it didn't require a descriptive container. This atmospheric availability of "good" took the pressure off the gender of God, facial hair of God, whether God is one or three, whether or not heaven exists, and if there is a heaven whether or not I'll have to play a harp, not to mention shrinking the issues surround-ing the DNA of the notable presumed descendent and the untouch-able literal truth of clearly metaphorical stories. It disappeared conflict with what humans are able to find out about the universe: allow the physicists and paleontologists to come unto me. As a result, I can be pretty unhappy in a church where the literalists want to mud wrestle.

When I returned to college after my daughter was born, I met Quakers who were very active in their communities and marvelous mud-wrestlers for a just society but held mostly silent church services— appealing to me at that point. When you sit in silence and look for the light in yourself and in other people, there is so much room to breathe. I was too antsy to look for the light very long, though, and my mind would stray to whether I'd taken the laundry out of the washer or whether I'd actually made all the corrections to the lit paper due that week. But my Quaker friends led me back to hymn singing. A small group of them sang a cappella shape-note hymns on Sunday nights for fun. The harmonies intertwined, and the theologies expressed in the texts were as divergent as door prize-winners drawn from a bucket. The poetry of the songs was personal and metaphoric at the same time:

> I will arise and go to Jesus
> He will embrace me in his arms
> In the arms of my dear savior
> Oh there are ten thousand charms.

While not understanding Quakerism or its history, I felt happy as soon as I started attending those singing sessions. Every week, six or ten people from the Hidden Hill Quaker Meeting, along with a few other esoteric music enthusiasts, would file through the doors of the rough wood common building and get themselves a cup of tea. The kitchen of that big cabin smelled like sweet spiced tea and wool sweaters and boots—there were usually a few long-term guests living at the community. Most of the singers brought their own Sacred Harp hymnals, sometimes in different versions so that we each had to find the next hymn we wanted to sing on different pages. When we got ready to sing we sat in a square, with the four parts facing each other. By the standards of punctual Quakers, we were slow to leave our greeting conversations to start singing, and, once we started, reluctant to leave the compelling songs to go home.

Shape-note hymns are from eighteenth- and nineteenth-century American singing schools; their heyday was in the rural Southeast. The shapes came from simple "fa so la" systems brought over from England to teach singers to read the names of the shapes—squares, triangles, circles—representing the intervals between the notes. Early on, these shapes didn't even have to be hung on a staff.

Surprising to me, the shapes don't represent any absolute pitch, and although they are now printed on a staff, the staff lines are just a rack to display the up and down movement of the notes, or "relative pitch"—and, of course, to store other important information such as rhythm and rests. This causes the appearance of a page in a shape-note hymnal to be both familiar and foreign. The names of the songs are odd, too, following an old English convention of using a place-name or keeping the name of the tune that preceded its present lyrics.

It's the leader of a song, usually the chooser and the "beater" of its rhythm for the group, who determines the pitch of the first note. In our Hidden Hill group, if the leader of the song started it by humming a note too high or too low, eyes would cross in mock suffering, short confusion would ensue, and then the leader had to start the group over with a more reasonably pitched *do* or *fa*. We'd sing the names of the shapes first, and then the words.

Many of the lyrics are intensely personal, which makes them hauntingly universal—as the father's grief in William Billings's "Daniel's Lamentation": "Daniel the king was griev-ved and mov-ved; he knelt in his chamber and wept. Would to God I had died, Would to God I had died for thee, O Absalom, my son, my son!" Some of the most vivid songs are fugued—where the different parts come in at different times with the same lyrics in strong echoes. In "Exit," one of the songs accidentally named appropriately, a unison "Death, like an over-flowing stream, Sweeps us away: our life's a dream" is followed by an echo from all the parts like a Greek chorus: "an empty tale, a morning flow'r." These words are repeated and entwined several times before falling into unison again to emphasize the song's point that human life is brief: "Cut down and withered in an hour." Shape-note lyrics are characteristically stark. Any comfort they provide has to come from singing them together.

Harmonies of older songs in the shape-note books are based on fourth and fifth intervals from ancient European modal scales and were not really harmonies at all but separate melodies. The harmonies do not come together by design but seemingly in spite of design. In the act of singing toward one another, the melodies are welded together by the rise and fall of the song leader's hand.

Because each part is actually a separate melody, when he joined me on shape-note evenings, Jim found his bass part incredibly busy and way too audible. No more hiding in the back row of the choir. The tenor, busiest of all the parts with frequent runs of eighth notes, sometimes even "crosses" the treble, or soprano, to soar on top. All the parts together spread out farther than hands on a keyboard can reach, which makes it fortunate there are no keyboards. The resulting sound is powerful and plain with a strong beat, and the effect is delightfully imperfect, even a little harsh if you have never heard it before. The tradition does not require that all of the voices hit their mark, shape-note chronicler Buell Cobb says, "But in the center, in the midst of the terrific volume, it is as if the imperfections are burned away."

Shape-note, a.k.a. Sacred Harp for its most famous publication and schools, spread to the rural West and South with itinerant singing masters decades before the Civil War. Although it is often identified with Primitive Baptist congregations, the teachers, book-compilers, and singers came from many different denominations—joined by the opportunities for singing, not dogma. Perhaps because of that, shape-note never caught on as a part of any denomination's church service. Shape-note singers gathered in any building large enough to hold them, their harmonies transcending differences in belief.

I'd like to think that shape-note singing transcended political differences too. North Alabama was and is part of the heartland for "fa so la" singing, reports Cobb. Winston County, where distant cousins of my father's family lived, famously tried to reject secession from the Union in 1861. Living in a hill country region without slaves and culturally opposed to slavery, many Winston residents agreed with a relative of my father's, like him named Bill Looney, that Alabama should not be a slave state and Winston County should remove itself from the secession effort. An iconoclastic friend of Cherokees and owner of a crossroads tavern that figured large in this conflict of ideas and loyalties, Bill took on the name the Black Fox, also the nickname of a Cherokee chief whose other English name was John Looney. This is a confusing detail that suggests relations closer than pen pals. Bill's notoriety spread as he smuggled unionists to the U.S. Army. Many of his own Alabama relatives disagreed with Bill and supported the state's decision to secede. I wonder if any of my old Alabama family members ever sat around their hearths in angry disagreement, then got out a Sacred Harp hymnal to try and heal the spreading wounds.

Historically, shape-note groups often splintered off and made their own books and started their own "singings." Individuals buy their own copies of shape-note hymnals so they can make notes in the margins and write in new verses, or bring in a verse they like better from a different edition or book. A fellow singer may have composed a new song. In Fairbanks with the Quakers, sticky notes and photocopied texts of new songs stuck out of everyone's books. The group put the words to "Rudolph the Red-Nosed Reindeer" on the tune "Winter," which was already a good fit for us Alaskans with its "liquid streams forbear to flow in icy fetters bound." And very much in the tradition, one of the singers added a spring breakup verse that we all scribbled into our books:

> The mud descends and covers all
> The ice drips from the eaves
> The rivers thaw and freeze once more
> And daylight we receive.

I immediately noticed that shape-note lyrics were fair game for continued interpretation and playfulness, if not civil disagreement. A hearty "He the Living God!" was simultaneously sung "She the Living God!" by some, and we supported a recently divorced member by singing "Leander" in the solidarity of revenge: "No longer will I ask your love, nor seek your friend-ship more / The happiness that I approve is not within your pow'r."

A shape-note singing is not a performance but an upwelling of music between singers. There was a night several of us met to sing in the crow's nest of the UA Fairbanks student union, far above the empty hall, where we rained down shape-note songs by heart. We didn't have a book, but singing to each other brought the songs out of us in waves. Four parts facing each other have no separate audience or congregation, which makes the center space not a podium or pulpit but an in-between, that place of potential transformation. One of the shape-note veterans told me that in some "singings" an errant youth might be asked to lead a song so that the music coming at him from all four sides could enter his heart.

It is loud enough to do the job. At Hidden Hill I asked William Walters why the quiet Quakers started singing this old, raw music. These are people who have the appearance of gentleness and typically let a little silence fall after a person speaks. They call this "letting the light shine" on what you have said. This startled me when I first experienced it. I grew up in a family where you had to "bumper car" what you wanted to say into the conversation even before the other person was done talking—if you wanted to be heard. I graduated to male-heavy summer jobs where a nearly rude assertiveness won you the leadership roles. Now I was suddenly with men and women who took time at the end of each of my statements to consider what I'd just said, took time to respond thoughtfully before they went on to express their own next thoughts. These people expected me to listen and respond in the same manner. It was a different kind of paying attention I've tried to learn.

William said he wasn't sure how Quakers started singing shape-note songs, as they now do in many places around the country, but he knows it happened recently, as in just a few decades ago. Perhaps this is no accident; singing this clamorous Babel of separate melodies is as free in its own way as the prayerful silence of the Quaker morning services.

My Sunday night friends were an uneven-looking crew, some with holey socks and torn Levi's, some in trendy outdoor clothing. Once in a while someone arrived with that nineteenth-century homestead-er look that accentuated a sense of backward time travel. Behavior was unpredictable. A man and woman sang bass together while their young son climbed on their heads. A young woman studying to be a doctor told us she'd give herself ten more minutes to sing before she returned to her physiology book. Whoever picked the song had to lead it—a fair bit of responsibility—so there was some hesitation for new members like me. But almost immediately I had favorites I longed to sing with the others, notably Billings's lovely song "Africa," so I'd try my hand and arm at summoning the flowing odd harmonies from our group:

> Now shall my inward joys arise and burst into a song
> Almighty love inspires my heart and pleasure tunes my tongue
> Oh shine on this benighted heart with beams of mercy shine
> And let the healing voice impart a taste of joys divine
> Oh for this love let rocks and hills their lasting silence break
> And all harmonious human tongues the savior's praises speak
> Angels assist our mighty joys, strike all your harps of gold
> And when you raise your highest notes this love shall e'er be told
> The generous fruits that never fail on trees immortal grow
> There rocks and hills and brooks and vales with milk and honey flow

Kari was three and four years old when I was learning to sing shape-note with the Quakers. She couldn't understand my hesitation when it came time to lead. She'd stand open-eyed in front of me and move her small hand in the air, showing me how. She would get bored after a couple of verses and go back to the toys and other kids. But I found out she never left the singing behind her when she wandered away from us. Later on in the week I heard her saying to herself, "Fly swift around ye wheels of time," an iambic echo from "Northfield."

A1: WAVE TO YOUR CORNER

It makes me sad to hear ninety-year-old "Berchman" (his given name is Bergman) Esmailka of Nulato say, "They are all gone now," about the oldest of the Athabaskan fiddlers, musicians who had been his downriver fiddle contemporaries. He says the younger musicians "don't like that fiddle—too hard." I'm watching a Youtube video of the November Athabaskan Fiddle Festival, a celebration that's been going on for over thirty years now in Fairbanks. The festival still requires each band to have a fiddle player, though, and another middle-Yukon player, Franklin Dayton, shrugs off the changes: "Kids like rock and roll but they mix it up with that fiddle anyway."

Alaska's urban places are stratified by race and income and age and other demographics people cling to when there's enough members of their own group to be able to ignore the others. What's invisible in urban Alaska is a flowing exchange of music still alive out west.

Fiddle music, mostly jigs and reels from French Canada and the British Isles, came up to Fort Yukon with the Hudson's Bay Company in the 1840s. G'witchin people along the tributaries made it their own. Fifty years later, the Alaska Gold Rush brought music from the American frontier, plus more instruments and square dances up the Yukon and the Koyukuk Rivers from the opposite direction. The music crossed the big portage to the Kuskokwim and came up all the creeks, wherever there was a banjo or a guitar or a fiddle to carry it. The downriver music moved up and the upriver music moved down until every village had its little dance band, often the same musicians who knew the indigenous songs and dances. A musical soul is a musical soul.

People still talk about the differences between the upriver and downriver fiddle music: the upriver music more austere, often just a fiddle, and the downriver music accompanied by a guitar or banjo or a cabin full of them. But the upriver and downriver tunes and dances are kissing cousins, with some of the same tunes meeting in the middle after traveling halfway around the world; "Soldier's Joy" and "Devil's Dream" are cases in point. As radio stations reached into the interior of Alaska, country western and popular tunes of the day also found fertile ground in the repertoires along the rivers. The radio brought Jimmy Rodgers and Ray Price, Ernest Tubbs and Hank in the 1940s and '50s: "Crazy Arms," along with "Waltz Across Texas."

Elvis is also alive and well in the school auditoriums and church halls, as is every other wave of music including rap and hip-hop. Music evidently travels along something as mysterious as plasma tubes, appearing suddenly in hands and voices thousands of miles away. Athabaskan diction and phrasing finds its way into these songs too. When we go to the fiddle festival in Fairbanks or bring fiddlers down to play at a fair, it is like standing in front of a crazy mirror to hear "Your Cheating Heart" born again through the Athabaskan musicians.

Through the queer "paradox of the periphery" noted by Athabaskan fiddle scholar Craig Mishler and others, an Athabaskan-composed fiddle tune like "Red River Jig" might preserve a rhythm and dance mannerism long extinct from its Orkney Island ancestor, while the American tune "Red Wing" has gathered up handfuls of the traditional singing and rhythms of its village practitioners all along the path north. Nothing stays the same, but you can hear the old strands in the mixing, very much like the way a clear stream runs into a muddier river leaving a transparent green swirl to play along the bank, far downriver from the confluence.

One of the mysteries in musical lineage cited by Mishler is the appearance of an ancient and obscure Shetland Island tune, "Wynadepla," reborn as "K'ooniit' aii Ch'aadzaa," the "Handkerchief Dance" in the Fort Yukon dance tradition, and now well known at the Athabaskan fiddle festivals and dances. Mishler speculates that "one of the Orkneymen who came to Fort Yukon with the Hudson's Bay Company may have picked it up from a Shetlander visiting his homeland." Other tunes and songs have purely Athabaskan names and origins, the antecedent traditions evident only in the dance tune forms or the occasions for playing them.

Like the reciprocal changing of the old fiddle tunes and reels and jigs, the popular Country Western and Rock and Roll songs brought new elements. The song "Eagle Island Blues" is played at every dance and Native fiddle festival in the interior of Alaska. This song brought a notion of the personal and intimate into the Native songs, according to Huslia elder Catherine Attla, who I remember said that her mother didn't want her singing "Eagle Island Blues" when she was a girl because it was too personal. A lonely Indian man, Tom Patsy, wrote the song at a trapping cabin in 1938 while thinking of his Nulato sweetheart. Now the song is performed as an instrumental or with its Native words at most village dances. All the bands play it, at Fairbanks or up and down the river and even way upriver into the Canadian Yukon.

Singers like Louis Demoski from Galena know all the old country and rock and roll standards from Chet Atkins to Chuck Berry, whose songs he said he learned from the radio and from Huslia musician Herbie Vent. Demoski added his own original songs to the mix, and his "Indian Rock and Roll," written for a Galena dance in 1974, is played by young and old along the lengths of the great interior rivers. When we came to Galena in the late 1970s, "Indian Rock and Roll" was just taking off in the middle Yukon River villages like Galena and Ruby and up at Huslia on the Koyukuk. Now you can find Joey Michaels's Innoko River Band on YouTube playing "Indian Rock and Roll" in the Kashim at Shageluk. It is a standard at the fiddle festivals.

Because Native languages and traditions have been submerged and tragically damaged by the ascendant white cultures and economies, ownership of the Athabaskan musical traditions is guarded, especially around performances, and does not often provide an open jamming venue for anyone who walks by with an instrument. Like all the other jagged edges of culture, this one can hurt. I found this out by being sorta invited and then sorta uninvited to a practice jam at the university in Fairbanks. The un-inviter was not unkind, but I still groan when I think of the moment—mostly because I should have recognized that I'd been invited to be a listener, not a participant. It wasn't just an issue of ethnicity; I could have been a white person who grew up playing the songs with the Native guitar player and I would have been a member of the group already. But issues of ownership and questions about how to preserve a fragile cultural treasure are all around this one like a picket fence. Ouchy moments will hopefully pass as the next generations take up the songs. But the Native words to the songs and old situations for singing and playing are passing out of the world. How can we feel about that? Berchman feels sad. I am an outsider who feels sad too.

In western Alaska's smaller towns and villages, there are so few musicians and music is so valued in all its forms that pickers can't be choosers. Normal jamming considerations tend to apply: join the group but sit back when a song comes up you don't know. Also, if you happen to be there—often so far from any road—there's probably some reason you belong. In the Alaska "outback," players still drag out instruments and chairs and swap songs with each other—with an energy that must be akin to what spread all those songs around the Interior in the first place. I taught a Shageluk kid how to pick "Billy in the Low Ground" and he taught me how to play along with "Indian Rock and Roll," though I've now forgotten it. Jim and I can hold down a background to "Eagle Island Blues" with that extra beat. At Russian Christmas in Nikolai or a basketball tournament in Lower Kalskag, if you show up with an instrument you will likely be invited to join the band. You will see more people at the dance than you ever imagined lived in the town.

At the Kashim in Shageluk, a round log building built a long time ago for men and traditional stories, there is dancing and a lot of Bingo for everyone. Visiting there once for the university, I had my mandolin along and was gathered into the band, a mostly Native hodgepodge of musicians playing old country western and dance tunes—including a schottische. At first, only the oldest people danced that one while the middle-aged and youngsters watched. But slowly, because elderly pairs were skipping and laughing and having all the fun, younger people grabbed partners and joined the dance, filling out the circle. I realized that there were likely always going to be people who could play a schottische and dance a schottische.

When we had some state fair money at McGrath, we tried to support the Athabaskan fiddling tradition by bringing musicians in from other Kuskokwim and Yukon villages. Something wonderful happened when Berchman Esmailka came to McGrath to play at the fair and stayed at our house. Jim's mom was visiting us from Wisconsin for a few weeks. Both of them were over eighty years old. They sat on the couch together and talked about popular songs from the 1940s—Glenn Miller and Tommy Dorsey songs, Bing Crosby and Andrews sisters songs, "Pennies from Heaven"—songs from both their youths. She learned the songs on a remote northern Wisconsin farm, off of a scratchy radio broadcast from Duluth or St. Paul. He learned them in a cabin in Nulato, a Yukon River village way out in western Alaska, from a scratchy radio broadcast from Fairbanks. Radio was brand new to him then. It was brand new to her then too. The forties were years when everything was ahead of them—a world war, marriages, children, all that would be thought and said and done in the next sixty years. Jim and I sat back and listened to the two of them talk, realizing that in terms of point of view from their generation, at the time they learned the songs, Lois and Berchman had a common background we could never share. Old music lovers, they were thick as thieves.

A2: BALANCE AND SWING

Passing through airport security on our way back from visiting family in the Lower 48, I braced myself for the same cold shower of dread I always feel when confronted with this advance guard of an increasingly uniformed society.

Yes, I know these people in starched shirts and epaulets are there for my safety, but as a driver of highways and shopper of supermarkets and goer of concerts, I also know they can't really provide safety except in a stiffly reactionary governmental kind of way.

There are threatening signs that make me feel queasy, telling me to stay in line and prepare my papers. In these lines I am not the protected citizen but the potential enemy. The Transportation Safety Administration seems made up of retired policemen, steadfast Walmart greeters looking for better benefits, discouraged business majors—people with clean, patriotic records and the ability to rivet any traveler with a suspicious gaze. In other words, I am profiling them as they profile me.

"You are the one," their looks say, "with the explosive toothpaste." All the innocent bottles of soap and beauty goop are now absurdly suspect, so I have stuffed them into my checked baggage where they will be jiggled and squeezed, ultimately spewing their contents into my wool socks and underwear, all the while riding in the belly of the same plane in which I am riding. What if the set of nefarious fingernail clippers I am now allowed to carry was a remote detonator?

The first TSA official is looking at boarding passes and identification. I fumble a bit because I have too many things in my hands: a small pack, a mandolin, my wallet, and these papers. She tells me, "ID on top, please." There is a cursory examination of my face, which somehow stops short of being eye contact.

At the next stop, though, there is eye contact. I am still in the sandals and shorts of a sweltering Midwest, so I don't have much to offer the x-ray machine except the pack and mandolin. As these go through and I head for the metal portal, another TSA woman tells me, "Stop! Put your wallet on the conveyor!"

I had forgotten I was still clutching it, and so I scuttle back like some small guilty animal to drop it in a gray rubber tub.

This lapse of ability to follow written instructions earns me a burning gaze all the way through the inspection corridor. When I've gathered up my stuff I still feel it, and I look up to the woman's eyes still pointed at me. Other people have passed through behind me, but she is still staring at me with what—accusation? Just for the infraction of being human and a traveler, I finger the potential for harm she sees in me as if it is a sore wound.

"What's in the case?" comes a voice from another TSA official, an older-than-me dark-featured man who strolls from the other side of the corridor. I jump a little, still filled with the gloom of a world in which people hate people they don't even know so much that they would blow themselves away just to get rid of them.

"It's a mandolin."

"I have my grandfather's violin," the man says, and there is no indication that he wants me to prove that the mandolin is really a mandolin, so I stand there holding it, along with my silly empty shoes and my backpack.

"It's a beautiful thing," he says, "very old. And when I had it looked at, the appraiser said the bow was even more valuable than the violin. Can you imagine that?"

"Do you play it?" I ask him, and he says no. His son is a musician, though. He tells me that he helped his son go to college for music and now the son plays the piano, gives concerts, teaches.

We stand and talk about music and kids while other passengers flow around us, get patted down for suspicious items, put on their shoes. After a few minutes the man looks at my mandolin case again and says, "I sure wish I could play my grandfather's violin."

"Want to see my mandolin?" I ask him. He nods yes, so I trundle my armload of stuff over to an unoccupied part of the inspection table and open the case. My tin whistle clatters out, dangerously long and metal. The man grins at me. We look at the smudged mandolin and I strum it, pointing out that it is tuned the same way as his violin.

By this time, the rest of my family is finished with the TSA line and looking slightly exasperated. But I'm putting on my shoes and my new friend lingers with me until I'm all done and ready for the B gates. "I might get that fiddle out and tune it up," he tells me.

B1: PASS THROUGH TO THE NEXT

Music is how you find your tribe. If you've ever sung harmony to someone else's melody, you can probably sleep on their floor anytime you want. Fussy and formal boundaries over who is what gender or who has what job melt like butter under the friction of a fiddle tune. In a gathering, it is just assumed that playing the next tune is more important than whatever spoken conversation is trying to start up. Even in the middle of some earnest political observation or a cute story, someone holding an instrument will throw in the starting phrase of a song and off we go, stranding the speaker in a puddle of mere spoken words.

Playing music is deeper in the brain stem than conversation. Ron Berry told us about a drunken clot of accordion players who'd just met at the Juneau Folk Festival. They followed each other back to the Alaska Hotel, blocking the hallway all night playing Rolling Stones tunes one after another.

Music is a suitably adult activity and besides that we can't help it. Jim will leave any conversation at the kitchen table and sprint across the room to the bass fiddle if a good three-chord song comes up on the radio. Our infant daughter slept on the pool table at KROA Lodge, next to babies belonging to our music friends, all the babies wrapped up in their blankets while we swapped songs around them. I never did tell my mom about the pool table. All of those kids grew into people who know homemade music is the real stuff. Al Koenig used to call his teenage son by starting to play the tune, "Dear Old Dixie." If Aaron was anywhere within earshot he'd come racing to his dad, grabbing any stray mandolin he could find along the way.

It's hard to tell which people have music wired directly to their hearts. They walk around in Clark Kent outfits until they hear a tune or a set of words that transfixes them. In the early '70s when I came "of age," I thought everything had been laid out for our use from the 1960s, like new clothes on the bed. Every folk singer, every rock and roll band was going to be put to use to make a better world. I've carried that idea around for half a century now; I still assume anyone packing an instrument case is not a gangster but a friend.

At Trapper's Den on a rare music night in summer, I probably know almost everyone. They have their kids with them, and a few dogs are enjoying the novelty of an open door. The dogs come in to check on their owners and get an ear rub from everyone before wandering back out to the mosquitoes. Mostly, we've been playing counterculture anthems from the 1960s: "Friend of the Devil," "Going Up the Country." Baker and Bruce and Becca rock the house with "White Freightliner Blues." Greg is playing rhythm guitar and sometimes throwing in a new song of his own with a driving texture. Jim is adding a bass heartbeat to it all, getting real good at divining the key of the song. He has to divine because the others forget to tell us, or it is too loud to hear what they are saying. Jim mouths "Dee!" or "Gee!" to me. Okay that I can't tell which, but I join in with the fiddle and find my place. I don't know all these songs, but the others will teach me to play them. People are dancing, sometimes yelling. Sweat is running off my forehead and into my eyes.

We are lucky that people younger than we are, especially our children of the infamous pool table, like so much of our music. Bob Dylan rolls on, and "A Hard Rain's A-Gonna Fall" is still a good summary of what's on the news. "Man of Constant Sorrow" from the Coen brothers movie *O Brother, Where Art Thou* stitched oldsters and youngsters together as soon as the movie came out; it seemed like teenagers in McGrath were singing it the next day.

Recently, "Wagon Wheel" from Old Crow Medicine Show can be heard at every bluegrass fest, wedding, or jam session, having traveled the mysterious connections between kindred hearts to a zillion radio programs. We played "Wagon Wheel" at Trapper's Den. My now-grown daughter and her partner sang "Wagon Wheel" in sweetest harmony at the farmers market in Homer last summer. Last week I heard them play it again, at a bar where an Alabama woman was pleading with them to pronounce "bouquet" as "bur-ket" so they'd sound more like the song's author, Willie Watson. I checked up on the Innoko River Band and found a YouTube video of "Wagon Wheel" being played in the Kashim at Shageluk. Ben Kardos, who once traded me his digging of an outhouse hole for a guitar of mine he wanted, now has "Wagon Wheel" on his rock and roll band website down in Washington. Jim and I went to the American Legion jam last month where a septuagenarian brought in the words to "Wagon Wheel." The night before, we'd been to a function at Glacier View School where twelve- and fourteen-year-olds were playing "Wagon Wheel." It's a musical shock wave moving through all the jam bands in America, and I'm not tired of it yet. After I joined in with the schoolkids on my fiddle, approximately approximating that double-stringed "Wagon Wheel" refrain, eight-year-old Isaiah asked me in complete friendliness and admiration for a gray-haired person knowing such a cool song, "How old *are* you anyway?"

Once at the Den, after several hours and almost all our songs, the electricity went out. It was early September and very dark, very late at night. The music stopped; the dancers stopped. A flashlight turned on and then a headlamp. When we could all see each other dimly, we started playing music again, but everything was changed because the power outage could have made us pack it up for home. But we didn't go home. There was a sense of having traveled magically into some warm dark Narnia. The music was quieter because there was no amplification but also because people were straining to hear the words. A few started singing along, helping out the band, so the boundary between band and audience dissolved. The heart songs came out—the ones you want to share with people you care about. Someone started the unaccompanied Stephen Stills song, "Find the Cost of Freedom." There's a high part that comes in with the harmonies, and it soars impossibly above the other voices. I don't know if Becca reached up there with her angel voice that night, or if my inventive memory hung that high harmony in the rafters. But just a few days ago when someone sent Jim a YouTube video of the young Crosby, Stills, and Nash singing "Find the Cost of Freedom" back in the day, I was surprised that the song no longer made me feel nostalgic, maybe because it has kept on teaching us its truth over these intervening years. Added to this bittersweet is present-time happiness about our friends in the Den—how heartfelt music can make ages and faces and hats and occupations and preoccupations dissolve in the dark.

B2: COME BACK HOME

It's 10:30 p.m. in July in Cordova, Alaska, and the sun is still above the horizon, casting an orange light through tall trees and buildings. We are playing music for a dance in the parking lot outside the library.

There are ten of us with guitars and fiddles, mandolins and banjos, two wings of musicians spread out from Francis Mallory's piano chords in the middle. Belle Mikkelson's fiddle, next to Francis, drives the tune. A slight wind plays with our melodies, so that I hear the bass fiddle thump in my bones a millisecond after I see the string being pulled. To keep our beats together instead of wavy as the ocean, we watch Jennifer's hands on the bass strings. Behind the piano, she and Francis are one heartbeat for us and one step in unison for the feet of the dancers.

The gill-netting fleet is still out in the salmon fields until the opener closes tomorrow, but some of the dads are here, swinging the moms, as children duck and prance under their arms. With this ruddy mid-summer light on their faces, the laughing and jostling of siblings and friends and the sure step of a grandparent or two in the mix, I think these fisherfolk are the loveliest people I have ever seen.

Fogs, rains, and gales are suspended for us. The greatest environmental hazards tonight are a few mosquitoes determined to land on busy left hand knuckles mid-tune.

An unaccustomed wealth of three dance callers takes turns giving the dancers long line contras like the Virginia Reel, along with squares and a few round dances. Genders are cheerfully reassigned when the dance requires, which is a nod to the absence of some fishermen and the shyness of teenage boys, or it is the plain recognition that this sort of dancing entirely deconstructs pairs of any sort. You don't just "dance with one who brung you" when you dance here. You dance with the town and with the light coming off the ocean.

Cannery workers and others walking up from the harbor below us hear the music and a few join our ranks. The callers fold them into a square or line then untangle them with patient voices and laughter until, by the end of each dance, the figures are moving together like colored chips in a kaleidoscope.

Because I have been playing my instruments all week, teaching easy first chords and notes to children at the 4-H camp during the day and jamming on heart songs with friends at night, my fingers on the fiddle strings are sore but agile. Most of the tunes I already know, and when a caller asks for something unfamiliar I duck behind the piano and take a peek at Francis's sheet music. By the end of the dance, maybe some forty times through the song, I'll know it well enough. I am a journeyman, a player in the band, an everyman.

I tell the children I'm teaching that there are several ways to "get songs" and none has special status—tablature or notes on a page or our amazing eyes and ears. I have only a workmanlike understanding of this too, humbled by the many young geniuses at this music camp who seemingly pick up notes and hand positions and styles through the pores of their skin. What I offer is basic, like the bringing of a stick to feed a fire. But who knows what a fire will do?

These fiddle tunes are built on the repeating frame of the eight bar A part, A part, B part, B part, and start again with the A. Sometimes there is a C or even a D part, also repeated because the figure must be "square" for the dancers. Whatever it is, the dancers pick up the structure immediately, or maybe it is that people who have this musical breathing inside them love to dance.

The caller turns them to the next moves as the musical phrases turn, and he throws in a bit of cryptic Civil War history when he sings a snatch of song in between dance instructions:

Twenty-five cents for whiskey, twenty-five cents for beer
Twenty-five cents for morphine, get me out of here.
I'm my momma's pride and joy
I'm my momma's pride and joy
I'm my momma's pride and joy
Sing you a song called the soldier's joy

Some of the songs I like go especially well to a minor key, like "The Banshee" or "Round the Horn," the latter evoking oceans and sailors. Although it is played in the key of G, it ends on a C chord—giving it an unfinished, reaching out kind of feeling. Open like the sea. Knowing this, when there are just a few of us playing these songs in someone's living room, my teasing Jim will play that last C chord, wait two seconds, and then hit a finalizing G chord just to slam the open feeling shut and watch me twitch. His grin acknowledges that I much prefer that unusual last IV chord to hang there like whatever it is that keeps sailors on the sea or people in love.

Often, with my favorites, one of the parts is low and one is high. "Cold Frosty Morning" is often played with the high part first, going low for the B part, that progression resembling your skin's alarm at the cold when you take off for a walk in winter—and then how it warms to the rhythm of your crunching steps.

"St. Anne's Reel," a tune from the American Northeast in the century before the last one and only God and the folklorists know from where before that, swings through the middle notes in the key of D like the dancers themselves are swinging. Then the B part kicks up to a refrain on the highest fiddle string. The high notes on a fiddle or mandolin, played exactly on the stacked harmonic of the pitch, are like honey tasted in the center of your head.

We play until midnight and the sun is down. The light will stay all night.

Bread

It's wild, and you have to learn to make it by making it. It's forgiving, and no matter what you do, almost, it will turn out to be food. When you are kneading, you are not tearing and mixing but letting the dough embrace itself again and again and again. I am thinking about a Native grandmother talking about the women's energy that gathers and joins. In her language, pronouns have no gender, but women are the ones who gather and sew and fold their families together. Around the wide earth, both men and women bakers tell their hands: "Now you are mother to the bread."

Breads from different flours—or the same flour in different conditions of warmth, liquid, sugars, duration of sponge, or proofing, or cooking—will turn out completely different loaves. Make a note about these things each time you make a loaf of bread, and then lose the note—so that you can discover the next bread as you make it.

Wild yeast lives in the air and can be coaxed into potato and sugar water. Instead of using yeast from the store, trust that wild yeasts live in your kitchen air and will breathe themselves into loaves of rising bread. It takes days and days to tame wild yeasts, luring them with a bowl of food, but then they are yours.

Bread is a gift—a thank you, a welcome, a hello. It doesn't have to match the curtains; it doesn't gather dust on a shelf or go to a yard sale. Its obligation half-life is a day only. It is of you and the time you have given to your friend, the people around your table. Here, have some.

I sometimes try to make bread recipes, but I'm drawn sideways by the sweet potato leftovers in the refrigerator, the dark beer, the molasses and honey, even the brussels sprouts. Try it, try it. You know it's going to work when your hands can feel the yeasts breathing on the floured board, stretching their tiny bubbles, the *boule* smooth as a baby's butt when you tuck each loaf into itself.

10
DON'T LET ME COME HOME A STRANGER

Will there come a time when the memories fade
And pass on with the long, long years
When the ties no longer bind, Lord save me from this darkest fear
Don't let me come home a stranger, I couldn't stand to be a stranger.
—"Don't Let Me Come Home a Stranger," *sung by Robin and Linda Williams,*
written by Robin Williams and Jerome Clark

One of the times I needed to hear Margaret's stories was after the Twin Towers fell in New York. I had been happy to live in a place so very far from a connected road system, a place where merely arriving required an airplane or a river barge. Lacking a gravel or asphalt highway, we turned for our local travels to the ancient highway of water, the Kuskokwim. Anyone in town knew when it rose four inches on a cloudy day because of rain upriver, or on a sunny day because far-off glaciers were melting. We went to the boats and pulled them up, or we pushed them farther down the sloping mud bank when the water dropped. I met the already-elderly Margaret during the flood of 1991 when I tried to help her move fifty-five-gallon drums of stove oil, but she had a tool she'd made herself—a tall bar with protruding stubs that fit over the top and bottom rims. It allowed one person to jack around a four-hundred-pound oil drum. She graciously allowed me to fumble with a few of the bright blue behemoths in the rising water, then she said, "That's okay, girl," and took back the job herself.

My husband and I had come to McGrath for forest firefighting, but we had a two-year-old daughter that first year, so I worked in the dispatch office only when there were active fires. I had time, with my daughter, to fall deeply in love with the messy layers of old-time residents and recent interlopers like us, everyone who had floated into town in waves and had stuck since 1906. I soon believed everyone necessary to solve the world's problems was there—Old Swedes and Sami reindeer herders, Inupiat from the north and Yupik from downriver, Lime Village people, back-to-the-land hippies who built odd houses in the 1970s, dog mushers, descendants of riverboat captains, trappers and miners still mining and trapping, drunks and school board directors and village council elders all mixed up and intermarried. It was half potluck and half potlatch all the time. If we—and I counted myself among the "we" by then—could get along, then anyone could.

I was told at the outset of our residency, only half-jokingly, that no one would really be regarded as an insider who did not have grandparents in the graveyard. Margaret was the one who kept the graveyard clear of brush. She snipped up the trunks of trees with her bow saw when the trees had grown rotten and fallen over in a windstorm. When someone died, townspeople came to ask Margaret where to dig the hole because she had the entire map of who and where in her head. She knew where the empty spaces were in the earth.

Like Margaret, I had a garden. Actually, she was the one who taught me to garden, though I had a childhood memory of seeds turning into squashes and had taken a gardening class and read my share of pamphlets and books. She and Ted lent me a few rows over at Ted's place by the airport, and Margaret cackled at me when nothing grew because I didn't know enough to keep it watered and weeded. Thanks to them, more than ten years later, I was standing in bright sun on a golden fall day with buckets of dug potatoes around me and beautiful fat cabbages still in their rows—on a day the sky was empty. The little airplanes of our town had already gotten the news: Super Cubs and Cessnas, along with every other large and small airplane in the country, would be grounded for at least a week. The silent sky was so strange and full of grief that I got on my knees in the warm dirt and cried. In the afternoon of the first day, two Air Force fighter jets roared through the silence for a few moments, then were gone.

It's not as if the violence of the world can't reach into the bush towns. McGrath, not a Native village but an old gold rush freighting town, was expanded and changed by World War II. The war brought

Ted, a civilian working at the army's gas plant, who had taught himself prospecting and flying and had dreamed of Alaska since he was a young man in Pennsylvania during the Great Depression. Other men and women came here after Korea and Vietnam. Western Alaska is not any safer than anywhere else, probably less so. People hurt each other, usually members of their own families. People die, too, and frequently—not just in their beds but in airplanes and trucks and wheelers and in the cold hands of the river. It was a revelation to me, in a place so inherently unsafe, to find how connected I was to faraway concrete and steel and the flesh and bone of strangers. Who knew that damage to them could choke down even our distant village? I felt pried open and raw. This was one of the many days I visited Margaret.

In McGrath, Margaret's couple of acres was like an island resistant to time's river, a rag and boneyard of pioneer dreams. Even in McGrath, which is itself nearly an island and a loop in time, Margaret's place was a remarkable eddy flowing backward: dog sleds leaning on ancient snogos leaning on track vehicles leaning on lumber leaning on boats leaning on barge containers. In summer, every margin of the property was filled with long grass and encroaching willows, punctuated by generous spills of leggy delphinium and calendula. Feral strawberries peeked out from between the flower stalks.

In the years after I met her, Margaret's Swede-blue eyes dimmed, becoming unfocused and more pale. In her house, always a crowded museum, she eventually became more curator than owner of her memories. Her still-busy hands sorted and stacked but had lost much of their purpose and organization. The center could not hold, but we, the randomly faithful, visited anyway.

She is keeping this tin can, so don't throw it away. Why? She is keeping this can, this box, this bottle. If those far-off factories making cans and bottles and cottage cheese containers are gone tomorrow, this tin can will be an object beyond price. Margaret and Ted always believed that the rest of the world beyond Alaska would someday disappear, but that they could live on what they could save or make themselves. When I brought Margaret water so that she wouldn't melt dirty snow, she patted my six-gallon plastic water container lovingly with a gnarled hand. "This is a beautiful jug," she said, "and a pretty blue." I was amused and honored.

Margaret sorted the boards and boxes every day, brought all her five-gallon buckets into the house so they would not be stolen—though I was sure there were enough five-gallon buckets in McGrath that every house had its share. Margaret's house was always best of show in the category of stuff.

Minus the now-shadowed and shrinking garden, her yard was stacked like a box of supplies for a camping trip, one that began in 1929 on the river steamer *Tana* that plied Alaska's Kuskokwim between Bethel and the upriver town of McGrath and had been continually appended during each new decade and for the new century. These old yards held the implements necessary to go river freighting, farming, trapping, hunting, or hard-rock gold mining.

Up at the Nixon Fork gold mine—once owned by Treadwell and then by Margaret's husband and his brother—were still-great Caterpillar tractors, cabins, the ruins of a hammer mill and mess hall. The structures had rotted into the tundra next to newer operations rising and falling with the price of gold. Out on the runway "down here" at town, Ted parked a new Arctic Tern airplane when he finally had the money but was by then too feeble to fly it. He also commissioned the construction of a gigantic river freighting boat that he and Margaret would never operate. They had done so many things in years past: mining, mushing, flying—all with lesser tools and all long before I met them.

In the McGrath house she called home for decades, Margaret now kept every pickle jar that ever passed through her hands. A small proportion of the can and jar collection resided in the outhouse, where barely enough room was reserved for visitors. In the yard, supplies of dried and canned foods and brand-new clothes and boots and tools filled several barge containers, each the size of half a railroad car. These goods waited to be of service in the next twenty years or at the Apocalypse, which would presumably drop the crowded and silly

Lower 48 back into the primal soup to start over and would leave Ted and Margaret on their own. This was both a fear and a hope.

Y2K was no big deal, either—Margaret and Ted had been expecting the big hammer for decades and they were ready, even a little disappointed, when the Janus head floated by without the world collapsing. But Margaret kept seed potatoes in her cellar; the latest batch had been down there for two years, so no matter what happened she said she would garden and eat. Ironically, as her memory grew uneven, Margaret occasionally recalled that she didn't like potatoes as a child, and this memory pushed aside sixty years of growing and eating her own tubers. When her friends brought potatoes for her supper, she'd sometimes take a bite or two to be polite and then quarantine the spuds from the rest of the food on her plate. At those times, she wouldn't even feed them to her dogs: "Dogs don't like potatoes, does they?" she'd croon to her black-and-white house husky and her Norwegian elkhound, both of them elderly and round as oil drums.

Margaret's home was a public bath house in the 1930s, so it was large by the old standards but so full of clothes, books, tools, paintings, paperwork, old radio sets, pots and pans and cans and crates of food and more food that visitors found it difficult to ferret out a place to walk or sit. Every grapple or carbide lamp or dog harness collar that hung from the beams had a story, though Margaret found it harder and harder to recall them.

When Margaret was ninety, she had been my time machine and friend for ten years. I would bring my packages of seeds over before I planted them, all for the rain of advice and stories that would fall on me when she saw them. In the winter, her amazing oil cookstove would fill the front room with warmth, even though you could never get the sticky front door entirely shut, and the wind flapped the ragged tarp around her open porch.

She was wrinkled and white and shaped like a question mark. She dressed like the fur trapper, river freighter, gold miner she was—in a plaid Pendleton shirt and denim jeans, some pairs with a red-and-white "WildAss" label on the back pocket. She had been big and strong but now had to cinch the jeans in with a broad leather belt, and she was a slight hanger for the woolen shirt that draped over her back. She was often dirty—because she worked in the yard with shovels and buckets, chopping, digging, and rearranging all day, winter and summer—and because she could not remember to wash up or change her clothes. One time when Margaret was in town ("town" for McGrath now means Anchorage, but years ago before the airplanes came it meant Fairbanks) for a doctor's appointment, a social worker took a look at her, talked with her just long enough to establish Margaret's confusion about why she was there and what she was doing, and was ready to call in the authorities for this homeless person. The fast talking of several friends was needed to convince the social worker that Margaret had a home, that she had money, that she could take care of herself if she was in her own place between the bed and the teapot and the garden.

At one time in her life not reluctant to drive a dog team a hundred miles to go to a dance and not allergic to a nice dinner in a hotel (after a haircut at Penny's department store), Margaret at ninety hated to go to town. She knew that the hospital and the old people's home would try to keep her. We, her friends, all said to each other that a move to town would kill her because her last mooring line from self to shore would be gone.

The kind of news I could bring to Margaret's house was not like falling towers. I could tell her that the river had risen or that I had seen a crane. Or I could sit with my new hurt of the world inside me and have it ease, slowly, with my hand on the head of an old dog. The hours suspended by Margaret's stories were gifts of places and people long dead and eaten up by trees and berries. They were live coals carried over inconceivable, unreachable distances to kindle my heart's recognition. When Margaret was gone, I knew, no one would ever tell me how that old life was lived, not through the eyes that actually saw it. No word on a page would ever be Margaret's voice again. What I knew was that if I could not go to Margaret's house and have a cup of tea, I, too, would be unmoored, and the woods, alive with people she had known, would recede to paper descriptions and ghosts.

Ted, though a few years younger, was often away at the hospital in Anchorage tending his own health problems. Margaret used to take care of Ted and anyone else in town who needed her. She used to deliver babies and sew up gashes from machinery and axes. She kept sutures and bandages and salves stacked in the bathroom, all around the toilet that hadn't worked since some decades-ago flood and the honey bucket, which had never been out of service. An ominous set of forceps hung from a beam next to a block and tackle—no relation, I always hoped.

Having been the most capable of persons, she was sometimes embarrassed when people came to help her do things she had always done by herself—laundry, dishes, cooking, garbage. She couldn't easily remember being a visitor, a helper, a medic, a midwife. But if you said to her, "Who taught you to stitch people up?" she'd say, "Oh, there were some people in the country who knew how, and I learned from them." Margaret couldn't recognize her own life from too far away, so you had to start the conversation with what you already knew about her. You had to name the names that helped her remember who she had been.

Margaret was propelled more by habit of will than by conscious intention or memory of what there was to be done. Sometimes when Ted was home she'd take the food he'd laid out for supper and feed it to the dogs, forgetting that the dogs had already been fed and that she and Ted hadn't eaten yet. Their years of cooperation and dividing the work of a bush household frayed and disintegrated like the old canvas on the porch, leaving them both confused and angry. If they were both in the room when I came to visit, they would tell their stories to me separately, sometimes at the same time and in a kind of competition that willfully ignored that the other one was also talking. But there were still moments of cooperation and grace that showed what kind of partners they had been.

Once, Ted told about a dance in the long-gone roadhouse across the river in old town. It was a big room with a stove made from the bottom half of a giant drum and a big steel plate welded to flatten the round top of it.

Margaret was there, dancing a waltz with Johnny Bishop. Her husband, Dolf, dead forty-five years now, was there too, healthy and full of humor, watching the dance. Ted was out on the floor, dancing with Rosie Winkelman. Johnny "had a pause in his kind of waltzing," Margaret said about him, and as he swung her around he lifted her up in the air and plunked her down, for a too long moment, on the hot flat of the stove. "Sat me right down on the stove!" she said.

"Boy, she was mad," Ted said.

"You bet I was mad!" said Margaret.

They laughed together and met eyes for just a second, and I caught a glimpse of their joined life. He was proud of her, the leggy independent dame.

Close to the time of her death, several people in town started a rotation of bringing meals and spiriting away garbage from Margaret's house. We wanted Margaret and Ted to live in the old age they had earned, in the clutter they gathered in the middle of the town they helped to build. All of us were newcomers but Sally, and none of us had family in the graveyard. Of Margaret's visitors, Sally was the only one who knew her in the 1960s.

Sally remarked that Margaret would be so upset if she could see herself—feeding the dogs too many times a day, changing a light bulb time after time because she didn't realize the lamp was not plugged in, shuffling endlessly through boxes and containers she was unable to throw away. Sally brought a picture from forty years ago, in which Margaret is up on her corrugated tin roof shoveling snow, ruddy faced, everything about her sturdy, and glad to be right where she is, doing what she's doing. You could see that she was long accustomed to the tool in her hands. If your house was on fire, she would have been the first person to arrive with a bucket of water.

Friendship is to some extent being a mirror for your friend; your regard for her and your memories of experiences and conversations constantly reinforce her picture of her past self, her continuity, her creation myths. If memory is like a wool sock—wearing out where you walk on it—then when the heels and the toes go, a friend can weave some yarn back and forth over the hole. Margaret couldn't remember if she'd had coffee in the morning, but if I came over and I reminded her that she was always a person who liked coffee in the morning, she'd answer back with a policy statement on coffee in the morning, and on tea in the afternoon, and it led her to the stove and the water and the tea and the honey of the present moment.

My own mother lost the keys to every memory of herself, and I was terrified, watching her die while she was still alive. I think she was in hell, wandering most of every day, the faces of her children fears among fears. I took her outside one warm March day—what a relief from her nursing home room—and she exclaimed over the yellow forsythia, "These are lovely! I remember these!"

I said, "You used to grow these. They hung over the fence in the backyard and they were beautiful." And she said, "Yes they were." And we were both satisfied for a while, mother and daughter again.

After my mother died I made my daughter, Kari, at age ten, raise her right hand and repeat after me: "No matter how crazy you may someday get" (No matter how crazy you may someday probably *giggle* get), "I will remember when I didn't think you were crazy" (I will remember when you weren't crazy), "and I will tell you about something you did" (I will tell you about something you did), "something that wasn't crazy and was nice" (That wasn't crazy and was nice). "So help me God" (So help me God). "I promise" (Okay, I promise!). "Amen" (Amen!).

A few years later my daughter asked me, "Well, if you forget what you are doing, and then you forget all the things you used to do, and all the people, then you aren't the same person, are you?" And, more to the point as only kids can get to the point: "If that happened to you, it would make you a stranger, wouldn't it?"

Well, yes. And being a stranger cuts ties of obligation. We say, "He's in the nursing home now" as if a man was put on ice and no longer needed visitors or friends. When there's a divorce, a death, a move, an illness, more than half of your friends unplug and leave the game. Of course this happens because you aren't there anymore. Can friendship be one hand clapping?

I brought Margaret some clothes from a Value Village secondhand store in Anchorage: jeans and wool shirts. Kari found her a green wool sweater with a zip-up front and a colorful geometric design around the chest. When she pulled it off the rack, she said, "This looks just like Margaret," and it did—it was a 1940s style, short-waisted and broad-shouldered with a collar, something an old woman of Swedish-German descent would wear outside on a crisp Alaska fall day. Not dressy enough for a dance but a fine sweater for doing a little yard work on a day that you feel good about yourself. Margaret liked the sweater but said it was too nice to wear. And then after a while she couldn't remember it was hers and finally she asked Sally who that nice sweater belonged to. I saw her hide it under a coat the next time I came over, because she couldn't remember who I was that day and was afraid I would carry it home.

I took dirty clothes and kitchen things away to wash them, and on one level Margaret understood that I would bring them back clean. But joined to that thought, like old paint on wood, was fear. There were so many people coming over and doing chores in her house, touching her things.

I hauled water and did laundry and cleaned up dog crap when Hansy the elkhound, the only dog left now, had to wait too long to go outside. We helpers had different skills, did different things. Israel made sure there was oil in the tank that fed the constant heat of the kitchen range and the stove in the back room, the one Margaret still thought ran on wood. Sally brought tea, honey, paper towels, bread, and cans of dog food when Ted, the constant shopper, was gone and Margaret was nearly out of one of these essential items.

Sally cleaned the floor too and did more—she spirited away dirty clothes and pots and she visited every day, sometimes many times a day, far more than anyone else. She had the license of the longtime friend to clean out the refrigerator, a place I never dared to touch, that sacred place of half-gone sour cream packages and Styrofoam containers of cheeseburgers or meatloaf from the restaurant. She put the pills in the plastic pill-sorter labeled Sunday through Saturday. Becky traveled miles from her upriver homestead to clean Margaret's house, and on one memorable and never-repeated occasion, to try and clean Margaret. She said she learned the full extent of Margaret's frontier vocabulary on that day.

We and others brought supper meals, organized on a schedule by Israel, and we all washed dishes, leaving big steaming pans of hot clean water sitting in the sink, hoping that Margaret would remember how to wash her body and hold off the indignity of being washed by strangers. Ted said hopefully one of us would get Margaret down to the clinic and give her a bath there, since Becky couldn't get her to take a bath at home. But he was dreaming. She would never have forgiven us.

We were not Margaret's children, but we were not strangers either. And in addition to having a shared affection for Margaret, we were joined together in the loyalty of an organized conspiracy. She didn't know we divided up the essential tasks that allowed her to stay in her own house. She just knew that she was getting more visitors than she ever used to have, and for the most part she was enjoying them. Supper magically appeared, and although she didn't remember that supper also had appeared the night before, the anxiety—an understated euphemism for this particular hell—of losing herself was reduced by the steady stream of people who came in the door like friends.

I enjoyed this conspiracy, which Ted was in on, because I like being the left arm to another's right, harmony to the melody. Leaks kept springing in the wall we built to keep out the inevitable move to a nursing home, but people kept stepping up to plug the holes, even though they were busy with their own leaking walls at home.

(Note to my daughter about something to tell me when I need to hear it: "Remember when you and Sally and Israel and Al and Linda and Joe and Becky were all trying to do little things for Margaret so she wouldn't have to go to Anchorage?" That would be a nice thing to have remembered to me.)

I had plenty of opportunity to sort my reasons for needing Margaret to need me. For one thing, I was the youngest child in my own family and tagged along as people in my family took care of the older ones. My mother also had a "trapline" of older people we visited around our eastern Oregon community. We would bring cookies or a meal and sit a minute and then head out the old screen door and back to the rest of life. But I noticed even from the earliest visits not only the old ones' hunger for company but my hunger to know who they had been.

Attracted to the attention paid by a child, an old woman in our town everyone called Granny Smith would hold me fast in a chair with the story of the wagon that rolled over her belly before 1900, or the fire that jumped the Snake River when all the fields were sagebrush. I'd ask for more stories until my mother dragged me home. Stories came from Mrs. Collins, Rudy Zimmerman, Harvey Otis—how to make a horseshoe fit a horse, descriptions of the empty wavering towns under the water of the Owyhee Dam, the Snake River sturgeon as big as canoes. Now, as a grownup of sorts and long a lover of stories, I know it is a part of me to want to hang onto the histories that slip away in separations and forgetting every day.

There is a healing stillness in an old house where an old person still lives. It is a privilege and a prayer to listen, and something else too. The pain we bring with us, when we come to listen, is not lessened but is put in context, as if we could grow up to it or surround it and learn something from it. Or if it is too strange and unknowable now, maybe we are just pried open enough by the gift of hearing stories from another's life to be able to trust that an inexplicable hurt is ours after all and will eventually take its proper place in us, a guest at our long table.

How I bless the collectors of first-person stories and letters, the patient gatherers of actual voices of people living their lives in their own times—what they ate, how they lived, who they loved. But what I wanted more than anything, when I visited Margaret, was not to write down the names of the great Kuskokwim stern-wheelers (though I did—the *Wallace Langley*, the *Tana*, the *Northwestern*) but to sit by her hissing stove holding the warmth of tea she made for us or I made for us—it didn't matter which. I wanted the moment when she was shaping the story for me, as if she would always offer the funny vignette from Nixon Fork mine of the big roan horse pushing his way into the cookhouse to get at the bags of flour, the door hitting the "Frenchie cook" in the ass. I wanted to watch her remember that story, rounding and crinkling her cloudy blue eyes, as she brought it out once again for telling to me. And if the silence grew too long, I could always ask her how to thin carrots. "You take your fingers like this," and she would make a gnarly backward "C" out of her right hand, "and you pinch and you pinch and you pinch."

I wanted the tale as it was in the moment of telling; I wanted to claim my half of my friend's story, to feel the warmth of living thought. One day I said to Margaret what I usually said when I came in her door: "It looks like you've been working outside." To which Margaret would always say, cheerily, "Oh, I work out every day." This was a policy statement, fit for any stranger. But on that day she said, wearily, "Is there anything else?" That was just for me, and she knew it didn't have any answer. When you want an answer to a question that doesn't have one, you can only ask a friend.

There is a children's story that haunted me from the first of many times my mother read it to me. I don't know what book it came from, which is just as well since I might not recognize a story I've reshaped in my need to remember it.

A young girl's heart is stolen by an old woman, that villainous old woman who is an invention of our fear, whose inscrutable betrayal of our trust in old women terrorizes childhood. She has taken the girl's heart and put it in an egg and put the egg in the bottom of a lake guarded by a great serpent. The location of the egg is a secret and the old woman dies without telling anyone where it is. Somehow, by accident, the watery serpent is killed, the egg discovered and nearly broken, and nearly broken again, and finally taken whole back to the girl. Does she have to break the egg to get her heart back? I can't remember.

I knew my mother in so many ways and from so many times that I have various moms distilled from my memories of her: tincture of disapproving Mom applied to teenage me, Mom's cool hand on my hot face when I was sick, Mom cooking twelve delicious things at once for a Sunday dinner with my aunts, Mom fishing in rolled-up pants, Mom holding my daughter. I can examine these memories. I can hear her voice. I can feel her love for me still.

My memories of my mother are all concerned with me, of course. But lying on her last bed she spoke words and dreamed dreams that didn't have me, or any of us, in them. She was wandering in a world by herself, looking for her first family. She was burned by fires, tossed by seas, held in arms whose names she couldn't say. I heard my homeless, courageous, frightened mother call out for her own mother. And get no answer. And I couldn't answer her because I wasn't even born yet.

It would make you a stranger, wouldn't it?

Well yes, I was a stranger to her, but she wasn't a stranger to me. I don't know everything that was inside that egg, but I knew enough of it to know I wanted to find it and give it back to her.

Knowing someone is simpler when you only know what you've been told. My Margaret is a composite of all the stories she ever told me about herself, selected by the self she most remembered and believed in at each session over tea. Over the years I came to know the west shore of Vashon Island, where Margaret was a child in 1920, from the post office at Lisabeulah two miles north of her grandfather's house to the Campfire Girls camp a mile south, and the path from the kelp beds and beach up through the giant fir trees to the orchards and gardens and the old house, even up to the spring that came from the hill above it. There were flowers planted along that path. I can see the two young sisters in the rowboat, one light-haired and one dark, and the little steamer that plied the west passage with Margaret's father, the captain, waving to the girls and saying to the passengers on the deck below him, "Those are my kids."

I know where "Old Town" McGrath was when Margaret came here—before the river changed course in the flood of 1935—because her stories sent me looking for it, pulling aside tangled willows and alders to find old cabins. I know how the spring up at the Nixon Fork mine made a little pond below the cookhouse, and how you had to carry the empty buckets down and the full buckets up and how your feet slipped on the mud of the steep path. Thanks to Margaret, I own topography I have never seen and will never see because it no longer exists. I have names and places enough to build a little one-dimensional Margaret from scratch.

I even know a few of Margaret's uncertainties—the sister-in-law who didn't like her, the road past her house she would have liked to look at but couldn't because of Ted and the "junk he's got out there." Oh that was an irritation: the horse-drawn grain binder three hundred miles from the nearest horse and the two-thousand-gallon oil tank hooked up to nothing and "sitting right there by the road so I can't see out."

I know some of the stories Margaret's silences told, too, but not many. Sally always knew more of those than I did, and those are Sally's to tell. The details we have each been entrusted with were good for holding a certain Margaret in front of us as we had tea, and each of us carried a handful of details home, like a gift of fish or berries. Still, I know we could never know enough about her, couldn't know and understand a "whole Margaret" even if we knew more. Even if we were her children.

I remember when Margaret lost the thread of a story for the first time ever. She was talking about dogs, her present dogs, and how Hansy knew he belonged to Ted. Then she switched the scene down to Vashon Island and her grandfather's dogs, and then she couldn't find the thread of either story anymore and she stopped mid-sentence. I patted Hansy and called him a good dog, and the moment passed.

That night, too, she looked right at me and said she was glad I was with her, and she thanked me for helping her. I felt a little shocked and exposed, since I was used to being invisible and regarded in sideways fashion as in when she would say to the dogs, "Mary always brings us something good, doesn't she?" I was happy enough to be invisible, my name never spoken directly at me. Addressed point-blank, I felt the too-familiar hurt of losing friends and family who care for me. "You are welcome," I said. And we both were.

Moments of love between people are exactly that: moments between us. This is where we live. We can come forward and claim our part in these days and claim our pain when the people have passed who loved us enough to tell us things.

And so it was that Margaret never quite became a stranger, and we sat in her warm house on the old cushions and became her friends again and again. She fell down on her floor and died on a summer day when she was ninety-three years old. I helped to wash her old body, remarkable that day for its peace and her absence from it. I spent the night in her silent house with the candles and the sad dog. If you don't think dogs know about losing a friend, you have another think coming. I don't know who told the men where to dig her grave.

So will I be a stranger when I've forgotten you?

Maybe not if you remember me, not if you are willing to fight the losing battle of teaching me to me again. Not if you understand that all battles are losing and beyond that, that the losing part isn't important. If I can't be taught, come have tea and try to teach me anyway. Hold what you wanted to say to me in the place in your heart where I am not a stranger. There, I promise, I will listen.

NOTES

Any person I could imagine protesting portrayal in these pages has had his or her name changed or omitted. Otherwise, I hope the people described here will bear the impertinence of my gaze, the burden of my affection.

"From the Air"

Amelia Hill's extensive collection of photographs, from the early 1920s to 1953, can be found in the Alaska State Library Historical Collections, Juneau.

"D-2 lands," as people commonly referred to them in those years, were on everyone's mind when we worked in the Brooks Range in the late 1970s. These lands were reserved under Section 17 (d) (2) of the 1971 Alaska Claims Settlement Act (ANCSA). This legislation was intended to settle Native claims, largely for the purpose of securing the lands along the Alaska Pipeline corridor for development, but this legislation also directed the Secretary of the Interior to withdraw millions of acres of lands for conservation purposes as "National Interest Lands." Protected status of these lands was due to expire on December 31, 1978, if they were not particularly designated. Congress failed to designate the D-2 lands, and their status was argued for much of the decade. As protected status was due to expire, President Jimmy Carter used the Antiquities Act to designate fifty-six million acres of the D-2 lands as national monuments, while Carter's Secretary of the Interior, Cecil Andrus, used the Federal Lands Policy Management Act to withdraw another forty million acres. The Alaska National Interest Lands Conservation Act (ANILCA) passed into law in December 1980 and created National Parks and National Wildlife Refuges from these withdrawn (from development) lands. Many Alaskans and their elected representatives opposed these conservation measures, so the terms "D-2" and "D-2 lands" were well known and often used pejoratively.

"Shape of an Egg"

Emily Ivanoff Brown is quoted from Eliot Wigginton's *I Wish I Could Give My Son a Wild Raccoon* (New York: Doubleday, 1976).

"People on the Ferry"

In *The Ascent of Denali*, Hudson Stuck describes Walter Harper setting foot on the actual mountain top in 1913: "Walter, who had been in the lead all day, was the first to scramble up; a native Alaskan, he is the first human being to set foot upon the top of Alaska's great mountain, and he had well earned the lifelong distinction." Stuck, Episcopal archdeacon of Alaska and the Yukon, should be widely read for his entertaining accounts of early travel in the territory and his advocacy of Native languages and cultures. His preface to *The Ascent of Denali*, first published in 1914, is an eloquent appeal for the "restoration to the greatest mountain in North America of its immemorial native name." Mary F. Ehrlander's book, *Walter Harper: Alaska Native Son* (University of Nebraska Press, 2017) chronicles the life and times of Harper and his adventures with Stuck, the Mt. McKinley ascent and the sinking of the *Princess Sophia*.

"My Life in the Service of Dog"

Lines quoted from Rilke as epigraph to this essay are from *Ahead of All Parting: The Selection Poetry and Prose of Rainer Maria Rilke*, Edited and Translated by Stephen Michell (New York: Random House Modern Library Edition, 1995).

"St. Anne's Reel"

A good resource for researching dances and fiddle tunes from America and the British Isles is the *Fiddler's Companion*, compiled by Andrew Kuntz. An online searchable wiki of this collection can presently be found at www.ibilio.org/fiddlers/ *Fiddler's Companion* entries for "Varsovienne" and "Put Your Little Foot" cite their entwined histories. Check out fiddler Vi Wickam's blog, "Fiddle Tune a Day, Day 103" for more on this old dance tune.

Bodie Wagner sang us a still immense but slightly different version of Captain Jack Crawford's song "California Joe." The original was first published in Crawford's book, *The Poet Scout: A Book of Song and Story*, in 1879. The song was recorded by Bill Jackson in 1941 at the Arvin Farm Security Administration camp in California, now part of *Voices from the Dust Bowl: The Charles L. Todd and Robert Sonkin Migrant Worker Collection, 1940–1941*, available through the Library of Congress, https://www.loc.gov/collections/todd-and-sonkin-migrant-workers-from-1940-to-1941/about-this-collection/. Jim Ringer sings the Bodie version on his recording, *Waiting for the Hard Times to Go* (1972).

A similar account of how Frank Hobson came to be a violin maker, with details about how he chose his materials, was published in the *Fairbanks Daily News-Miner*, Saturday, April 10, 1976.

For the history of shape-note music, I relied on Buell E. Cobb Jr.'s *The Sacred Harp: A Tradition and its Music* (Athens: University of Georgia Press, 1978).

Read much more about Alaskan and Canadian Native fiddling traditions in Craig Mishler's *The Crooked Stovepipe: Athapaskan Fiddle Music and Square Dancing in Northeast Alaska and Northwest Canada* (Urbana: University of Illinois Press, 1993). For a first stop that will lead to others, seek out the music of Bill Stevens, an iconic Alaska fiddler and teacher. Music of many Native Alaskan fiddlers, as well as highlights and interviews from the annual Athabaskan Fiddle Festival, held in Fairbanks, Alaska, can be found on Youtube.

ACKNOWLEDGMENTS

Here are names of some of the people who encouraged these essays: Louie Attebery, Frank Soos, all the kind members of my long-ago cohort at University of Alaska Fairbanks's MFA program, Cole Clancey and Sally Collins for reading the wildfire and McGrath essays and providing details, Stephen Corey at *Georgia Review*, Ron Spatz at the *Alaska Quarterly Review*, and my smart and kind family members who gave insider views on the events and people we've shared: David and Shawn Looney, Cliff Looney, Bill Looney, Teri Looney, and Pat Looney for sharing her peach-canning day with me.

My daughter, Kari Odden, was an insightful "inside" reader who also offered objective advice to help the writing. A graphic artist, she gave me design and format ideas I was able to use as the book developed. My husband, Jim Odden, patiently read and listened to many drafts of these writings.

As this book took its shape, these readers looked at scenes or details with me: Althea Hughes, Chantelle Pence, Israel Nelson, Trista and Al Koenig, Richard Hoffman, Dan and Patti Billman, Tom and Lisa Smayda, Barb and Ken Deardorff, Linn Clawson, Harley McMahan, Janelle Eklund, and Nigel Young.

I want to thank Robin Williams and Jerome Clark for permitting me to use lines from their beautiful song, "Don't Let Me Come Home a Stranger."

In addition, I'd like to express appreciation to Peggy Shumaker and Boreal Books for gently nudging the book toward publication and to the Rasmuson Foundation Individual Artist Award for support and encouragement. I'd like to thank the 49Writers organization, the Alaska State Council for the Arts, and the extended community of writers and artists who nourish each other in these interesting times. Thank you to Alaskan artist Sara Tabbert for her beautiful tile piece, 'A Small Mystery,' which is the base art for the cover of this book. Big thanks to editor Joeth Zucco for her help with the manuscript and to the talented folks at Red Hen Press for all their work in giving this book a home.

With thanks to those who first hosted them, these are essays previously published, some in substantially different versions:

"Going to the Hills," in *Northwest Review*

"March," in *Alaska Quarterly Review*

"From the Air," published as "Rivers from the Air," in *Nimrod International Journal Points North*

"Shape of an Egg," "Sound of a Meadowlark," and "Don't Let Me Come Home a Stranger," in the *Georgia Review*

"Seeing the River," appeared in *Under Northern Lights: Writers and Artists View the Alaskan Landscape*, edited by Frank Soos and Kesler Woodward (Seattle: University of Washington Press, 2000).

BIOGRAPHICAL NOTE

Mary Odden's essays have appeared in the *Georgia Review*, *Northwest Review*, *Nimrod*, the *Alaska Quarterly Review*, and *Under Northern Lights*, an anthology of contemporary Alaska art and writing. Born in eastern Oregon, she traveled north to work on forest fires in Alaska. She studied writing at the University of Montana and the University of Alaska Fairbanks. She has worked as an aviation dispatcher, village teen counselor, writing teacher, and as publisher/editor of a small newspaper in Alaska's Copper River Valley. In 2015, she received a Rasmuson Foundation Individual Artist Award to work on the essays gathered in *Mostly Water*. She lives with her husband in Nelchina, Alaska.